TRANSFORMING TRADITIONS:

Women, Leadership and the
Canadian Navy, 1942-2010

Editors:
Stéphanie A.H. Bélanger and Karen D. Davis

CANADIAN DEFENCE AC

D0905947

Canadian Defence Academy Press
PO Box 17000 Stn Forces
Kingston, Ontario   K7K 7B4

Produced for the Canadian Defence Academy Press
by 17 Wing Winnipeg Publishing Office
WPO30555

Library and Archives Canada Cataloguing in Publication

Transforming traditions : women, leadership and the Canadian Navy, 1942-2010 / editors: Stéphanie A.H. Bélanger and Karen D. Davis.

Produced for the Canadian Defence Academy Press by 17 Wing Winnipeg Publishing Office.
Issued by: Canadian Defence Academy.
Includes bibliographical references and index.
ISBN 978-1-100-14938-7 (bound)
ISBN 978-1-100-14939-4 (pbk.)
Cat. no.: D2-258/1-2010E (bound)
Cat. no.: D2-258/2-2010E (pbk.)

1. Canada. Royal Canadian Navy--Women--History.   2. Canada--Armed Forces--Women--History--20th century.   3. Canada--Armed Forces--Women--History--21st century.   4. Women sailors--Canada--History.   5. Canada. Royal Canadian Navy--History.   6. Canada--Armed Forces--History--20th century. 7. Canada--Armed Forces--History--21st century. I. Davis, Karen D. (Karen Dianne), 1956- II. Bélanger, Stéphanie A. H III. Canadian Defence Academy IV. Canada. Canadian Armed Forces. Wing, 17 V. Title: Women, leadership and the Canadian Navy, 1942-2010.

UB419 C3 T72 2010   359.0082'0971   C2010-980068-0

Printed in Canada.

3 5 7 9 10 8 6 4 2

ACKNOWLEDGEMENTS

This volume was planned in recognition of the Canadian Navy Centennial to commemorate, celebrate, and learn from the experiences and perspectives of the women who have contributed to the navy over the past several decades. Congratulations and thank you to each of the authors. The women who contributed to this volume came forward and committed their voices and knowledge to the professional development of others, as well as to the future of the navy. They have generously shared challenges, insights, reflections and hope for those who follow in their footsteps, and we believe that many will benefit from their example.

A special thank you is extended to each of the Wrens who provided input to this book. Your tireless commitment to this project and others that contribute to the naval community is inspiring. We are particularly indebted to Chief Petty Officer 1st class (retired) Shirley Brown and Margaret Haliburton, WRCNS, for their extensive knowledge and all of the information that they made available to this project. Karen Davis is especially grateful to Edythe, Shirley, Gwen, Doreen, Pat, Bernice, Eleanor, Ruth, Betty, and Joyce in Nova Scotia for their kindness and sharing their experiences. This volume has been enriched by your contributions and the insight gained from the memorable time that Karen spent with you.

The origins of this project can be traced back to 1988 when Karen Davis was an officer cadet with the University Training Plan for Non-Commissioned Members (UTPNCM) in the Canadian Forces. Under the tutelage of Dr. Linda Christiansen-Ruffman, Saint Mary's University, the world became full of possibilities. Karen is indebted to the inspiration and encouragement of Dr. Christiansen-Ruffman, at a time when the future of women in operational roles in the Canadian Forces was anything but *fait accompli*, and at a time when Karen was naively unaware of the contributions of those women who served before her. Although this volume could not have been imagined at that time, it is equally true that the first steps in the journey to its fruition were made possible by the insight and support of Dr. Christiansen-Ruffman.

The realization of many aspects of this project were made possible with the Academic Research Programme of the Royal Military College of Canada. Dr. Bélanger is very thankful for the support received from Dr. Joel J. Sokolsky, Principal, for his inspiring encouragement in all of her academic endeavours, including her participation to the publication of this book. She would also like to acknowledge the support of Commodore William S. Truelove, Commandant, for the activities surrounding the Naval Centennial. Many thanks to Dr. Bélanger's research assistant, Michelle Moore, for her constant and enduring efforts. Finally, Dr. Bélanger would like to thank her Commanding Officer at HMCS CATARAQUI, Lieutenant-Commander Susan Long-Poucher, a truly inspiring role model, as well as the Executive Officer, Lieutenant-Commander John Leighton, who introduced her to so many "salty dips".

We would also like to acknowledge the valuable contributions of the Navy Command Historian, Richard Gimblett, and of the Canadian War Museum Historian, Andrew Burtch, for providing us with precious information. Similarly, we would like to say thank you to the *The Salty Dips* Committee of the Ottawa Branch of the Naval Officers Association of Canada.

The opportunity to create a volume such as this simply would not exist without the leadership and logistical support of the Canadian Defence Academy (CDA) Press, and the Canadian Forces Leadership Institute (CFLI). Since 2004, the editor of the CDA Press and former Director of CFLI, Colonel Bernd Horn, has supported numerous initiatives regarding women and leadership in the Canadian Forces under the auspices of CFLI. Colonel Horn is keenly aware of the importance of providing an opportunity to all members of the CF to share their experience and knowledge, and has provided ready access to the resources of CDA Press to see this volume through to completion. Our sincere appreciation is extended to both Colonel Horn and the current Director of CFLI, Lieutenant-Colonel Jeff Stouffer, for their support of this project.

Melanie Denis is a critical CFLI resource who has been available to the editors in completing this volume. An outstanding Project Manager by profession, Melanie is by nature an exceptionally cooperative, innovative, resourceful and industrious individual. Her guidance and expertise have kept us on course throughout this project, and we are very grateful.

As editors, we are very proud of the final product. The 17 Wing Publishing Office staff have once again demonstrated their expertise and professionalism. The edit, layout and design of both the content and cover of this manuscript have resulted in a volume in which we can all take great pride.

TABLE OF CONTENTS

FOREWORD

Anniversaries are times for celebration and contemplation, and the navy centennial is no different. This year we look back on 100 years of our navy's accomplishments in peace and war, even as we look forward to consider the implications of what the next 100 years may hold for us. *Transforming Traditions: Women, Leadership and the Canadian Navy*, is also a work of celebration and contemplation, on an issue of great importance to the navy as a national institution.

Today, every sailor is a sailor, regardless of gender, sexual preference or race. But it wasn't always so. It took great courage on the part of many individuals and persistent leadership to make it happen, and the journey wasn't easy. But today's navy is stronger, more effective, and more relevant because we embraced what society deemed to be important and successfully integrated it within our culture as a fighting institution.

This is the major lesson I draw from the stories in these pages, told by women who are proud of their service and accomplishments, even if their contributions weren't as valued once by their navy as they are so clearly valued now.

Women have served in the navy for almost 70 years, the full span of which is represented in this volume. By bringing even a small sampling of that collective experience within one cover, the editors have done our navy a great service— permitting us to celebrate women's experiences and achievements in the navy, and to contemplate what their collective contributions have truly meant to our institution.

Vice-Admiral P. Dean McFadden, CMM, CD
Commander Maritime Command

she describes her experience as a female in a hard sea trade as one characterized by constant reminders that women were still not fully valued and accepted in the seagoing environment, an absence of female role models, and a surplus of poor leadership. She enrolled in university to prepare herself for release and transition to another career. As a result, she found herself on a journey of discovery, one that provided her with the knowledge and tools to further develop her leadership ability based on a clearer understanding of her potential and identity as a woman and member of the CF. Today, she believes that the operational culture of the navy still has some catching up to do with CF leadership doctrine. As a PO1, she also believes that she has a responsibility to contribute to that change by sharing her leadership experiences and supporting junior women to ensure that they have every opportunity to develop to their full potential.

One of the well established traditions in the navy is the seven toasts of the day. When LCdr Nancy Setchell joined the navy in 1995, the original toasts were still in practice. In Chapter 15, she describes the old toasts as well as the new toasts that were introduced in 1997 upon recognition by the Naval Board that the old toasts were no longer appropriate and did not reflect the reality of today's navy. One of the new realities they were referring to was, of course, the integration of women. Although three toasts were changed and two were altered slightly, LCdr Setchell notes that in some cases leaders continue to support the use of the old toasts. She maintains that such practices not only undermine the progress that has been made in integrating women into the navy, but also presents a challenge to the values that the navy represents to its members and Canadians today.

In Chapter 16, Sub-Lieutenant (SLt) Louise Walton's testimony of her experience as a PO1 Main Propulsion Supervisor in the Naval Reserve reflects the challenges undertaken by servicewomen who have led the way in male-dominated domains. She acknowledges the difficulties, but importantly, she has not let them stand in her way. She believes that women in leadership roles owe it to themselves and the CF to maximize their personal and collective leadership potential. Her advice: self-reflect and take an honest inventory of your strengths and weaknesses; make the decision to address shortcomings; encourage each other to pursue challenges; and remember that people are always watching when you are in a leadership position. Similar to PO1 Mondelli, SLt Walton's advice and experience reinforce the importance of acknowledging and sharing your leadership challenges and strategies to strengthen not only your leadership but contribute to the development of others – think of all the things that infuriated and discouraged you as a junior sailor and try not to repeat them; treat people how you expect and demand to be treated; and perhaps most significant, be the change you want to see.

LS Geneviève Jobin and Private (Pte) Lorraine van Rensburg are those serving members that have the "last word". With approximately 10 and 3.5 years military service, respectively, these authors are the only junior NCMs to contribute to this volume. Chapter 17 reflects what they have learned about leadership during their time in the CF, primarily from the example and input of senior NCMs and officers. The chapter also reflects their pride as members of the navy and the CF, their respect for the positive leadership that they have experienced among navy women, and their optimism for the future. Their analysis considers navy policy and doctrine as it has developed and impacted the integration of women in recent decades, as well as the experience of women. LS Jobin and Pte van Rensburg acknowledge the progress that women have experienced, and also suggest that the navy could be more innovative in its efforts to recruit and retain women; provide support to families; and enhance morale by reducing barriers between NCMs and officers. Regarding women and leadership, they believe that leadership is gender neutral; however, leadership is still often judged based on traditional gender stereotypes.

In Chapter 18, Dr. Stéphanie A.H. Bélanger explores female leadership in the Canadian navy through the analysis of ten testimonies of naval officers, serving either in the Reserve or the Regular Force. She illustrates the tension between the will of these women to serve the navy first and the need to impose themselves as serving female members by practising leadership in ways that draw on their strengths as women. Whether they consider their role to be gender based or neutral, they all strive to be gender neutral, without losing their identity as a woman. Dr. Bélanger's analysis explores whether the negative relation of femininity to war, that she attributes to various studies, is evident through the experiences of women in the navy. She concludes that such negative attributions are no longer present, although cautions that her sample is limited and thus may not represent the broader naval and CF experience. As such, Dr. Bélanger is hopeful that further study will be conducted to learn more about gender and soldier/sailor identity in the CF.

Chapter 19 presents research that was originally conducted by the Chief of Maritime Staff (CMS) in 2001/2002 in an effort to better understand the lessons that had been learned from the first decade of mixed gender crews on HMC Ships. As the primary research officer, LCdr Lynn Bradley conducted 26 interviews with Commanding Officers, Executive Officers and Cox'ns (all male at the time), to collect and synthesize "best practices" that could be used to assist future leaders of mixed gender ships. From the perspective of senior leaders in the navy, she concluded that the presence of women on ships was simply no longer an issue. However, as the interviews included only senior leaders, and from the perspective of these leaders themselves, these findings cannot be generalized to all serving personnel in the navy. As a result, LCdr Bradley recommends that her research be considered no more than a mid-course review to be followed by further research and analysis of the changing culture of the navy as women become more integrated and increasingly visible in leadership roles.

The research presented by LCdr Lynn Bradley and LCdr Debbie Pestell in Chapter 20 was originally conducted by the CMS in 1999 to inform senior leaders regarding the employment of women in submarines. Although a number of important factors such as crewing and bunk management, privacy, health and medical care issues, and the psychological aspects of mixed gender crews needed to be carefully addressed during a transition period, the study concluded that there was no longer sufficient reason to exclude women from submarine service. With the acquisition of the new VICTORIA-class submarines in the late 1990s, some of the original concerns regarding privacy on the previous OBERON-class submarine no longer applied. A decision was made in 2001 to permit women to serve on Canadian submarines and in 2003 the first two women joined a submarine crew. Based on the experience of female submariners since that time, the authors discuss numerous lessons learned, including those in regard to medical and health practices.

The inclusion of women in submarine service represents entry into the "final frontier" from a naval perspective. Women are now eligible to serve in all naval occupations and sub-occupations and have qualified to serve and are serving in most. Women have become a permanent presence on board all HMC Ships; however, there are still domains in which very few women have qualified and served, leaving the contribution of women in those areas inconsistent over time. The ultimate frontier is, of course, the senior leadership of the navy. Women are commanding ships at sea. In 2003, Lieutenant-Commander Marta Mulkins became the first female Commander of a Canadian warship when she took command of **HMCS KINGSTON**, a coastal defence vessel; and in 2009, Commander Josée Kurtz became the first female to command a major warship when she assumed command of **HMCS HALIFAX**, a HALIFAX-class multi-role patrol frigate. The future of women leaders in the navy remains to be seen; however, it looks very positive. The leaders who have contributed to this volume convey a sense of the high quality of leadership that has led women to their current status in the navy, and will capably contribute to the future of the navy.

1   Veronica Strong-Boag and Anita Clair Fellman (1991) Introduction, in Veronica Strong-Boag and Anita Clair Fellman (eds.) *Re-thinking Canada: The Promise of Women's History*. (Toronto: Copp Clark Pitman Ltd.), 2.

2   The term "Wren" originated with the initials of the Women's Royal Naval Service (WRNS) in Britain. The addition of 'C' in Canada to signify the WRCNS made no difference – members of the WRCNS were still referred to as Wrens. Rosamond "Fiddy" Greer *The Girl's of the King's Navy*, (Victoria, BC: Sono Nis Press, 1983), 11.

CHAPTER 1

Once a Wren, Always a Wren: The Experience and Contribution of Canada's Wrens, 1942-2010

Lieutenant-Commander (retired) Karen D. Davis

Lieutenant-Commander (retired) Karen D. Davis, CD, MA, is a defence scientist with Defence Research and Development Canada, currently assigned to the Canadian Forces Leadership Institute. She holds a Master of Arts in Sociology from McGill University and is a PhD candidate in the War Studies program at the Royal Military College of Canada. Karen served in the Canadian Forces from 1978-2000 as an oceanographic operator and a personnel selection officer. She has published numerous papers on gender in the Canadian Forces, including the experience of women in the combat arms in Canada in the early 1990s. She is a contributing writer and the editor of *Women and Leadership in the Canadian Forces: Perspectives and Experience* (2007), and *Cultural Intelligence & Leadership: An Introduction for Canadian Forces Leaders* (2009).

> …women, like men, need their history. The sense of self depends on having a sense of one's past, and to the extent that modern women have been denied, in the historical canon, all but the faintest glimpses of their own history, they are like victims of amnesia. *Alison Prentice and Ruth Pierson*[1]

As the Second World War ended, a chapter in the history of Canadian women came to a close. During the war years nearly 50,000 had served in the women's services of the Canadian armed forces,[2] including over 7,000 women who served in the Women's Royal Canadian Naval Service (WRCNS)[3] as Wrens. The end of the war meant that like many other Canadian women who had gained employment outside the home in support of the war effort, their services were no longer required. The Canadian Women's Army Corps (CWAC), the Royal Canadian Air Force Women's Division (WD), and the WRCNS were disbanded. Although the WRCNS was a relatively short-lived organization, the WRCNS contribution to the Canadian war effort was significant. As a result, the legacy of those first Wrens[4] has been with us since 1946. In spite of the CF dark green uniform, which was common across the Canadian Forces (CF) sea, land and air

1

environments throughout the 1970s and 1980s, women in the navy were referred to as Wrens well into the 1980s.

In 1989, with approximately 10 years of service in the CF sea environment, I was given an opportunity to explore some of the history that had a direct impact on me as a woman in the military. In partial fulfillment of my Bachelor of Arts (Honours) in sociology at Saint Mary's University in Halifax, I interviewed ten women who had served in the WRCNS and Royal Canadian Naval (Reserve) (RCN(R)). This chapter draws on that experience to provide an introduction to those women who served in uniform as Wrens during the Second World War, Korean War and postwar period leading to the permanent presence of women in the Royal Canadian Navy in 1955. The contributions of those women who served in the military during the Second World War continue to impact the growing legacy of women within the military. In addition, their experience has impacted the historical literature regarding the participation of women in the Second World War, and many Wrens continue to support the naval community through their affiliation with Wren Associations and other organizations that support veterans across Canada.

The opportunity to meet and learn about the Wrens who came before me occurred at the same time that the role of women in the military was under debate in Canada. In 1985, the National Action Committee (NAC) on the Status of Women in Canada took a stand that did not support the participation of women in the military; however, NAC did concede that if women did serve in the military, they should be treated equal to men.[5] Within the military, the suitability of women to serve in all roles was contested. Canadian Forces Administrative Order (CFAO) 49-15, issued in 1986, clearly articulated the potential negative impact of women on operational effectiveness,

> ...in order not to jeopardize the operational effectiveness dictated by the needs of national security, the composition of some units will remain single-gender male...in a number of others, there will be a minimum male component.[6]

The Wrens that I spoke to in 1989 in Halifax reinforced my sense of belonging within the CF, as well as my sense of pride and identity in my naval roots, in spite of the debates regarding women and operational effectiveness. Although these Wrens believed their experience was quite different from currently serving military women, they were interested in opportunities to be more involved with them. In particular, they believed there was a lack of esprit de corps among military women in comparison to that which existed among the early Wrens. They were also interested in the future of women in the navy and asked me many questions about my own experience and the opportunities available to me in the navy. In addition, I was asked several times how I felt about women going to sea. Although some were skeptical, I imagined that most of them would have jumped at the opportunity if presented with it at a different time. And although the context was different, I also discovered that there is much that we can learn from their experiences. What follows is but an introduction to their contributions to the navy.

Six of the ex-Wrens that I interviewed served in the WRCNS between 1942 and 1946, with periods of service varying from 20 months to just over four years. Out of these six, three also joined the RCN(R) between 1951 and 1954, and one of these women continued to serve from 1955 to 1958, as a member of the RCN(R). In addition, three of the Wrens initially joined the RCN(R) between 1951 and 1954 and served on Continuous Naval Duty (CND) for approximately three years. The tenth Wren served in the Women's Royal Naval Service (WRNS) in Great Britain from 1948 to 1955, subsequently moved to Canada with her family and served in the Royal Canadian Navy (RCN) from 1956 to 1961. These Wrens shared many similar experiences and memories; however, the brief introductions that follow provide a glimpse into those experiences that were also unique.

Edythe served in the WRCNS from 1943 to 1946, and spent much of her time working at the Central Victualling Depot in Halifax. She is proud of her navy background, admits that Wrens are a "clannish group", even today, and chuckled as she told me that she married a fellow in the army who did not like the navy!

Shirley joined the WRCNS in 1943 and served as a Sick Berth Attendant (SBA) until 1946. Although she has mostly fond memories of her land-based experiences in the navy, she did not think too much of a long boat ride across the Sydney harbor, and remembers being called a "prairie gopher" during the ordeal!

Gwen joined in 1944 and, unlike many of the women in the WRCNS, she was sent to Saskatoon where she worked in supply until 1945. She told me about a Petty Officer who liked to push his weight around; she did not always go along with him and as a result, she told me that she was "in the you know what" all the time!

Doreen was among one of the first drafts of Wrens to arrive at Stadacona in 1943, and subsequently served in the WRCNS as a Captain's Office Writer ("COW" as she humourously pointed out to me) until 1946. She takes her naval service in her stride, and is proud Wrens were able to show the men what women could do. Doreen also trained with the RCN(R) in the early 1950s.

Pat served in the WRCNS as a Wardroom Assistant from 1942 to 1946 and also served in the RCN(R) on CND as a paywriter from 1951 to 1952. She remarked that it was crazy that she had to get out when she had a family. By 1989, she had worked for the navy for 24 years as a civilian employee, in addition to her naval service…as she said, she might just as well have stayed in!

Bernice served in the WRCNS from 1942 to 1946, in the RCN(R) on CND from 1951 to 1955, and continued to serve in the RCN from 1955 to 1958 after a permanent women's division was established. Her experiences, which include travelling to Newfoundland on the "Lady Rodney" in 1945 as she (the ship) was chased by an enemy submarine, and representing Canadian Wrens at Queen Elizabeth's Coronation in 1953, made her navy experience both harrowing and rewarding!

Eleanor joined the RCN(R) and served on CND as an Engineer Officer's Writer from 1951 to 1954. Her naval service was a good experience, and she enjoyed meeting many people. Eleanor says it was kind of a "skylark" really, but she admits that she is envious of the improved pay and greater freedom which servicewomen enjoy today.

Ruth experienced the Second World War as a child and since that time had wanted to join the navy. She served in the RCN(R) on CND from 1951 to 1955, with most of that time spent working in Communications in Coverdale, New Brunswick. Her free time was often spent with navy friends and participating in sports such as basketball and softball…or a last minute detour to Halifax on the way to the laundromat when the mood struck her and some of her friends!

Betty joined the RCN(R) in 1954 and served on CND until 1957 as a Medical Assistant. She remembers that it was quite different than going to an office job at 9 o'clock in the morning, and still thinks that the military is a good experience for women. By 1989, Betty had worked for the air force as a civilian for 16 years.

Joyce served in the Women's Royal Naval Service (WRNS) in Britain from 1948 to 1955, and in the RCN from 1956 to 1961. Her service in Canada took her to various spots in Nova Scotia, as well as to the Canadian National Exhibition in Toronto to represent Wrens at the naval display. Joyce's memories include a brief posting to a ship. She reported on board with her posting instruction and suitcase, much to the surprise of the ship's Captain! Although a well-planned joke that lasted less than one day, it was also a foreshadow of the future.

There's a Spot for You in the Wrens[7]

The WRCNS was established in July 1942, following the establishment of the Canadian Women's Auxiliary Air Force (CWAAF) in July 1941 (which became the RCAF WDs in February 1942), and the CWAC in August 1941.[8] The WRNS, which was originally established in Britain in 1917 and reorganized in 1939, provided the initial leadership of the WRCNS.[9] In January 1942, in anticipation of the establishment of the WRCNS, the RCN sent a request to the British Admiralty for assistance, and three British Wren officers arrived in Canada in May 1942.[10]

Although the WRCNS was based largely on the WRNS example, there was one notable difference. The British WRNS was an auxiliary service, distinct and separate from the Royal Navy, but members of the WRCNS were members of the RCN. Officers and ratings of the WRCNS were subject to the same chain of command and rank structure as well as entitled to the same marks of military respect by all members of the RCN.[11] However, there were differences. Although Wren officers received the King's Commission and held the same ranks as men, Wren officer rank was signified by sky blue stripes and a diamond shaped loop rather than the gold stripes and circular loop that designated rank for male officers.[12] Also, payrates for Wren officers and Wrens were lower than those of RCN men.

The WRNS officers toured Canada to select a group of Canadian women who were deemed suitable to form the foundation of the WRCNS: British subjects, in good health, between the ages of 18 and 45 (officers 21 to 55), and without dependents or children under the age of 16. Sixty-seven Canadian women were selected to undergo training at Kingsmill House in Ottawa in September 1942.

The above criteria continued to influence the recruitment of Wrens; however, Aboriginal women and members of other immigrant communities were recruited to serve in the women's services. It is estimated, for example, that by the end of the Second World War 72 Aboriginal women from the Yukon had served in the women's services.[13] It is difficult to determine the number of Aboriginal women who served overall or within each of the women's services, as race or ethnicity was not included on enlistment papers. Also, not all Aboriginal women admitted or were even aware of their Aboriginal heritage.[14] In any case, it is unlikely that the first class of officers and Leading Hands from Kingsmill House that were prepared to take on the task of building the WRCNS,[15] included women of non-British descent.

In October 1942, the first class of 70 probationary Wrens started basic training in HMCS CONESTOGA in Galt Ontario, under the guidance of two of the British WRNS officers and Canadian Training Officer Isabel Macneill, who had graduated in the first class at Kingsmill House. Isabel Macneill later served as the Executive Officer and Commanding Officer of HMCS CONESTOGA, rose to the rank of Commander, and was the first Canadian Wren to receive the Order of the British Empire (OBE) on June 8, 1944.[16] In January 1943, WRCNS officer Betty Samuels took over the leadership of HMCS CONESTOGA from the WRNS officers, and in September 1943 Commander Adelaide Sinclair was appointed as the Director of Women's Naval Services in Canada, thus becoming the first Canadian woman to be in charge of Canada's Wrens and the first Canadian woman to wear the four executive stripes of the RCN; she became a member of the OBE in January 1945.[17] Phyllis Sanderson, also a member of the first class of Wrens at Kingsmill House, served as the Master-at-Arms at HMCS CONESTOGA for two years, before serving as the first Wren Master-at-Arms at the Canadian Naval Base, HMCS NIOBE, in Glasgow, Scotland; Chief Petty Officer Sanderson received the British Empire Medal on June 14, 1945.[18]

Initially established for a complement of 150 officers and 2,700 ratings, the WRCNS grew throughout the war. The largest number serving at any one time was 5,893, with over 1,000 serving overseas in the United Kingdom (Londonderry; HMCS NIOBE, Scotland; Plymouth; and London) and Newfoundland, as well as New York and Washington, D.C.[19] Most Wrens served in one of over 35 locations in Canada, with the largest concentration at HMCS STADACONA in Halifax.[20] By the end of the war, Wrens were serving in 39 different branches, most of them as messengers, cooks, messwomen, general duty writers and wardroom attendants.[21] Although rare, several Wrens were required to board Allied naval military and coastguard vessels, accompany RCN staff on trial runs or inspections of corvettes, frigates, minesweepers, coastal vessels, or to man harbourcraft, as part of their duties.[22]

According to many Wrens there was never any discussion of the pay and allowance inequities between the Wrens and male members of the RCN.[23] By the end of the war Wren pay rates had increased from two-thirds to four-fifths of the equivalent RCN pay, and was still less than comparable rates of pay for civilian jobs. The difference in pay was originally attributed to the assumption that it would require three women to replace two men, but when analysis proved this incorrect the pay ratio was increased. The remaining difference in pay is attributed to military philosophy, including the fact that women were not permitted in combat roles. For their part, the Wrens were pleased to be able to contribute to the war effort and were satisfied that they could demonstrate their ability to learn quickly and perform their work as well as their male counterparts.[24] When the WRCNS was disbanded at the end of the war, Wrens received almost all of the same allowances and post-discharge benefits as their male counterparts, including support for re-training.

Many believed that in a time of great need Canadian women had joined the services out of a sense of patriotism, and continued service on the part of women was not considered.[25] The WRCNS, like the WD and CWAC, was a temporary organization designed to fulfill manpower shortages with a reserve of womanpower.[26] Rosamond "Fiddy" Greer cites a report given to the Chief of Naval Personnel by the female Director of the WRCNS in 1946 that says that women have served "cheerfully in a time of emergency, but it is doubted whether they would do so readily in peacetime."[27] At the end of the war the Canadian Department of Labour set up vocational training programs for ex-servicewomen which emphasized pre-war traditional roles.[28] Most postwar planners believed that "for most women the primary role should be the one of wife and mother, a role not to be combined, except in the direst of circumstances, with paid employment outside of the home."[29]

In spite of the significant departure from pre-war gender roles and social values that women's military service and labour market participation represented, many historians have concluded that women made very little progress toward equality during the Second World War.[30] For example, Ruth Roach Pierson, in her book *They're Still Women After All: The Second World War and Canadian Womanhood* examines the participation of women in the military services and concludes,

> …the disturbing prospect of female sexual independence led to a tightening of the hold on women of respectable femininity…the immediate legacy of the Second World War was an indisputable reaction against war's upheaval, including the unsettling extent to which women had crossed former sex/gender boundaries. The war's slight yet disquieting reconstruction of womanhood in the direction of equality with men was scrapped for a full-skirted and redomesticated post war model…[31]

Indeed, the title of Pierson's book, *They're Still Women After All*, is borrowed from the title of an article written in 1942 by a Canadian foreign correspondent, expressing men's fears at the wartime sight of many British women taking on formerly male jobs.[32]

Canadian historian Jeff Keshen[33] argues that much first-rate research and analysis has been conducted to explain the basis of social continuity regarding gender roles in spite of war-time blips; however, not enough historical analysis has been devoted to understanding historical change. He acknowledges that Canadian newspapers and magazines in the 1940s do provide evidence of widespread concern regarding the migration of women into the labour market and a desire to restore the patriarchal order once soldiers returned. However, Keshen's analysis concludes that the experiences of women during the Second World War established a wider and stronger base upon which later generations of women could launch more substantial, successful initiatives for gender equity.[34] In fact, in the opinion of at least one woman who served in the military during the war, "… the women's movement was a backlash by women who had taken some part in winning the war and were not prepared to be relegated to the home again." [35]

Women Return to the Navy

Regardless of the emphasis on pre-war gender roles, by the early 1950s Canadian women were once again called upon to participate in the military in support of the Korean War effort. In 1951, approval was given for the establishment of a Women's Reserve in the RCN(R) and approximately 60 officers and 650

Wrens joined.[36] Women have served in the Naval Reserve since that time. In February 1955, the Minister of National Defence announced the establishment of a women's component in the regular force of the RCN,[37] following the Royal Canadian Air Force and the Canadian Army who began enrolling women into their Regular Forces in 1951 and 1954, respectively.[38] This was the first time that Wrens were integrated as members of the Regular Force rather than through a separate organization for women; these Wrens were now members of the RCN and Wren officer rank was signified with gold braid, rather than the sky blue braid previously worn by Wren officers. The first women in the regular RCN were a small group of 35 officers and 365 Wrens, many of whom had come from the RCN(R). Some members of the WRCNS also returned, including Commander Isabel Macneill who, upon request, returned in 1954 as Staff Officer (Wrens) to assist in the creation of a permanent force of Wrens.[39]

By the early 1960s, the future of women in the Regular Force of the three services was in doubt as a result of changing defence policy and a sharp reduction in the need for women with the introduction of more automated equipment in trades where women were concentrated. However, in 1965 the future of women in the Regular Forces was secured with the establishment of a fixed ceiling of 1500 women across the three services, primarily in administrative and support roles. This policy remained in place until the early 1970s when the recommendations of the Royal Commission on the Status of Women in Canada resulted in expanded roles for women and the elimination of the fixed ceiling of 1500.[40]

Clearly, by 1951, those women who pursued non-traditional options such as military service challenged social ideology and postwar economic planning which had expressed a collective sigh of relief when women returned to their roles as housewives and mothers after the war. In addition, those who joined the military in the early 1950s were living in a world which would undoubtedly remember the "whispering campaign" of the Second World War which caused "…fear that servicewomen, removed from parental control and thrown together with men on military bases, would lose their sexual respectability."[41] For example, regarding her decision to join the RCN(R) in 1954, one of the Wrens that I interviewed (Betty) explained,

> It was something I had always wanted to do from the time I was ten or
> eleven. I saw a movie once and it had servicewomen in it and it seemed

exciting. I had always said I was going to do this and I'm not sure my mother was really in total agreement with it. I mean it was what I wanted to do but I'm not sure she thought it was nice for a girl because…and I don't really know why. I think there were a lot of things from wartime with Wrens. You know. I don't know whether it was all talk. I don't think there was much to it really.[42]

Regardless of the challenges and opportunities, by 1951, servicewomen, including the Wrens had become firmly established within public memory.

Once a Wren, Always a Wren

In her address to the Wren reunion in Halifax in 1975, Commander (retired) Isabel Macneill remarked, "A few days ago I celebrated the 33rd anniversary of becoming a Wren. I have been a Wren for half my lifetime."[43] Toward the end of her address, she recited the following:

Blue Smocks
Long talks
Marching around the park
Pork pies
Wrong size
Undressing in the dark
Sick Bay
Wrong Day
Aspirins all expended
Gathering gash
Time for hash
Lines that never ended
Pay parade
Troubles fade
Never felt so well
Gone now
But how
Steaks at the hotel
Now drafts

All laughed
Just got what I wanted
East West
Home's Best
The Bytown draft's undaunted

Little Wren
Now a hen
Pride of all the Navy
Say when, if again
Yes, No, or Maybe

For most of us it is NO

If again
Little Wren
Now a hen
Won't be seen
Wearing Green![44]

She immediately adds, "However the spirit will go on – as long as there are Armed Forces.[45]

Upon disbandment of the WRCNS in 1946, Wren Associations were established in communities across Canada. In May 1946, Lieutenant Frances Parson drafted a letter suggesting that a Wren club be formed and offered her support. As a result of the initiative of several Wrens and the support of serving male officers at CHIPPAWA, the first general Wren Association (Chippawa Division) meeting was held on board HMCS CHIPPAWA, in Winnipeg on the 27th of September 1946. Officers and Convenors were identified for the roles of President, Past President (as the group was initially inaugurated in May 1946), Vice President, Secretary, Treasurer, Social Convenor (and assistants), Hospital Convenor (and assistants), and a News & Publicity Editor. It was agreed that money would be collected at each meeting for candy, cigarettes, etc. for the ex-Wrens at the Deer Lodge Hospital,[46] as a key purpose of the group was to provide support, care, and establish contact with ex-Wrens. Also, Wrens leaving the WRCNS in the Winnipeg area found that they had lost contact with civilian friends, but found many friends and welcome support at HMCS CHIPPAWA.[47] At the time Wren groups were forming across Canada and meeting notes indicate that these groups would be known as Wren Associations (Local Division), and therefore the Winnipeg group would be the Wren Association (Chippawa Division).[48]

In its first few years the Wrens at Chippawa Division were very active. From 1947-1952 there were 175 members, a number that dwindled to 30 by 1992. In early 1949, for example, they organized a dry canteen to care for underage sailors; the canteen was turned over to the RCN in 1955 with the repeal of prohibition. Fundraising activities included teas, the first of which was opened by the wife of the Lieutenant-Governor of Manitoba, and Sadie Hawkins dances that were held on the parade deck at HMCS CHIPPAWA. In 1950, during the Winnipeg flood, over 150 Wrens stood volunteer shifts to keep the canteen open 24 hours/day for military members who were assisting with dyking and pumping water. Over the years, Chippawa Wrens have also been involved in Ship's Company Christmas parties which supported underprivileged children, organized three Wrens Reunions (1963, 1988 and 2006),[49] and numerous other naval-related celebrations and commemorative events.

The Wrens that I interviewed in 1989, with the exception of one, were contacted through an inquiry to the Royal Canadian Naval Association (RCNA) in Halifax; nine of them were active in the Wren Association of Nova Scotia. The Wren Association of Nova Scotia was an informal social group which gathered for what was described to me as "eating meetings" and socializing. The Association became more formal when called upon to organize and support specific events. In 1989, for example, they were beginning to organize a Canadian Wren Reunion in 1992 in Halifax, which would celebrate 50 years from the first service of females in the navy in Canada (1942-1992). Although Wren Associations are not formally affiliated with the RCNA, the Wren Association frequently used the facilities of the RCNA in Halifax. Several of the Wrens that I interviewed, along with their husbands, were also members of the RCNA.

The shared experiences and characteristics of the Halifax Wrens, since their active naval service, are very particular to this group and as such cannot be generalized to the broader experiences of Canadian Wrens. Regardless, their experience did provide me with a glimpse into the history and experiences of women in the navy in Canada. The continued contact which these women enjoyed with other ex-Wrens both reflected their past naval experience and shaped their experience. From varying Canadian backgrounds, these women had grown together over the years as they shared many experiences, recounted their experiences as serving Wrens and added to their shared experiences through participation in meetings, reunions, etc. Being an ex-Wren, for these women, represented not only their time in uniform but also participation in ongoing Wren activities. Their active military service years remained a highlight in their lives, but being a Wren did not stop when their naval service ended.

Many of those who did not serve again after the Second World War were not able to do so because they were married with children by 1951. One of the ex-Wrens admitted that she felt a bit of jealousy toward those who were able to join the RCN(R) for CND. Another ex-Wren expressed lingering resentment regarding her medical release in the 1950s due to pregnancy; in her case, she lost not only employment but all entitlement to unemployment benefits as pregnancy was considered medically unfit at that time. It would be another 20 years before women could serve after the birth of child. This was one of the recommendations that appeared in the report of the Royal Commission on the Status of Women in Canada in 1970; beginning in 1971, servicewomen in Canada were permitted to serve after the birth of a child and could be enrolled if they were married.[50]

In spite of widespread social objections to women in military service and the moratorium placed on women's services at the end of the war, many of the women who served during the Second World War and Korean War took great pride in their contributions as Wrens and continued to distinguish themselves as Wrens in the years and decades following their military service. Since the first Wren Reunion held in Toronto in 1950, Wren reunions have been organized and hosted by Wren Associations across Canada. Over 1,000 participants were seated for dinner[51] at the first reunion and 15 reunions followed;[52] the last reunion, held in Winnipeg in 2006, was identified as the "final" reunion. In support of ongoing reunions, the Toronto Wren Association raised $2,000 and made it available as seed money to Wren Associations for the reunions that were hosted after the first one in 1950. This continued until the last reunion when it was left with the Wren Association (Chippawa Division), and contributed to commemorative and other initiatives regarding Wrens.[53]

In 1972, as part of the Wren reunion hosted by the Wren Association of Toronto, over 600 Wrens gathered at the site of HMCS CONESTOGA in Cambridge, Ontario (formerly Guelph) to witness the unveiling of the Jenny statue commemorating the WRCNS and celebrate the 30th anniversary of the WRCNS in Canada. Former Director of the WRCNS, Adelaide Sinclaire, and former Commanding Officer of HMCS CONESTOGA, Isabel Macneill, were among those who participated.[54] The Wrens were also taken on a tour of the Grandview School for Girls, once the site of HMCS CONESTOGA. In speaking with the girls at the school, Wren Jean Brodie (Nugent), discovered that they thought that the Wrens were former inmates of the correctional school for girls, that was converted to become HMCS CONESTOGA in 1942![55]

Those who celebrated in Cambridge also enjoyed a performance by the *Jenny Wren Revue*. The *Revue* was formed in 1972 to entertain at the banquet following the unveiling of the "Jenny Wren" statue[56] and since then the group has performed across the country, including singing and dancing at Wren Reunions (11 in total), naval functions, legions, and other events. All of the women in the *Revue* served in the Second World War or in the immediate postwar years.[57] In December 2009, for example, the *Revue* performed for the St. George's Society in Toronto and were applauded and cheered heartily. According to *Revue* member, Margaret Haliburton, the age of *Revue* members impresses their audiences. Those who performed at the St. George Society ranged in age from 70 to 89. The average age of the Second World War Wren members was 87, and the two post-Second World War Wren members were 70 and 75 years old. As result of their December performance, the *Revue* was approached to appear on a seniors' TV program.[58]

The Wren Association of Toronto has published approximately 10 newsletters every year since its first meeting in 1946, which are sent to ex-Wrens across Canada, the United States and the United Kingdom; the newsletter has been considered the "tie that binds" for ex-Wrens who live in distant and isolated communities. Through the Toronto association, the Canadian Wrens have also maintained contact with international Wren associations including the WAVES (Women Accepted for Volunteer Emergency Service) in the United States and the MARVA in the Netherlands.[59]

In 2002, Wren associations across Canada celebrated the 60th anniversary of Wrens (1942-2002), marked by the establishment of the WRCNS in 1942.

Fewer than 500 Wrens attended the reunion in Edmonton in 2002 compared to approximately 1,000 who attended the reunion in Kingston in 1995.[60] The ex-Wren associations are experiencing increasing difficulty with sustainment, as most of the original Wrens who were members of the WRCNS have passed away. Wrens who served in the Naval Reserve since 1950 have been instrumental in ensuring the continued life of the ex-Wren associations. In 2006, the Wren Association of Toronto reported "We look forward to more years of fellowship, as so many of our newest members are postwar, young and energetic."

In the program of the *Final Wren Reunion* in 2006, Wren associations from Toronto, Nova Scotia, Vancouver, Ottawa, Chippawa Division in Winnipeg, Ottawa, and Edmonton, as well as the "Wrenship" from London, Ontario reported on their recent activities. Group memberships at the time ranged from eight members in the London Wrenship to 112 members with the Vancouver Wren Association.[61] Wrens also continue to meet in Kingston, Ontario at the naval reserve unit, HMCS CATARAQUI.[62] In some cases such as Kingston, the Wren Associations maintain contact with the naval reserve and other naval-related organizations. In addition, some of the Wren Associations are reaching out to broaden membership and participation. For example, the Wren Association of Toronto, welcomes the membership and participation of all former members of the WRCNS and of women from the RCN and Sea Element of the Canadian Armed Forces and its reserves, the WRNS, Commonwealth and other Allied forces.[63]

The Wren/ex-Wren associations across Canada have devoted considerable effort to ensuring that the history of the WRCNS as well as the spirit of those who served in the WRCNS, live on as they take their place in naval history.[64] Ex-Wrens and Wren Associations have raised funds, organized, and coordinated with other organizations to ensure the dedication of numerous commemorative plaques,[65] statues,[66] stained glass windows,[67] etc. to individual Wrens, the WRCNS, the three women's services, nursing sisters, and sailors. In 2008, on behalf of the Wrens across Canada, the Wren Association of Toronto began the process of introducing and promoting a commemorative rose in recognition of the centennial of the Canadian navy, 1910-2010. The Wrens chose a dark red velvet rose developed by Agriculture and Agri-Food Canada and grown exclusively by J.C. Bakker and Sons Limited.

The Navy Centennial rose is named "AC™ Navy Lady" as a dedication to the women who served in the WRCNS and the women who continue to serve today in Canada's navy. In 2010, the Wrens dedicate the rose as a tribute to all of the men and women who served at sea and ashore in the Canadian navy, past, present and future.[68]

Commemorating the Past to Build the Future

The legacy that Wrens offer us today as a result of their military service and their continuing service to the naval community is substantial. While much effort has been dedicated to ensuring their place in military history, through the activities of Wren Associations in particular, there is much more to be done to capture and integrate the experiences and contributions of Wrens into the cultural memory of the navy. As I explored the early experiences of naval women in Canada, there were few references regarding Canadian military women and just one documented experience of a Wren was available to me in 1989. My personal copy of *The Girls of the King's Navy*, published by WRCNS member Rosamond "Fiddy" Greer in 1983, became my close companion. Since that time, several important sources of Wren experience have been published. In 2001, the Department of National Defence published the experiences of 58 civilian and military women during the Second World War, under the cover of *Equal to the Challenge: An Anthology of Women's Experiences During World War II*; 10 of these entries reflect the experience of women who served in the WRCNS. In 2006, Wren Audrey Sim Shortridge published *On the Double Matilda: One Woman's Story of Life as a Wren*, and Anne Kallin's 2007 history of the training of Wrens during the Second World War, *Proudly She Marched Volume 2: Women's Royal Canadian Naval Service*, draws on the experiences of some 300 Wrens. Available documentation of the experiences and contributions of Canadian military women, including those who served in the navy, from 1951-1967 remains quite scarce.

The Wrens who served in the WRCNS, the RCN(R) and the RCN between 1942 and 1965 – the Wrens and the postwar Wrens who served before the permanent presence of women was established – took great pride in their contribution to the Canadian navy. Although many of them were denied anything beyond a few years of full-time service, through ongoing membership in Wren Associations across Canada, they continued to develop their identity as Wrens, support and commemorate Wren veterans, and continue to contribute to this day in numerous ways to the navy and naval veterans in Canada. For example, as a result of funds remaining after the 2006 Wren Reunion in Winnipeg, primarily due to the fundraising and coordinating efforts of the Wren Association (Chippawa Division), the Naval Museum of Manitoba is establishing a permanent exhibit dedicated to the women who have and are still serving in the Canadian navy. It is their hope that women who served in the Canadian navy 1942-1945; 1951-1967; and 1967-present, will contribute their stories and memorabilia to this exhibit.[69]

Today, women have access to all roles in the navy and most operational roles have been successfully filled by at least one woman. Those who serve today participate in the cultural processes of the navy which are, for the most part, practiced as gender inclusive rites of passage and traditions that build identity, belonging, and acceptance. Such customs and traditions are deeply revered and honoured, but also taken for granted by many. As the navy celebrates its centennial, it is important to remember that although women in uniform are not fully integrated into 100 years of history in the same way as men, women have contributed to the Canadian navy for many decades.

There is no doubt that the first women in uniform contributed to the status of women in the navy and CF even though many who served, during the Second World War in particular, were not interested in service beyond their contribution to the war effort. In 2010, the picture in the rear view mirror is a linear and logical history of the increasing inclusion of women into all aspects of military naval service in Canada. However, the post-Second World War social and economic climate emphasized pre-war domestic roles for women, including those who had served in the military. In spite of what seemed to indicate the end of women in the navy, Canadian Wrens established postwar organizations and continued to contribute to the naval community. Concurrently, the participation of women in the uniformed naval community became more permanent and significant. It is not likely that anyone imagined that sixty years later women would not only be serving on Her Majesty's Canadian Ships at sea, but would be commanding those ships at sea![70]

1   Ruth Pierson and Alison Prentice, "Feminism and the Writing and Teaching of History", in Geraldine Finn & Angela Miles (eds.) *Feminism in Canada: From Pressure to Politics.* (Montréal, QC: Black Rose Books, 1982), 110.

2   Ruth Roach Pierson, *They're Still Women After All: The Second World War and Canadian Womanhood*. (Toronto: McClelland and Stewart, 1986), 9.

3   Nancy Miller Chenier, "Canadian Women and War: A Long Tradition," *Oracle*. No.54, National Museum of Man. (Ottawa, ON: National Museums of Canada, 1984).

4   The term "Wren" originated with the initials of the Women's Royal Naval Service (WRNS) in Britain. The addition of 'C' in Canada to signify the WRCNS made no difference – members of the WRCNS were still referred to as Wrens. Rosamond "Fiddy" Greer, *The Girl's of the King's Navy*. (Victoria, BC: Sono Nis Press, 1983), 11.

5   *Feminist Action Feministe*, "Women in the Military: NAC takes a stand," (October 1985).

6   Canadian Human Rights Commission. (1989). Tribunal Decision 3/89 Between: ISABELLE GAUTHIER, JOSEPH G. HOULDEN, MARIE-CLAUDE GAUTHIER, GEORGINA ANN BROWN Complainants and CANADIAN ARMED FORCES Respondent (Decision rendered on February 20, 1989), 32.

7   Slogan on a W.R.C.N.S. Recruiting Pamphlet, presented in Anne Kallin, *Proudly She Marched: Training Canada's World War II Women in Waterloo County, Volume 2: Women's Royal Canadian Naval Service*. (Kitchener-Waterloo, Ontario: Canadian Federation of University Women, 2007), 70.

8   Ruth Roach Pierson, *They're Still Women After All*, 95.

9   Rosamond "Fiddy" Greer, *The Girls of the King's Navy*. (Victoria, BC: Sono Nis Press, 1983), 11.

10   Rosamond "Fiddy" Greer, *The Girl's of the King's Navy*, 14.

11   Anne Kallin, *Proudly She Marched*, 62.

12   Rosamond "Fiddy" Greer, *The Girl's of the King's Navy*, 32. According to Greer, this was a carryover from the design of the British Wren uniform in 1918, after the British Treasury forbade the use of gold for members of the WRNS (considered it a waste of gold because gold was the prerogative of men. See Vera Laughton Matthews, *Blue Tapestry*, (London, England: Hollis & Carter, 1948).

13   Janice Summerby, *Native Soldiers: Foreign Battlefields*, (Ottawa, ON: Veteran's Affairs Canada, 1993), 20.

14   Grace Poulin, *Invisible Women: WWII Aboriginal Servicewomen in Canada*. Unpublished Master's Thesis submitted in partial fulfillment of Master of Arts, (Peterborough, ON: Trent University, 2006); Poulin's research draws on the experience of 14 Aboriginal Servicewomen who served in the CWAC, two who served in the RCAF WD, and one who served with the WRCNS (Gertrude Fraser).

15   Rosamond "Fiddy" Greer, *The Girl's of the King's Navy*, 15, 18.

16   Rosamond "Fiddy" Greer, *The Girl's of the King's Navy*, 39.

17   Anne Kallin, *Proudly She Marched*, 124.

18   Rosamond "Fiddy" Greer, *The Girl's of the King's Navy*, 42. In total, 22 Wren Officers and Ratings became a member of the Order of the British Empire or were awarded the British Empire Medal or a King's Commendation. See Rosamond "Fiddy" Greer, 151-156 for all citations; see also Anne Kallin, *Proudly She Marched*, 125.

19   Rosamond "Fiddy" Greer, *The Girl's of the King's Navy*, 18.

20   Anne Kallin, *Proudly She Marched*, 99.

21   Rosamond "Fiddy" Greer, *The Girl's of the King's Navy*, 16. Although not an exhaustive list, other trades included visual signaler, wireless operator, sailmaker, draftsman, librarian, photographer, naval operations plotter, coder, driver, sick berth attendant, steward, quarters assistant, mess caterer, supply assistant, stenographer, confidential book corrector, postal clerk, secretary, paywriter, telephonist, switchboard operator, teletype operator, and dispatch rider. see also Anne Kallin, *Proudly She Marched*.

22   Anne Kallin, *Proudly She Marched*, 100.

23   Anne Kallin, *Proudly She Marched*, 62.

24   Anne Kallin, *Proudly She Marched*, 62.

25   For discussion of considerations leading to decision to demobilize the WRCNS see Gilbert Norman Tucker, *The Naval Service of Canada: Its Official History. Vol II. Activities on Shore During the Second World War*, (Ottawa: King's Printer, 1952) (published under the authority of the Minister of National Defence), 482-483; This discussion also appears in Rosamond "Fiddy" Greer, *The Girls of the King's Navy*, 147-148.

26   Ruth Roach Pierson, *They're Still Women After All*, 129-130; Rosamond "Fiddy" Greer, *The Girls of the King's Navy*, 147.

27   Rosamond "Fiddy" Greer, *The Girls of the King's Navy*, 148.

28   Ruth Roach Pierson and Marjorie Cohen, "Women for Work: Government Training Programs for Women, before, during, and after World War II," Michael S. Cross and Gregory S. Kealey (eds.). *Modern Canada 1930s – 1980s* (Toronto: McClelland and Stewart, 1984) 206-243.

29   Ibid., 223.

30   See for example, Karen Anderson, *Wartime Women: Sex Roles, Family Relations and the Status of Women During World War II*. (Westport, Connecticut: Greenwood Press, 1981); Sherna Berger Gluck, *Rosie the Riveter Revisited: Women, The War and Social Change*. (New York: Meridian – New American Library, 1987); Maureen Honey, *Creating Rosie the Riviter: Class, Gender and Propoganda During World War II*. (Amherst: University of Massachusetts Press, 1984); Ruth Roach Pierson, *They're Still Women After All*; and Ruth Roach Pierson and Marjorie Cohen, "Women for Work."

31   Ruth Roach Pierson, *They're Still Women After All*, 220.

32   Ibid., 129.

33   Jeff Keshen, "Revisiting Canada's Civilian Women During World War II," *Histoire sociale/ Social History*. 30 (6, November, 1997): 239-266.

34   Jeff Keshen, "Revisiting Canada's Civilian Women During World War II," 266.

35   Anonymous, *Equal to the Challenge: An Anthology of Women's Experiences During World War II*. (Ottawa, ON: Department of National Defence: Assistant Deputy Minister (Materiel), 2001), 517.

36   Naval Museum of Manitoba, The Naval History of Manitoba, WRENS – A Proud Heritage, A Brief History of the Woman's Royal Canadian Naval Service, <http://www.naval-museum. mb.ca/history/exhibit10.htm>, accessed 30 Nov 2009.

37   Ibid.

38   Suzanne Simpson, Doris Toole, and Cindy Player, "Women in the Canadian Forces: Past, Present and Future," *Atlantis* Vol 4 (spring, Part II, 1979), 226-283.

39   Rosamond "Fiddy" Greer, *The Girls of the King's Navy*, 149.

40   Suzanne Simpson, Doris Toole, and Cindy Player, "Women in the Canadian Forces."

41   Ruth Roach Pierson, *They're Still Women After All*, 170.

42   Interviewee cited in Karen D. Davis, *Women Join the Navy, 1942-1946 and 1951-1954: Social/ Historical Processes and their Decision to Join*, Unpublished paper submitted in fulfillment of the requirements for the degree of Bachelor of Arts (Honours) in the Department of Sociology. (Halifax, NS: Saint Mary's University, 1989).

43   Isabel Macneill, "Talk to Wren Reunion – Halifax Aug 30th, 1975" Copy provided by ex-Wren Shirley Wolfe.

44   "Won't be seen Wearing Green!" refers to the tri-service green uniform that was worn by all Canadian Forces members, regardless of environmental affiliation, after unification in 1969. In 1986, the Canadian Forces began issuing separate environment uniforms, and by 1989 all members were wearing distinct navy, army and air force uniforms.

45   Isabel Macneill, "Talk to Wren Reunion – Halifax Aug 30th, 1975".

46   Minutes of THE FIRST Wren's Association (Chippawa Division) meeting held on board HMCS CHIPPAWA, Winnipeg, MB, on September 27th, 1946, copy provided to author by Chief Petty Officer 1st class (retired) Shirley Brown, December 2009.

47   Lorine Hodgson, undated, "Chippawa Division," provided to author by Wren Association (Chippawa Division) through executive member Shirley Brown, December 2009.

48   Minutes of THE FIRST Wren's Association (Chippawa Division) meeting.

49   Lorine Hodgson, "Chippawa Division."

50   The report of the Royal Commission on the Status of Women in Canada was released in 1970, and included five recommendations specific to the employment of women in the Canadian Forces, including the recommendation that married women be permitted to enroll in the CF

and that servicewomen be permitted to continue service after the birth of a child. This two part recommendation was implemented in 1971. Suzanne Simpson, Doris Toole, and Cindy Player, "Women in the Canadian Forces: Past, Present and Future."

51   E-mail correspondence, Margaret Haliburton to author, 27 November 2009.

52   Subsequent reunions were held as follows: 1958 in Vancouver; 1963 in Winnipeg; 1967 in Hamilton; 1970 in Victoria; 1972 in Toronto/Galt; 1975 in Halifax; 1979 in Ottawa; 1982 in Vancouver; 1985 in Toronto; 1988 in Winnipeg; 1992 in Halifax; 1998 in Kingston; 2002 in Edmonton; and final reunion in Winnipeg in 2006. Date and location of all reunions provided to author by Wren Association of Toronto through Margaret Halifburton.

53   E-mail correspondence, Margaret Haliburton to author, 14 December 2010.

54   Anne Kallin, *Proudly She Marched*, 115.

55   Anne Kallin, *Proudly She Marched*, 115.

56   The "Jenny Wren Statue", located beside the Library in Galt/Cambridge was sculpted by ex-Wren Frances Gage who now resides in Coburg, ON. Frances also grows poppies for the seeds and sells them for the legion, e-mail correspondence, Margaret Haliburton to author, 13 January 2010.

57   Wren Association of Toronto, News Release "60th Anniversary of the Wren Association of Toronto," May 2006. <http://www.thewrens.com/canada/toronto/activities/60thann-toronto.html>, accessed 4 January 2010

58   E-mail correspondence, Margaret Haliburton to author, 5 December 2009.

59   E-mail correspondence, Margaret Haliburton to author, 14 January 2010.

60   CBC Digital Archives, <http://archives.cbc.ca/war_conflict/second_world_war/clips/4979/>, accessed 8 December 2009.

61   Program of the *Final Wren Reunion*, held in Winnipeg, Manitoba, September 15-17, 2006.

62   A WRCNS (Wren) Association announcement for an upcoming meeting on Jan 13, 2010 at HMCS CATARAQUI appeared in a local paper. See for example, *Kingston This Week*, "Community Digest," Thursday, January 7, 2010, 27.

63   The Wren Association of Toronto: <http://www.thewrens.com/canada/toronto/index.htm>, accessed 13 January 2010.

64   See for example, Barbara Duncan, "Serving Canada and Remembering the Women Who Served" Chapter 4 in this volume.

65   See, for example, Barbara Duncan, "Serving Canada and Remembering the Women Who Served."

66   For example, the Wren Association of Toronto led the fundraising efforts for the Jenny Wren statue that was erected and dedicated in 1972 in Cambridge (previously Galt, ON) at the previous site of HMCS CONESTOGA. Documentation provided to author by the Wren Association of Toronto through Margaret Haliburton, December 2009.

67   For example, in 2005 the Wren Association of Toronto funded the installation of a stained glass window in memory of Mary Sweeney at the University of Toronto Hart House Soldier's Tower. Documentation provided to author by the Wren Association of Toronto through Margaret Haliburton, December 2009.

68   The Wren Association of Toronto web site: <http://www.thewrens.com/>, accessed 13 January 2010; and, Canadian Naval Centennial web site: <http://www.navy.forces.gc.ca/centennial/3/3-c_eng.asp?category=121&title=236>, accessed 11 January 2010; the Wren Association of Toronto is holding a ceremonial planting of the Centennial Rose at the "Jenny Wren" statue in Cambridge, 16 May 2010, to be followed by a reception in the nearby Cambridge library, e-mail correspondence, Margaret Haliburton to author, 14 January 2010.

69   Correspondence, Anita Chapman, Ex-Wrens Association Representative, Board of Directors, Naval Museum of Manitoba to Shirley Brown, Wren Association (Chippawa Division), August 2009.

70   In 2003, Lieutenant-Commander Marta Mulkins became the first female Commander of a Canadian warship when she took command of HMCS KINGSTON, a coastal defence vessel with a crew of approximately 37, followed by command of HMCS SUMMERSIDE, also a coastal defence vessel, in 2005. In 2009, Commander Josee Kurtz became the first female to command a major warship when she command assumed of HMCS HALIFAX, a HALIFAX-class multi-role patrol frigate with a crew complement of 225.

CHAPTER 2

Reflections of a Wren:
I Would Do it Again "at the drop of a hat"

Wren Margaret Los (Haliburton)

Margaret Haliburton served in the Women's Royal Canadian Naval Service as a Telegraphic Special Operator from 1942-1946.

I was born in Saskatchewan and moved to Ontario before I was two years old. All of my schooling was completed in Toronto and when I graduated from grade 13 in 1940 I worked for the Bell Telephone Company as a Telephone Repair Clerk. University did not interest me and although I was interested in joining the military, it was not possible for women to join in 1940. In 1942, when the women's services were established, I read the recruiting ads for the army and the air force but somehow could not get enthusiastic about joining. When the navy started recruiting women, I was interested but my mother was quite old and not well. One day she said, "I don't know what's the matter with my daughters. They have no get up and go. If I was young enough I would have been first in line." The next day I joined up! When I get the usual question – why did you join – I say my mother told me to! I think I'm the only one who can say that. Many of the other girls tell me that their families objected to their decision to join and some most violently.

After basic training at HMCS CONESTOGA in Galt, Ontario (now Cambridge) I was sent to HMCS ST. HYACINTHE in Quebec to be trained as a Radio Operator. The camp was being renovated and enlarged and the living conditions – through no fault of the navy – were to put it mildly, primitive. We – some 25 Wrens – were the first girls posted there and lived a most interesting life. Because of the austere living conditions we learned (if we did not already know) how to cope with cold, heat, dust, long hours, homesickness, and especially how to adapt to any circumstance. In spite of the housing problems there were no serious complaints, only the healthy grumbling that is common to service life. In retrospect, I still think it is remarkable that 25 or more women from all walks of life, of all ages and all strangers to each other, lived in such harmony.

After graduating as a Wren Telegraphic Special Operator (Tel so) I worked as a High Frequency Direction Finding (HFDF) Operator known as Huff Duff,[1] responsible for tracking German Submarine Radio Traffic. I was first stationed at #2 Radio Station Gloucester, Ontario, located in a very isolated wooded area. The only "outside" contact was the supply truck that came in every Wednesday. After a few months I was posted to Naval Radio Station Coverdale, New Brunswick, which was the only naval presence in the area. It was in the middle of a cow pasture near the small town of Gunningsville and across the Pedacodiac River from Moncton. The people of Gunningsville offered us friendship. We played baseball with the Royal Canadian Air Force Women's Division (RCAF WDs) and went to dances at the Royal Air Force (RAF), British Air Training Scheme, Manning Pool in Moncton.

The work at Coverdale consisted of spending hours and hours searching the airwaves for a German transmission and seconds of excitement when such a transmission was received. To get to work we one had to cross the pasture rife with cowpats in the summer, and much blowing snow in winter. The HFDF operators of the world were the first to receive the news of Hitler's death and German capitulation. One of our girls could read German and as these messages were sent in plain language, she translated for us as they were transmitted and picked up.

After the German conflict was over, I volunteered to continue with the Japanese war. I was sent to HMCS ST. HYACINTHE to learn Japanese Morse code, which consisted of a few more characters than English Morse code. The problem was that we were expected to use typewriters. It didn't matter that we could copy faster by hand than the others could type. As I was having great difficulty with the typewriter, I wanted to ask for a change of trade. Five others agreed, wrote up the request, and appointed me as the spokesperson. We went to the appropriate officer, I gave our spiel, the officer listened, and said "request denied." Right turn quick march, then I smartly made a quick left, with the others following, into the largest broom closet we had ever seen! I don't remember how we got out or his reaction. He probably laughed. The war ended shortly after, the Wrens disbanded and I went home.

How did I (and others feel) about returning to civvy life? Lost is the best word. We had three years of independence, and in many of cases, we had authority and experiences that we were unable to explain to civilians. But the families, friends and employers expected you to be, and treated you as if you were, the young naïve person who left home. The men tell me they had the same problem. We came back women and men, not the boys and girls who had left home to join the military.

I came home in January 1946 and was married in August 1946. My husband, who was still in the Air Force, was posted that September to the Yukon to take over a Telephone/Telegraph station from the American Army. As the highway was a military road and not open to the public, there was no accommodation at this isolated station for women. Also, one had to obtain military and Royal Canadian Mounted Police (RCMP) security clearance to be there. I was not happy about the prospect of being left behind, so I called the RCAF Commanding Officer (CO) in Edmonton, to whom my husband would report to as the manager of the station in the Yukon. The CO said that it was so far north and so lonesome that he didn't believe it was appropriate for women to go there. I told him I had been born in the far north and he didn't seem interested. When I told him I was a telegrapher he decided that I could go. I spent from October 1946 to June 1947 as the lone white woman for hundreds of miles. My husband found a storage shed, and fixed it up. It was so small we could not insulate from the inside so we insulated on the outside and covered it with tarpaper. Up there one used what was on hand as there were no stores, not anything! I can honestly tell people that my first home was a tarpaper shack. My life on the highway is another story.

As the wife of the station manager I was expected to be able to manage any family needs. Some of the problems that I was expected to handle were far beyond my expertise but I knew who to ask, and where to go for help – a lesson I learned in the navy. Although I was never given a promotion when I was a Wren I was asked (told) many times to take positions of authority and the other Wrens often came to me for solutions to problems. …And thank goodness my family believes heartily in teaching household skills of all kinds. This knowledge has been a lifesaver more than once.

My naval and northern life experiences left me with the feeling I could accomplish almost anything I put my mind to. There is something about being in the navy that is different from the other services. I can't quite put it into words. It is the knowledge that wherever I go in the world, if there is a naval veterans club or association I will be welcome and will be able to get help. I wouldn't even be shy about approaching a naval base if I could not find anything else. This includes foreign lands. You are always "one of us."

The Wren Association has given me a "family." As a result of moving so often, I found it hard to belong. Not so in the Wrens. Through my association with the Toronto group I have found friends, companionship, and people who put up with my foibles. Mostly because of their acceptance I have had the confidence to take on the office of President of the Wren association, as well as various positions with the Wrens and other associations that I have had held and still hold today. Also, my involvement in the Wren association has given me introduction to aspects of government, and other associations and events I otherwise would not be privy to. I really feel that my experience in the navy – and most of all being raised as an independent woman by a very independent woman, gave me the tools I needed for the northern experience and the rest of my life.

My presentation to the Battle of the Atlantic Parade in Toronto, 7 May 2006, provides a synopsis of my relationship with the Royal Canadian Navy which has now spanned over 68 years. My hope, along with other Wrens and members of the naval family, is that the past sacrifices and contributions of various members of the naval family, including the contribution of the WRCNS to the admirable record of women in Canadian navy, will always be remembered.

Presentation to Battle of Atlantic Parade (Toronto 7 May 2006)

We are here to honour those of the Royal Canadian Navy, the Royal Canadian Naval Volunteer Reserve fondly known as the Wavy Navy, the Women's Royal Canadian Naval Service – Wrens, the Canadian Merchant Navy the RCAF sub searchers and Allied personal who fought the Battle of the Atlantic.

This was the longest battle in WWII lasting 75 months. The casualties in the Canadian Navy alone amounted to 2000 men and 6 women. Those who have no crosses row on row, those who still bravely bear the scars and those who have since cros't the bar are remembered on this first Sunday in May every year.

You have seen us women proudly marching and no doubt there are women in the crowd who also served. No we did not go to sea or fly a plane or shoot a gun but we served our country well. To quote Milton, "They also serve who only stand and waite."[2] Not that we did much standing around. Whatever our duties were – technician, cook, signals, pay master, clerk, messenger etc. We worked often in very difficult circumstance, sometimes at isolated stations, for odd and long hours, for very low pay. Many of us traveled over dangerous waters to reach our postings. We gave up a lot of creature comforts living in naval barracks – known as Stone Frigates – under naval restrictions, to release a sailor for sea duty.

We saw the results of war at first hand and in those days there were no grief counselors and most of the time we couldn't seek comfort outside. We learned to handle life. Like the boys who became men in the service we changed from girls to women in a very short time. We learned, if we didn't already know, that equality meant equality for both the good and for the bad.

My personal introduction to the worse aspects of equality came when I arrived at HMCS ST. HYACINTHE with a duffle bag, a large suitcase, a small suitcase and a purse. I asked the sailor at the gate house if there was any help or transportation for me to the Wren hut about three quarters of a mile away. He looked at me and said "You're in the Navy now sailor." So I picked up my luggage and marched off. Yes – I learned how to pack efficiently and now travel the world with only the baggage I can handle all by myself!

The Wrens made lifelong friends in the navy – grew both socially and intellectually. They came home with confidence, marketable skills, wonderful memories, and some with husbands. If asked if we would do it again the answer most of the time is "at the drop of a hat."

---

1   Refers to HFDF, high-frequency direction-finding radar application. *Equal to the Challenge: An Anthology of Women's Experiences During World War II*. Lisa Bannister (producer) (Ottawa, ON: Department of National Defence, 2001) 537.

2   John Milton, "On His Blindness," in *The Oxford book of English Verse, 1250-1900* A.T. Quiller-Couch (ed.) (Oxford: Claredon, 1901).

CHAPTER 3

From the Second World War to the 21st Century: Reflecting and Reconnecting

Petty Officer Kathleen McCormack (Best)

Kathleen McCormack served with the Women's Royal Canadian Naval Service from December 1942 to March 1946 when she was demobilized as a Petty Officer.

I officially became a member of the Women's Royal Canadian Naval Service (WRCNS) on 31 December 1942. Prior to joining up, I was a member of the Legionettes, 10 young dancers from C-I-L who entertained the troops at least once a week after work. I worked at C-I-L as a stenographer/secretary in the General Chemicals Division for two years. We were asked to be part of the entertainment at the Montreal Forum for a New Year's Eve celebration, and so I was granted permission to fulfill that commitment, and thus commenced my naval career in Galt one day late! Basic training at HMCS CONESTOGA in Galt started January 1, 1943, and lasted for a month. Immediately after basic training, I spent another month in Toronto marching and washing windows, then a few days in Ottawa before going off "on foreign service" to the USA.

Two of us from basic training were posted to Washington D.C. in March 1943, and others followed sometime later. We worked in a building shared with the Canadian Army and Royal Canadian Air Force (RCAF) as liaison with our British and American counterparts. I was in Washington from March 1943 until March 1946. At the Naval Military Canadian Joint Staff (NMCJS) we were a small group, and I was not aware there were any other Canadian Wrens serving in Washington. "The Silent Service"!! We had two Wren officers and about ten ratings working in Communications or the Executive Branch, plus two Wren drivers who worked shifts taking the Admiral to meetings and various social functions. As writers, our duties were general office work, having knowledge of the King's Rules and Admiralty Regulations (KR & AI),[1] and I remember sending dispatches to Ottawa, closing top secret documents with red wax and an official seal. Some of us were in the Signals section, and I was in Administration. I also worked with the Engineering Officer, arranging for the refit of Canadian ships in US ports.

The rest of us did not do shift work. Once a month we got one 24-hour and one 36-hour pass, as well as annual leave to go home. During my time in Washington I was granted leave at Christmas to go home once. We were given a subsistence allowance and had to find our own accommodation and food. I actually shared half of a bungalow with three other Wrens. We had little contact with the members of the Canadian Women's Army Corps (CWAC) or RCAF Women's Division (WD) as their offices were on different floors.

As there were no women in the US Navy when we arrived in Washington (the WAVES were formed several months later), we were quite a curiosity with the CANADA flashes on our shoulders. We were often asked which ship we had come over on!

Although we were not privy to many top-secret matters, there was an aura of tension in the air prior to D-Day. It was an exciting time to be in Washington and to feel, in our own small way, we had contributed to the ultimate Allied victory in Europe.

Upon demobilization as a Petty Officer in March 1946, I was employed as a secretary at the International Air Transport Association (IATA), an association of international commercial airlines. Headquartered in Montreal, their focus was on technical, legal, financial and traffic regulations throughout the world. For me, this entailed attending meetings in Brazil, the Netherlands, California and Brussels, taking minutes, assembling documentation and so forth. (If you look at your airline ticket, IATA regulations still prevail.)

After five years with IATA, I resigned to get married and raise a family, but continued to work on a voluntary basis in various ways. My organizational skills in the navy stood me in good stead. That experience gave me confidence to plan a large centennial Brownie/Girl Guide program in St. Bruno, Quebec in 1967. Later in Toronto, for more than ten years, I taught English as a Second Language to newcomers to Canada. In fact, I am still in touch with one of my Vietnamese students who arrived here as a boat person with her husband and year-old daughter, who now has a Masters Degree in Pharmacy. It is with pride that I have helped new arrivals become upstanding Canadian citizens.

I joined the Wren Association of Toronto by chance, as I happened to attend a meeting where the Jenny Wren Revue[2] was performing. I expressed my interest and as a consequence joined the Wren Association of Toronto in November 2008 and am now a member of the Revue. I did not attend any reunions over the years because I had no contact with any Wren Associations. However, it was a wonderful experience being a Wren, and I am proud to have been part of the Royal Canadian Navy in the Second World War. I did keep in touch with six other Wrens from my Washington days, but sadly all but one have now passed away.

---

1   King's Regulations and Admiralty Instructions, originating with the British Naval Discipline Act of 1866, also applied to the Royal Canadian Navy during the Second World War; a predecessor of today's Queen's Regulations and Orders.

2   The Jenny Wren Revue was formed in 1972 to entertain at a banquet after the unveiling of a statue of a Wren at the site of the former HMCS CONESTOGA, a Second World War training establishment for the Women's Royal Canadian Naval Service in Galt, which is now Cambridge. Since then the group has performed across the country, including singing and dancing at Wren Reunions, naval functions, legions, and other events. All of the women in the Revue served in the Second World War or in the immediate postwar years. See the Wren Association of Toronto, News Release "60th Anniversary of the Wren Association of Toronto, May 2006. <http://www.thewrens.com/canada/toronto/activities/60thann-toronto.html>, accessed 4 January 2010.

CHAPTER 4

Serving Canada and Remembering the Women Who Served

Wren Barbara Duncan

Barbara Duncan served with the Women's Royal Canadian Naval Service as a Sick Berth Attendant from 1944-1946. In 2006, she was awarded a Minister of Veterans' Affairs Commendation for her contribution to the care and well-being of veterans.[1]

At the age of 17 I tried, but was too young, to join the Women's Royal Canadian Naval Service (WRCNS). I was desperate to get out of high school! Instead, I completed high school (which served me well in the years to come) and in September 1944, the minute I turned 18, I joined the WRCNS. The parting words from my parents were, "Now don't you disgrace us!" I wasn't sure exactly what they meant by that at the time. My first stop was three busy weeks of basic training at HMCS CONESTOGA where our stay as Probationary Wrens included, among many other things, receiving needles [injections], learning military regulation, learning to march, and seeing a film about what young Wrens should avoid…I was beginning to understand what my parents were talking about.

In October 1944, I was sent to HMCS PROTECTOR in Sydney, Nova Scotia to learn to be a Sick Berth Attendant at the naval hospital. When training was completed in January 1945, I was stationed at HMCS PEREGRINE in Halifax to work in an 18 bed sick bay. The men that we cared for at PEREGRINE came off of the ships, most of them suffering from upper respiratory problems. Those who required acute care were transferred to the hospital at HMCS STADACONA, also in Halifax.

It was during my time in Halifax that I was introduced to cockroaches. I opened the sick bay medicine cabinet one morning to discover, to my horror, unidentified long legs, which my colleagues assured me belonged to cockroaches. As sick bay was located next to the galley, I complained to one of the cooks in the galley about the cockroaches. His jovial response was, "Hell, you should see them when I come in and turn on the lights at 5 a.m. – they're on the floor having morning divisions!" This struck me as quite humorous at the time and stands in my memory as one example of the important role that humour played in dealing with the challenges we encountered along the way.

Very early (5 a.m.) one spring morning in 1945 I was loaded into a truck to travel to Digby, Nova Scotia where I would cross the Bay of Fundy on the ferry – the first leg of the journey to my next station, HMCS DISCOVERY in Vancouver. In Digby, another sick berth attendant joined me as we had both been assigned to staff a Wrens sick bay at DISCOVERY. The trip was quite exciting to think that in 1945 I would be travelling all the way across Canada and through the Rockies to Vancouver by rail. As it turned out I left Halifax just one week before word of Germany's surrender and the VE-Day riots which took place in Halifax, 7-8 May 1945.

In October 1945, the other sick berth attendant that had travelled from Nova Scotia with me, Mary Greenwood, and I were transferred "on paper" to HMCS GIVENCHY. However, we were actually assigned to the hospital at HMCS NADEN where I worked on the wards. By this time many men were being discharged from the military and it was a very busy time in the hospital. Petty Officer (PO) Wright was responsible for medical-related lab work and needed help. He took me into the lab and taught me to do many things that were new to me and I loved it. I learned, for example, how to do white blood counts and urinalysis. I had little more than one year of military service at this time and was still very naïve. The sailors were treated with sulfa drugs and given soda bicarbonate to prevent crystallization of the sulfa drug in the kidneys. As a result, samples had to be checked to make sure that crystallization had not occurred. One day I had a sample under the microscope and discovered little "tadpoles" moving around. I began shrieking, "Something is alive!" Don't worry about it, the PO responded – it's sperm.

On another occasion, I remember taking a blood sample from a British sailor who was gravely ill and not expected to live. I wrote a letter to his mother to tell her about her son's situation. Soon after, the medical officer came by and said he was going to try a new drug, called "penicillin," on this sailor. I was amazed with the result. In a few days the sailor was up and walking around. I stayed at

HMCS NADEN until March 1946 when I was discharged from the WRCNS and sent home.

After the war, men and women who were discharged from the military were entitled to retraining with the support of the Department of Veteran's Affairs (DVA). Initially, I applied to St. Michael's hospital in Toronto to be trained as a lab technician; however, there was a one-year waiting list for the training. I took an aptitude test through DVA, which suggested that I should consider becoming a physiotherapist. DVA paid me $60 per month and paid my tuition for a three year diploma course in physiotherapy at the University of Toronto; $40 per month was used for room and board and the remaining $20 was all that was left for books, bus transportation, etc. As this left little to no money for clothes, I took the badges off my Wren uniforms and continued to wear them. In the second year of my program, I got married and by the beginning of the third year of my program I was pregnant. I attended graduation, received a baby carriage for a graduation gift and had my first baby just one week later.

Although Wren Associations were established across Canada soon after the WRCNS was disbanded, the next several decades would keep me very busy raising five children (four girls and one boy) and working as a physiotherapist in the Toronto area. I had never forgotten my time with the Wrens in Vancouver so once my children were grown and on their own I moved to Victoria. In 1991 or 1992, I ran into a Wren while I was working. She invited me to a Wren meeting, which was held at the old wardroom outside of Naden at the time, and I have been with the Wren association since that time. I have also been a member of the Ex-Service Women's Legion, Branch #182, and maintained involvement as a service officer with the Royal Canadian Naval Association (RCNA). Until very recently, Wren meetings were held at the Naval Museum at CFB Esquimalt.

I feel very strongly about the activities of the Wren association, the Women's Legion and the RCNA, in particular in regard to their role in establishing the historical memory of women's contributions during the war. During my five- to six-year tenure as the President of the Victoria Wren Association I focused on keeping in touch with other Wren branches as well as coordinating our efforts and resources with like-minded organizations. In 2002, the Vancouver Island Merchant Navy Association established a large memorial gazebo and plaque in Veterans' Memorial Park, Langford, BC, dedicated to the memory of the eight women who lost their lives on board merchant ships in the First and Second World Wars. While I was the Sergeant-at-Arms of the Women's Legion, I coordinated a double plaque dedication ceremony, which took place at the gazebo on 21 September 2008. The first plaque was dedicated to all of the women who served Canada during the Second World War, as members of the WRCNS, the Canadian Women's Army Corps (CWAC), and the Royal Canadian Air Force Women's Division (RCAF WD). As a result of funding provided by the Women's Legion, a second plaque was dedicated to the memory of nursing sisters who served Canada during the First and Second World Wars. The service was conducted by Reverend Diana Spencer of the Women's Legion and included an all women's Legion colour party, a female piper, and the unveiling of the plaques by the serving Presidents and Past Presidents of the Women's Legion and of the Nursing Sisters of Victoria.

In addition to my years as President of the Wren Association and Sergeant-at-Arms of the Women's Legion, I served as a service officer, through the Wren Association and the RCNA. As a service officer, I maintained contact with my Legion branch veterans to ensure that they received appropriate veterans benefits and care. The Victoria Wrens no longer hold formal meetings but about 15 Wrens in the Victoria area do get together for lunch about three times a year. The Wrens also continue to participate in memorial activities such as candle light tributes at the Veteran's Cemetery in Victoria and laying a wreath each year at Remembrance Day ceremonies. I am very proud of the efforts of the Wren Association, and in particular the double plaque dedication ceremony which I coordinated. However, there is so much more to do, including the establishment of additional memorial plaques, and the documentation and sharing of the experiences and contributions of Canadian women veterans, including those who served as Wrens.

---

1   As a result, I was also featured in "Volunteer preserves the past: Veterans Affairs recognizes retired Wren's commitment to veterans", *Esquimalt News*. (Friday 7 July 2006).

CHAPTER 5

The Good, The Bad, and The Royal:
The Challenges and Opportunities of Being a Wren

Petty Officer 1ˢᵗ class (retired) Rosalee Auger (van Stelten)

Petty Officer 1ˢᵗ class (PO1) (retired) Rosalee Auger, CD, QGJM, enlisted in the Royal Canadian Navy (Reserve) (RCN(R)) at HMCS CHIPPAWA, Winnipeg, in 1951, transferred to Continuous Naval Duty (CND) in 1952, and to the Royal Canadian Navy (Wrens) in 1955. She served in the RCN (W) at HMCS STADACONA, HMCS NADEN, HMCS SHELBURNE, HMCS CORNWALLIS, HMCS BYTOWN and HMCS NIOBE, London, England. Petty Officer Auger was awarded the Canadian Forces Decoration in 1964 and honourably released in 1965. In addition, she was awarded the Queen's Golden Jubilee Medal in 2002 in recognition of her volunteer work with the RCN Benevolent Fund.

It was a career that took me from the Canadian prairies to Buckingham Palace and from a stone frigate[1] to the decks of the Royal Yacht Britannia. It all began in 1950 when Winnipeg experienced a major flood and the Red River rose 32 feet above datum. My schoolmates and I volunteered for sand bag duty. However, I was too slight of build for such heavy work and was sent home. I registered with the Central Volunteer Bureau and was called to assist in galley duty at HMCS CHIPPAWA, instead, washing dishes in the super-sized sinks. I was then about 5'2" tall and the sinks were almost up to my armpits, so I was dismissed after a day's labour.

A few days later, because of my shorthand and typing skills, I received a call to work in the Flood Liaison Office at CHIPPAWA. Between phone calls and shorthand dictation Lieutenant Carter, who was a former Royal Navy officer, regaled me with salty dips. Canada was not recruiting Wrens at the time, and I was too young in any case, but I went home and told my mother, "As soon as I turn 19, I'm going to Britain to join the Wrens." It was the call to adventure, the opportunity for travel, a life different from that which beckoned me, and the opportunity for service which drew me to the navy.

By the time I started work as a stenographer for a chartered accountants' firm in Winnipeg, the Korean War was heating up. The RCN had begun recruiting Reserve Wrens. I joined the Reserves at HMCS CHIPPAWA in October 1951. After my new entry training at HMCS CORNWALLIS the following summer, I talked incessantly about my experience. One evening my Mom said, "Oh, if it means that much to you, go!" She was referring to "go" on full-time naval service. My stepfather, who had been in the Air Force said, "Over my dead body!" My mother and I won that discussion. She was very progressive.

Very shortly thereafter, in 1952, Sub-Lieutenant (SLt) Ellen Lang interviewed me for my transfer to Continuous Naval Duty (CND). Later, she also transferred to CND and was my divisional officer at both HMCS SHEARWATER, Nova Scotia and HMCS NADEN in Esquimalt, British Columbia.

In the Reserves, I was a Communications Crypto rating but did not want to do that full time. One of the other options was Engineer Officers Writer, which SLt Lang and I concluded must be a stenographer for Engineer Officers. I chose that branch and later received my training at HMCS STADACONA in Halifax, Nova Scotia.

In 1955, Wrens had the opportunity to become part of the Regular Force with pension rights, although we could not advance beyond trade group 3 because we did not serve at sea. There was some discussion at the time about not being able to marry during our first term of service, a condition that did not bother me unduly, despite press coverage to the contrary.

When Lieutenant Jean Crawford-Smith, later Staff Officer (Wrens), was in Winnipeg drumming up recruits, I was on compassionate draft to CHIPPAWA and was interviewed by the local newspaper. The resulting headline read: "Her Problem: Navy Interfere with Marriage?" The question presented in this headline really riled my feminist soul. The column said, "One drawback to permanent service is the stipulation that a girl must finish her term before leaving the Wrens even though she marries. Rosalee wonders if she likes that." Rosalee didn't wonder at all!

I returned to HMCS NADEN in the fall and signed up for five years in the Royal Canadian Navy (Wrens), or RCN (W). My branch choice was Naval Stores but I was placed in the Administrative Writers branch and drafted to HMCS SHEARWATER awaiting course.

In the meantime, the Photography branch opened to Wrens and I requested a transfer, which was granted. However, before I was given my trade course, I was asked to join the Wren Personnel (Regulating) branch. From 1956 until 1965 I was a Personnel rating, first as a trainee and then as a Leading Wren and Petty Officer responsible for the welfare and discipline of the Wrens and management of Wren Quarters.

I found the Wren Personnel branch socially isolating, since I was discouraged from fraternizing with lower ranks and was not supposed to consort with commissioned officers. Female petty officers and single males in the non-commissioned officer ranks were often few and far between. On the east coast, Wren Personnel rates travelled back and forth to each other's establishments for friendship and moral support. I also took part in a lot of sports such as softball, basketball, bowling and curling and participated in inter-establishment sports meets, where I could be one of the gang.

When I was promoted to Petty Officer on the west coast and joined my male counterparts to wet down, or celebrate, our promotion from Leading rank, I was taken aside by the Mess President. He told me I was not to frequent the mess unless I was accompanied by a male petty officer.

In HMCS SHELBURNE, on the other hand, I was one of the boys. We lived and were messed in Quonset huts. When first I arrived on base, the air in the chiefs and petty officers' mess could be blue with a certain expletive used as noun, verb and adjective, except when there was a lady present. I devised the routine of shouting, "Ding! Ding!" at the entrance door, so they could clean up their vocabularies. One day after work I was seated at the bar spinning salty dips when someone shouted, "Ding! Ding!" I looked up. There in the door stood the ship's padre.

HMCS CORNWALLIS was especially hard for me because of its geographic and social isolation. "The Wren petty officer" seemed to be the object of much conjecture and gossip. A Reserve petty officer with whom I went out ruefully said of his cohorts, "They want to know if you have hair under your arms." I felt like the girl in the goldfish bowl and retreated accordingly.

Because I was billeted in Conestoga Block with the new entry and ship's company Wrens, I never got away from the job. My cabin door was just off the quarterdeck, where I could hear duty watch mustering and feet pounding along the gangway. There always seemed to be some evening "emergency" which my Duty Block Petty Officers (DBPOs) could not cope with. They were Able Wrens, or sometimes older Ordinary Wrens, because we had no one of Petty Officer rank or even Leading Wrens in ship's company. Some were very tentative about carrying out their responsibilities.

The Duty Wren Officers were only in the block for rounds and inspection at 20:00 and lights out at 22:30 otherwise they were on base on call. It was easier for the DBPOs to bang on my door than to phone the Duty Wren Officer and wait for her arrival. I stood watch as Duty Wren Officer, often one-day-in-three when there were no Wren officers' leadership courses in session. The outcome of all this was that I eventually suffered burnout and was mercifully drafted to HMCS BYTOWN in Ottawa, where I had both service and civilian friends and all the amenities and anonymity of a city.

To be fair, HMCS CORNWALLIS was equally difficult for the one single male petty officer in the ship's company. He had a good buddy in married quarters but, unless there was a leadership course in progress, he was billeted by himself. I at least could watch television with the ship's company Wrens in their lounge. In addition, he was expected to volunteer to stand watch at Christmas and holidays so that the married men could be home with their families. We both felt overburdened.

In HMCS CORNWALLIS and elsewhere I was known as "Pusser Auger" because of my adherence to spit and polish and naval regulations. I strived to treat the Wrens with a level hand and morale was usually high. Trying to get around me was often a game with them. For example, when preparing for Captain's inspection in Naden one group of Wrens only buffed their dormitory deck, instead of first applying paste wax on their hands and knees. They felt they had gotten away with a major coup. Decades later, one bragged to me about this event (which did not exactly equate with the mutiny on the Bounty).

In the fall of 1958, while I was serving at HMCS NADEN, I was called with my divisional officer to report to the Manning Commander of the Pacific Fleet.

"Auger," he said, "You are going to London and you are going to work for the Queen." The position was top secret until the news was released by Buckingham Palace in January 1959. In the meantime, I nearly burst with suppressed excitement. Even the members of my family didn't know the purpose of my draft to HMCS NIOBE.

When it was announced that I was to be the secretary for Canadian Esmond Butler in connection with the upcoming Royal Tour of Canada, I became an international celebrity. In palace parlance, I was a member of the Royal Household with the title Lady Clerk to The Assistant Press Secretary to The Queen. Mr. Butler was a retired Lieutenant-Commander, RCN(R) and had suggested the Palace choose a Wren for the position. Naval Headquarters announced that I was selected because of my "stenographic ability, tact; capacity for work, and appearance."

During my tenure, I had the good fortune to be billeted with the British Wren Chiefs and Petty Officers at Furse House near Kensington Palace. I enjoyed their camaraderie and basked in the sights and sounds and life of London. My British messmates, meanwhile, kept me well grounded despite my heady working conditions.

On the six-week tour of Canada I travelled by Royal flight, yacht and train, working many long hours as we went. The highlight of the tour for me was service on Her Majesty's Yacht Britannia.[2] I was called to the bridge on my fourth day aboard. Flag Officer Royal Yachts, Vice-Admiral Peter Dawnay, presented me with the Royal Yacht cap ribbon and shoulder flash for my uniform. I had been sporting a tally from HMCS NIOBE on my cap. With this generous gesture I became, and am to this day, the only female "Yottie" in Britannia's history.

I am a lifetime member of the Association of Royal Yachtsmen and had the pleasure of attending a reunion in Portsmouth, England in 2003, when I was presented to Her Royal Highness Princess Anne, the Princess Royal. Throughout the evening, in formal proclamations and toasts, and in the address by Her Royal Highness, the salutation was "...Royal Yachtsmen and Lady" to the point of it becoming a running joke. Princess Anne is Rear Admiral and Chief Commandant for Women, Royal Navy, so I was especially pleased to meet her. Her warmth of feeling for the Yachtsmen was palpable, as was theirs for her. In conjunction with my attendance at the reunion, I was invited to be a special guest of Britannia, which was decommissioned and is now a floating museum in Leith, Scotland just outside of Edinburgh. It was fun to have a private tour and to learn that my old cabin has become a stationery closet! This gives you an idea of its size.

For over 40 years, in and out of the Service, I was a volunteer with the Royal Canadian Naval Benevolent Fund and was honoured to receive The Queen's Golden Jubilee Medal in 2002 in recognition of this work. I am a Member Emeritus of the Fund.

My years in the navy provided me with many challenges of leadership and service, with opportunities for travel, and with friends that have lasted a lifetime. In what other career could I have gone from palace to Quonset hut, sailed the St. Lawrence Seaway and Great Lakes, and served from the Atlantic to the Pacific oceans?

---

1   In the days when shore establishments were called HMCS, or Her Majesty's Canadian Ship rather than Canadian Forces Base, they were known colloquially as "stone frigates."

2   For a detailed account of my experience as Lady Clerk to The Assistant Press Secretary to The Queen, and as a member of the Royal Household during the six-week Royal Tour of Canada in 1959, see Rosalee van Stelten, "In Her Majesty's Service," *Legion Magazine.* September 1, 2002, <http://www.legionmagazine.com/en/index.php/2002/09/in-her-majestys-service/>, accessed 17 December 2009.

CHAPTER 6

Wren Chief Leading Wrens into the Future...One Challenge, One Achievement at a Time

Chief Petty Officer 1st class (retired) Shirley Brown

Chief Petty Officer 1st class (CPO1) (retired) Shirley Brown, CD, CCM, served with the Royal Canadian Navy (Reserve) from February 1955 to May 1985. She was the first woman to become the Coxswain of a dry land Naval Reserve unit when she was appointed as the Coxswain at HMCS CHIPPAWA in Winnipeg in 1980.

I joined the Naval Reserve on February 9th, 1955 at 21 years of age. The summer of 1955 I requested two weeks leave of absence from my job at Eaton's department store to take my required New Entry Training at HMCS CORNWALLIS, Digby, Nova Scotia. It was my very first time travelling out of the province of Manitoba. On the two and one half day train ride from Winnipeg to Saint John, New Brunswick, I was train sick; and on the ferry crossing the Bay of Fundy from Saint John to Digby I was sea sick. Upon disembarking from the ferry, they threw our duffle bags into the back of the transport trucks and we climbed into the back with our bags for the trip over the hills and around the winding roads to Cornwallis. By the time we arrived at Cornwallis, I was car sick! What an initiation!

Two weeks later, I cried because I didn't want to leave. We all enjoyed the training and meeting gals from all over Canada. There were approximately 40 women in our New Entry Class. I chose the Administrative Trade, became a Pay Writer and underwent trades training at HMCS STAR in Hamilton, Ontario as well as at HMCS HOCHELAGA at Ville La Salle, Québec. Once I had completed all the trades training requirements for several years, my next commitment was a Leadership Course at HMCS NADEN. The course included all women students who, among other things, learned how to fire a sten gun, a pistol, and a 303 rifle, and experienced the use of a gas mask in a gas filled chamber. Successful completion of the course qualified us for classroom instruction, parade square responsibilities, and promotion.

With the exception of the New Entry Training and the Leadership course, men and women were trained together. For the most part, the training went smoothly, although Regular Force personnel were not always cooperative with Reserve Force personnel. In my experience, this was more likely to be the case among the ranks of Petty Officers and Chiefs. Once I had completed all of the required examinations as a Pay Writer I served at HMCS CHIPPAWA in Winnipeg in a support capacity in the Ship's Office, Recruiting, and as the Executive Officer's assistant. Over those years, I was sent to Maritime Command and HMCS STADACONA on the East Coast several times to relieve Regular Force personnel taking holidays, I served as a Petty Officer of a New Entry Class at HMCS NADEN in Victoria, attended an Instructional Technique course at HMCS NADEN, and took the Chief Petty Officer's Refresher Course at HMCS NADEN.

On one of my trips to Halifax when I was a Petty Officer, I arrived at HMCS STADACONA very late one night (midnight) expecting to be directed to the Chiefs and Petty Officers (Chiefs and POs) building for accommodation. To my surprise, they billeted me in the Lower Deck building. I was too tired to argue, but the next morning I requested an appointment with the Commanding Officer (CO) of HMCS STADACONA to plead my case. It was explained to me that they did not have female accommodation in the Chiefs and POs building. I indicated that if this was the case, I would be returning to Winnipeg on the next plane. They accommodated me with a reservation at the Holiday Inn in Dartmouth for the two-week duration of my stay. The next time I travelled to HMCS STADACONA they had modified the third floor of the Chiefs and POs accommodations to include billeting for females…a step forward for women in the navy!

In 1980, I attended the Cox'n's course at HMCS STADACONA. There were 12 Chiefs on the course: eight Regular Force members off ships, and four Reservists from Reserve establishments across Canada. The weekend within the course I decided to fly to Sydney, Nova Scotia to visit my brother and his wife, and planned to return to Halifax on Sunday night. However, the fog rolled in and I could not get a flight until Monday. Consequently, I was AWOL[1] from class for a day. Being the only female on the course I certainly received a lot of ribbing for that incident! Upon successful completion of this course, I became the first female Cox'n of a dry land Reserve establishment in Canada – HMCS CHIPPAWA – another mark on the wall for females!

During my three year term as the Cox'n at HMCS CHIPPAWA, my main responsibility was the dress and deportment of all of the ship's company as well as the security of the ship. It was my responsibility to write up charge reports and present the person on charge to the CO, who was Commander W. Fox Decent during my tenure as Coxswain. Once the CO had heard both sides of the story and delegated disciplinary measures, it was up to the Cox'n to see that the punishment was carried out. The cox'n was a member of the inspection party whenever the ship's company had a parade inspection. In addition, my office oversaw the evaluation of weekly attendance sheets and my staff followed up with a phone call if a company member missed three consecutive parades. Our office issued an absent report and distributed it to all of the Divisional Officers for follow-up. We also set up a watch system so that all of the ship's company could be contacted upon the receipt of a directive from Naval Headquarters in Ottawa, in the event of an emergency. This might mean that all personnel would be required to report to the ship for further instruction. Fortunately this directive was never required in the 30 years that I was a member of HMCS CHIPPAWA.

After thirty years with the Naval Reserve, I retired on May 18th, 1985. There were certainly many changes at HMCS CHIPPAWA over the 30 years that I was there. Of course, changing the uniform to green was certainly not popular. The numbers have decreased dramatically in the Reserve. We had a complement of approximately 100 Reserves in the Chiefs and POs mess during my time, and now there are only a dozen personnel in the mess. While serving at CHIPPAWA, it was very evident that female recruiting was on a par with the males. In fact, on some occasions they had to put a limit on the number of females recruited until the male complement increased.

In 1990, I joined the Ex-Wrens Association – Chippawa Division and have been on the executive ever since. When I have tried to move off of the executive, the Wrens insist that they have been there, done that, and now it is the postwar gals' turn to take the lead. I have held the position of Secretary, Treasurer, President, Past President and now have stared over again as Treasurer. Throughout my years in the navy, and now the Ex-Wren Association, I have made many friends from coast to coast. I certainly feel that the navy offers an experience that is beneficial to any young person wanting to gain independence, accept responsibility with a degree of discipline and, above all, see Canada.

---

1   Absent Without Leave.

CHAPTER 7

On Board HMCS NIPIGON, 1989-1992: Living a Dream?

Leading Seaman (retired) Rose Tanchyk

Leading Seaman (LS) (retired) Rose Tanchyk, CD, joined the Regular Force in 1979 after serving two years with the Naval Reserves in Winnipeg. She originally joined as a firefighter but as she was too short she served as a member of the Military Police for about two years, and then served as a Postal Clerk for the next eight years. She really enjoyed working in the Post Office but when the opportunity came for a chance to sail on ship, she took it. LS Tanchyk became a Boatswain and sailed on HMCS NIPIGON, MARGAREE, and PROTECTER on the east coast, and then on board HMCS ANNAPOLIS on the west coast. Due to a car accident, she had to retire from the Canadian Forces (CF) in 1999. She moved to Calgary and really thought this was the end of her military career. LS Tanchyk had the fortune of meeting a member of King's Own Calgary Regiment (KOCR) band and volunteered as a retired member, just as she had always played in volunteer bands while serving in the Regular Force. From there she became involved with the HMCS TECUMSEH band. While playing with both bands, she has had the opportunity to teach the Navy League Band as well as the Sea Cadet band from Royal Canadian Sea Cadet Corps Calgary (RCSCCC), and is now helping with an Air Cadet band. When not teaching music, she makes costumes and does theatrical make up. In addition to all of her volunteer activities, she works full time job as a Service Writer for Brandt Tractor and renovates her house in her spare time. Although very sad to leave the CF, LS Tanchyk's involvement with the military in Calgary has made her transition to civilian life a lot less abrupt.

Since I was very young, I had a dream to serve on a ship. Before I joined the Regular Force in 1979, I was a navy league cadet, a sea cadet, and a member of the Naval Reserves. I was self-motivated, and I also believe that being in the military for 10 years before I did serve on a ship made me a very strong person. My first experience serving on a ship was on board **HMCS NIPIGON** from 1989 to 1992 as a member of the first group of women to serve on a Canadian combat ship. As a result, I was a member of **HMCS NIPIGON**'s crew in 1991 when she became the first Canadian warship with a mixed gender crew to participate in exercises with NATO's Standing Naval Force Atlantic (STANAVFORLANT).

Women were not initially welcomed by the men on board as our presence challenged a long held belief that it was bad luck to have women at sea. The men also believed that women were not as strong as men and, therefore, were not able to do the job. My job as a Boatswain (Bos'n) consisted of a lot of heavy lifting and working long hours. I held the rank of Leading Seaman. Some of the other women on board included naval acoustic operators (Nac Ops), naval combat information operators (NCI Ops), supply technicians (Sup Techs), cooks, stewards, signalmen (now called signal operators or Sig Ops), and administrative clerks (Adm Clks). The females on board included Lieutenants, Petty Officers, Able Seamen, and Ordinary Seamen. My estimate is that about 35-40 women were part of the total crew of approximately 245 sailors and officers.

As there was not a female Master Seaman on board, I was the highest rank in my mess and was quickly appointed "mess mom". So, not only did I have to prove myself to the guys, I also had younger women looking up to me for guidance. The military Junior Leadership Course (JLC) that I had taken at Canadian Forces Base (CFB) Borden in 1985 prepared me for challenges on the ship. The course taught me time management, which was really important. While at sea, we were given extra tasks, some of which were high-priority safety-related jobs that had to been completed in addition to our every day duties. For example, a loose guardrail would have to be repaired immediately or it could lead to the possibility of someone falling overboard. Even today in my civilian job, I am able to time-manage and organize various events. The JLC also introduced me to various types of leadership, which I was able to use when I was in charge of men that were not very happy about reporting to a woman. I was able to lead without barking out orders or making them feel less masculine. Many of the men I was leading had more sea experience than I, so I also learned to use my experts. I listened to what they had to say and if they had a good idea on how to do a job, and if I agreed with it, I would do it their way. However, if they did not have a better idea, then my orders stood. This made my job a lot easier and resulted in a better relationship with my peers and junior team members. The leadership training also gave me the confidence to take charge without second-guessing myself.

Honestly, there were times when the men were brutal toward the women, but I kept my strength. They made me work when I had the flu and hypothermia, and stand duty watches with my arm in a sling. I did not complain but rather did the job the best I could. I think this shocked the men even more than the fact that I could do the job under normal conditions. When I worked long hours, I stayed cheery and cracked jokes; humour helped me on the job, and I think that it contributed overall to the integration of women on ships. If the men insulted me, I would insult right back. They teased me to see if I would break down and cry, but I would not give them the satisfaction. Instead, I teased them back. I won their respect, not only because I could do my job, but because I did not fall apart as they expected a woman would. I never thought of myself as a role model, but one of the other women on the ship told me that I was. She said women like me made it easier for other women to be in the navy. I did my job to the best of my ability. Fortunately, I had tough skin and would not let the guys get under it. I will admit it was not always easy to do. I did have to work twice as hard as the guys to prove I was as good as them. I had to hide my hurt feelings and just go about doing the best job that I could.

I also had to be strong for the younger and junior women on board. It just would not do for me to fall apart when they looked up to me. I cannot tell you how many times I had a girl cry on my shoulders because the men were picking on her. I let the junior women vent to me about how the guys were treating them. I told them to not let the men get to them, and to do their job to the best of their ability. Instead of getting mad I suggested that they just ignore the attempts of the men to try and upset them. Basically, my message to women was to show the men that you belonged there and not to let them scare you off the ship. That meant that they could not let the men's comments break them down and they certainly could not give them the satisfaction of seeing a woman cry. I let the girls vent as I knew I could not fix their problems for them. Most of the time that was all they needed to go on.

The guys found ways to torment us as much as they could. For example, when they had to come through our mess to do rounds, they would yell "man on deck" at the top of their lungs and wake us up every hour. They thought this was great fun. However, after a while the women decided to reciprocate and eventually this practice ended. Our mess was number one mess, located right in the bow of the ship. It was very rough up there and not the place to be if you were sea sick. Also, the odd time the anchor cable would come loose and the clanging would keep us awake.

On my NATO cruise in 1991, I was the only female quartermaster for our port visits. The guys knew I could hold my own. They did have some fear that some rather large European males might get out of hand, but they knew I could handle them. This was a very high compliment to me – to know that they trusted me to do the job. It was a hard job to be on the first crew of women on a ship but as I think back on it now, it was well worth what I went through. I am now a civilian but still think back to those days when I served. To this day, I have women thanking me for my contribution to making their lives easier on ship.

Sadly, due to a car accident, I had to leave the Canadian Forces in 1997 with a medical category. I learned many skills in the military. I learned how to paint and use power tools, so I am able to complete renovations to my house. The military taught me how to teach others and now I teach music to cadets. I also volunteer as a musician in a Reserve band and I am able to help the new members adjust to military protocol. The military taught me discipline so I do not procrastinate in my work. I have learned that I can do anything I put my mind to.

CHAPTER 8

How I Spent My Summer Vacation

Commodore Jennifer Bennett

Commodore (Cmdre) Jennifer Bennett, OMM, CD, BPE, MEd, enrolled in the Naval Reserve in 1975 in HMCS STAR as a Naval Communicator. Cmdre Bennett was commissioned as a Sub-Lieutenant in August 1979. She was promoted to Captain (Navy) on January 1st, 2000, upon appointment as Director Reserves, under the Chief Reserves and Cadets at National Defence Headquarters. In September 2003, Cmdre Bennett joined the Headquarters staff of the Canadian Defence Academy, as Director of the Ottawa detachment. Concurrent with these duties, she also served as a Naval Reserve Regional Coordinator for the Laurentian and Pacific Regions. Cmdre Bennett was promoted to her current rank on December 1st, 2007, upon her appointment as the Commander Naval Reserve.

Every September as students head to school after their summer holidays, they look back over the time since they left their classrooms and come up with the answer to that classic question: "What did you do this summer?" Some will have had a summer job; a few will have been travelling; others off to camp, family cottages or vacation spots and many will have simply spent the time "hanging out". The stories we remember best were those that were different or more exciting than our own and in 1975 I made a decision that changed not only my response to that age old question, but the direction of my eventual career path and future opportunities.

Between the 1970s and the 1990s the military and the government sponsored a number of Youth Employment Programs that provided an interactive and fun introduction to military training. These included Summer Student Training Program (SSTP), Summer Youth Employment Program (SYEP), Youth Training and Employment Program (YTEP) and Katimavik. In May 1975, I opted to join the Naval Reserve Summer Student Training Program (NRSSTP) and I started what was originally to have been an eight week commitment with the military July 3, 1975.

We completed an introduction to Basic Military Training at home units in a less intimidating environment than recruit school and at the end of the summer, some of the participants were offered the opportunity to continue training and join the unit. Something clicked during that introductory program and since that time, I've continued to serve as a Primary Reservist, working evenings, weekends and holidays with the military while concurrently pursuing a civilian career in education. I could easily use the phrase "How I spent my summer vacation" to describe my career that began as a high school student, only interested in spending eight weeks of my summer learning a bit about the navy with no intention of making this a career, to my rise through the ranks to command the Naval Reserve. My civilian jobs as a teacher and school administrator have allowed me the flexibility to pursue two concurrent careers, each with leadership opportunities and challenges, unique to the environment in which I was operating but linked and connected because in both I was dealing with people, individually and in teams.

I've experienced some of the most challenging and rewarding leadership opportunities and developed skills that have led to my success in both my military and civilian careers. As well, I've seen many changes – not the least of which has been opportunities for women.

Women have played an essential role across the history of armed conflicts in which Canada has taken part initially serving as nurses, stenographers, camp cooks, mechanics, drivers, and airplane pilots. It was only at the end of the 1980s that women were able to take their place in positions that were directly linked to combat. Women asked for this right in 1942 but were only initially allowed to serve behind the scenes: "We, the Women of Canada, have demanded and won the right to participate in public affairs with our votes. Today, we ask our fathers, our husbands and our brothers for the honour of standing by their sides to defend our country and our liberty."[1]

The full integration of women in operations and leadership positions within the military is similar to that of the rest of society as women have shifted from more traditional roles to careers outside the home in business and industry. The First and Second World Wars allowed women to slowly gain recognition and build esteem both inside and outside the military as they assumed roles left vacant by the men who served on the front lines. Our nation saw women proudly wearing the uniform and serving their country in the fields of transport, communications, supply and administration, medical and limited operations.

I owe my success and acceptance in leadership roles to the determination, proud service and success of the nursing sisters, Women's Royal Canadian Naval Service, The Canadian Women's Army Corps and the Royal Canadian Air Force Women's Division. Although these women did not set out to challenge society's perceptions of the roles of women, they blazed the trail for those of us who serve today.

While changes since the Second World War were impressive and comprehensive considering the restriction to service for women up to that time, there were still many barriers to overcome and the navy I joined in the mid seventies was still very traditional in its thinking. Upon enrolment, I was assigned what was considered an operational trade in the navy as a Communicator, but I could only sail in ships during the day as women were not allowed to be at sea overnight. There was no accommodation for females on board ships and the training focused on a support role that could normally be conducted ashore. The Naval Reserve was considered progressive in those days as females were taken to sea for training and exercises but again, only during the day and not far from shore to allow return to dockyard or shore accommodations for the night. When I did my navigation training on the West Coast, we sailed each day on an auxiliary vessel, came into a port in the late afternoon, left the ship, got on a bus and returned to Victoria to stay overnight while the male Commanding Officer and crew stayed aboard the ship. The next morning, we travelled by bus to meet the ship again and the same pattern repeated itself. We could only go to ports that were within a reasonable bus trip back to Victoria.

Women did not march in platoons with men because our uniform skirt was tapered and did not allow us to step out with the same length of pace as men. We were not issued trousers as part of our dress uniform until the late 1970s. My first dress uniform was very stylish and modeled after stewardess uniforms but highly impractical for military service. The green, tri-service uniforms were designed by a Montreal designer with a short jacket, a blouse with an elasticized neck tab, and a slim tailored skirt just above the knee. Our number one uniform also included white gloves and a purse, carried over the left forearm. Our green bowler hats styled like those of European flight attendants came with a plastic hood that tied under the chin in the event of inclement weather and we had a mink hat with a pom-pom top knot for the winter. We were not permitted to parade with weapons so there were no female honour guards. Since there were no pockets in our skirts or blouses you had to carry your ID card and money in your shoe or tucked into your bra if you weren't carrying your purse. This made it a little awkward when you went to pay for something….. Years later when we got pockets on our shirts and in our trousers and skirts, a celebration could be heard across the female members of the Canadian Forces (CF)!

Ranks were also differentiated for male and females indicating in the case of the navy that you were a Wren (Able Wren, Leading Wren, etc). As an officer we also carried a "W" to designate "woman" so when I was a Navy Lieutenant, I was Lt(N)(R)(W) – (N) for Navy, (R) for Reserve and (W) for woman.

Basic training was conducted separately for men and women and trades were limited for female non-commissioned members and officers. When I transferred to the officer corps there was no choice of occupation for female Naval Reserve officers at that time. I was assigned one of two support trades for female officers – Personnel Administration or Logistics. Although I was trained in Sea Logistics, there were no billets for us at sea. That was only three decades ago and seemed quite normal for the day. I can only imagine the experiences of the first women to integrate into the CF.

We can look back across more than one hundred years to see women contributing to and making their mark on Canadian military history. There are many examples of women throughout history who have made significant contributions during conflicts and opened doors for those of us who now serve.

Francoise Marie de Saint-Etienne de la Tour came to the defence of her husband against a rival for the governorship of Acadia in 1640. Not only did she travel widely to find help and funding for her husband's troops, for three days she held off an attack of their fort at the mouth of the Saint John River in New Brunswick.

At age 14, Marie-Madeleine de Verchères followed the 1690 example of her mother by defending her seigneury near Montreal against the Iroquois. After taking refuge behind the barricades, she armed the women and children with muskets and fired the only cannon, thereby warning neighbours of a possible attack.

During the War of 1812, Laura Secord travelled a great distance on foot through enemy lines to warn troops of a planned American invasion.

The Canadian version of the American "Rosie the Riveter" was Elsie MacGill, a war heroine who became known as "Queen of the Hurricanes" and our symbol of wartime transformation for women. In 1938, the 35-year-old woman became Chief Aeronautical Engineer at Canadian Car and Foundry.

Nurse Hallie Sloan, a Naval Lieutenant, cared for thousands of wounded during a 1945 33-day attack on the Rhine Region in the Netherlands Campaign. In one month, the hospital where she worked received 18,000 wounded and doctors performed 1,600 operations. In 2005, Princess Margriet of the Netherlands presented a Dutch medal to Lt(N) Sloan in recognition of her contribution.

I did not set out to be a trendsetter or "first" in any of the positions to which I aspired and ultimately achieved. I was inspired and encouraged by many other leaders, some of whom have been female, and I was given a series of progressive challenges and opportunities to develop my abilities as a leader in this institution and my civilian career. I feel extremely proud and somewhat intimidated to consider myself part of that history and a role model for future female leaders of this institution.

My military career has given me much more than can be listed on a resume including challenges and opportunities that are completely different from any other environment. The practical experience I've had, the courses, and the hands-on leadership have led to success in my civilian career and my life. The military differs from the civilian sector in a number of ways but one that has been the most positive for me is the way that decisions are made about your career. The tendency of the military to tell people when they are ready for advancement sets this career apart. In civilian careers, we tend to look at opportunities that might be a challenge and decide whether or not to pursue or apply. Occasionally someone recommends you for a position but you have all of the control to apply or turn it down. In the military, someone else says "This will be your next job" and pushes you forward. While you may be second-guessing your ability, you are given the challenge because you are ready and able and need this to further develop professionally and personally. I am convinced that I am where I am in my military and civilian careers because people did this for me. I have also tried to do the same for others to improve their potential.

The military provides progressive professional development, training and experiences that prepare you for greater responsibility and leadership through career management and annual performance appraisals and merit boards. However, in the same way that networking gives one a competitive edge in the business world, the same can be said for the military, and in particular, for women in the CF. Opportunities can be a twist of fate and I have been fortunate to have a number of those in my career that had me in the right place at the right time to demonstrate my abilities and have them noted by someone who recommended me for a higher position or a particular challenge that would build my skills and develop my leadership. Interesting and unique challenges are a component of life in the CF and they help us to grow and develop as leaders. I have learned from successes and failures and have had to make tough and sometimes unpopular decisions. Adversity builds not only character but resilience and wisdom.

Experts and current CF leaders agree that success in handling difficult challenges is essential for leadership development and prepares leaders with greater self-confidence and skill. Learning from experience means facing failures as well as celebrating success.[2] Leadership research concludes that those "who experienced failure and adversity earlier in their careers were more likely to develop and advance to a higher level than those who experience only a series of early successes".[3] Learning from failure must involve accepting some responsibility or acknowledgement of personal limitations and looking at ways to overcome this situation in the future.[4]

The Naval Reserve has always been progressive in encouraging and facilitating women in leadership roles and was the first to introduce "conversion courses". We have always had a higher percentage of female members than the Regular Force and there is something to be said about "safety in numbers" and positive critical mass. We had our first female command team members in the 1970s and the first female Flag officer in the CF was a Naval Reservist from Calgary – Cmdre Laraine Orthleib, CMM, CD who was appointed the Senior Naval Reserve Advisor (SNRA) in 1989. The Naval Reserve has achieved a number of significant milestones for females ahead of the navy or the CF including the first female in command of a Naval Reserve Division when Commander (Cdr) Marilyn O'Hearn served as the Commanding Officer (CO) of HMCS HUNTER in Windsor August 1981 to October 1985, the first female Flag/General Officer with the appointment of Cmdre Orthleib as SNRA 1989-1992, the first female CO of a Minor Warship, LCdr Marta Mulkins, CO HMCS KINGSTON in July 2003 and the first female Formation Commander with my appointment as Commander Naval Reserve in December 2007.

While I was the first female CO in HMCS MALAHAT, Victoria, I was the sixth female CO in the Naval Reserve, preceded by Cdr Marilyn O'Hearn in HMCS HUNTER, Windsor, Cmdre Laraine Orthleib in HMCS TECUMSEH, Calgary, LCdr Jacie McCrae in HMCS BRUNSWICKER, Saint John, Cdr Yvonne Hepditch in HMCS CABOT and Captain (Navy) (Capt(N)) Christine Newburn in HMCS DISCOVERY, Vancouver. These women served as role models and mentors for me and I take great pride in now doing the same for those who have served with and for me. I'm very grateful for the opportunities that I have been afforded in both areas of my professional life and I am pleased to now be able to "pay this forward" to the next generation of female leaders. Throughout history, there has always had to be someone who's the first and I appreciate those who have gone before me to open doors. I've always strived to be a mentor, coach and role model and I am pleased when people refer to me as such. People opened doors for me in my careers and I hope that I can do that for someone else. I look forward to the future when the current generation of female leaders in this institution will have put the "firsts" behind them and it will be commonplace to strive for and achieve the highest of leadership goals and ranks in the CF.

As women enter any new occupation or position of authority, they break new ground and become the focus of attention, not only from the media but from their male colleagues. Most do not want to be the centre of attention and would prefer to be recognized for their achievement based on qualifications and experience, not gender. That was certainly my preference – to be treated and respected as an equal, qualified and competent.

When I was appointed to command the Naval Reserve Division, HMCS MALAHAT in Victoria, I had been a Department Head and the Executive Officer amongst a team of male and female members for many years but I was going to be the first female CO of that particular unit and that was considered "newsworthy". While there had been other female COs of units across Canada including five in the Naval Reserve, the press continued to focus on the gender issue and the first drafts of press releases suggested the headline "MALAHAT gets lady Commander". I was able to shift the focus by pointing out that the selection criteria for command did not include chromosomes and I was considered by the navy to be "an officer and a gentleman", not necessarily a "lady". When asked, my Ship's Company commented that their new CO was Cdr Bennett not referring to my gender or the change from the past trend of male COs.

In comparing notes with my female colleagues who have endured "firsts" for women in leadership positions, we all have stories of "boldly going where only men have gone before" and we all agreed that we wanted the focus to be on our abilities and experience, and we wanted to protect those whom we were leading from the extra scrutiny that might come with a new, female leader.

When I was promoted to Cmdre and appointed as Commander Naval Reserve, I may have been the first to hold this position in the navy but I was not the first female General/Flag officer. However, when the Chief of Maritime Staff (CMS) promoted me, I was not able to wear my new rank immediately because the supply system did not carry female versions of all the kit. Summer shoulder boards were available in the shorter female size but slip-ons were not. My cap had to be ordered and then the embroidered oak leaves on the brow had to be sewn on by hand. Adaptations have been made to use what was available in the system, tailored to female sizes and styles. The good news is that I was told that the supply system is planning ahead with boards and slip-ons with two and three maple leaves for future use.

Again, I am not the first female Cmdre in the navy or the Naval Reserve but there was increased media interest and attention because I was the first female, non operational trade officer to command a Formation of the CF. However, this time, the stories did not concentrate solely on the aspect of being a "first" and were very positive in delivering a message that encourages other women to strive for goals that they once thought were out of reach or unattainable.

I am encouraged that women are finding their place in the CF in increasing numbers, roles and domains. Today, 35 per cent of the 4200 members of the Naval Reserve are female and we serve across a range of leadership positions in every military occupation. In my personal career in the military, I have been fortunate to have been unaware or unaffected by gender blindness for the most part and the navy as an institution has been out in front in terms of integration and acceptance.

There are however, some advantages and anomalies about being one of a very small group at this rank. When I attend meetings with my peers in the CF, there isn't a line up for the ladies' room at break time. This is probably the only place in our society where this happens!

In terms of my succession and leadership development, I have had a number of leadership opportunities and experiences in both my civilian and military careers that have built up my confidence in my own ability to lead and guide others. Working as a youth leader in sports, athletics and youth groups gave me some initial exposure to leadership development and I enjoyed working with people. While teaching Physical Education and coaching a variety of sports with students from preschool to Grade 13, I applied the same principles of leadership as we use in the military to encourage, develop and lead. Teaching in a classroom that didn't have the structure of desks and a consistent routine taught me to think on my feet, anticipate a variety of scenarios and always have a back up plan. That also served me well on my Junior Leadership Course, Basic Officer Course and command positions.

Team dynamics and organizational behaviour have always been of interest to me and I soon learned that the human dimension of leadership was the most challenging but also the most influential. As I worked with children in my teaching career and adults in my military career, I stumbled into leadership opportunities and was very fortunate to have been presented with some unique experiences along the way. Never overlook an opportunity to advance or challenge yourself. Even those experiences that might seem "out of your league" initially will provide you with experience to improve and apply your skills. I have made it a point to encourage civilian and military subordinates and peers to find experiences and qualifications that will set them apart from others. I'm often considered to be the "non-traditional" candidate for positions, which has led to interviews and employment offers in a wide range of leadership roles.

I have not followed the typical path of my military classification or civilian career and that's what has kept me engaged and moving forward for so many years. I have looked for interesting and challenging opportunities and have had success and failure along the way. When there were no jobs in my field, I opted for an alternative and learned new skills. I aligned myself with good coaches and mentors and paid attention to both good and bad leaders over the years. Those whom I considered to be strong leaders taught me as many lessons as those whom I considered to be less than ideal and I always hoped that I would serve as a good example for others to emulate. "Appropriate values and behaviours can be learned from competent superiors who provide positive role models to emulate."[5]

I come from a family with a tradition of military service. My father served in the Naval Reserve for 30 years, retiring with the rank of Cmdre, and my sister and brother are serving members of the Naval Reserve. When I joined, my father was the Commodore of the Naval Reserve (SNRA) so history was made when we became the first father/daughter team to achieve the same rank and position in the navy. My personal style of leadership was influenced heavily by my father and I have great respect for his ethics, values, wit, putting people first and his ability to maintain his personality and sense of humour within the military context.

One of his favourite quotes and words to live by comes from the *Laws of the Navy*, written by a very wise Royal Navy Captain who later rose to the rank of Admiral – Rear Admiral (RAdm) Ronald A. Hopwood. First published in the 23 July 1896 issue of the British *Army and Navy Gazette*, RAdm Hopwood presented lessons for life that apply to not only those who serve at sea, but in all professions. While there are many excellent lessons the one most often quoted in our family is verse five:

> On the strength of one link in the cable,
> Dependeth the might of the chain.
> Who knows when thou may'st be tested,
> So live that thou bearest the strain![6]

I also like the lessons in verses eight and eighteen:

> Count not upon certain promotion,
> But rather to gain it aspire;
> Thou the sightline may end on the target
> There cometh perchance the miss-fire.

> Dost think in a moment of anger
> 'Tis well with thy seniors to fight?
> They prosper, who burn in the morning,
> The letters they wrote overnight.

My personal style of leadership has always been one in which I would rather earn respect than demand respect because of my rank or position. I am probably not typical of military leaders in my style and approach and I recently received the highest compliment by one of my officers when I was introduced as one who exemplified "servant leadership". I took this as a compliment because the following are considered qualities of servant leaders: listening, empathy, healing, awareness, persuasion, conceptualization, foresight, stewardship, growth and building community. Servant leaders are considered to be "stewards" and value based, transformational leaders.[7]

The concept of servant leadership was developed by Robert Greenleaf in 1970 and roughly means that servant leaders serve the people they lead. The characteristics are that they

> ...devote themselves to serving the needs of organization members; focus on meeting the needs of those they lead; develop employees to bring out the best in them; coach others and encourage their self expression; facilitate personal growth in all who work with them; listen and build a sense of community. [...] Servant leaders are felt to be effective because the needs of followers are so looked after that they reach their full potential, hence perform at their best. A strength of this way of looking at leadership is that it forces us away from self-serving, domineering leadership and makes those in charge think harder about how to respect, value and motivate people reporting to them.[8]

CF leadership doctrine defines effective CF leadership as: "directing, motivating, and enabling others to accomplish the mission professionally and ethically, while developing or improving capabilities that contribute to mission success."[9] This is better aligned with my philosophy and style of leadership than the old definition of "convincing people to do things that they otherwise might not do".

Kouzes and Posner provide good advice for leaders in *The Leadership Challenge*. "When getting extraordinary things done in organizations, leaders engage in these Five Practices of Exemplary Leadership: Model the Way; Inspire a Shared Vision; Challenge the Process; Enable Others to Act; Encourage the Heart."[10] Another message that I have applied personally in my leadership is the importance of "modeling the way" by letting followers know and see your personal values, ensuring that leaders live what they preach. "People first follow the person, then the plan.[11]

I am proud of my achievements in the CF and for the leadership challenges that have contributed to my personal and professional development but my greatest accomplishment and legacy will be having opened the doors to those who will follow. I am fortunate that as a leader in the CF, I have been accepted and respected and each new appointment has been met with positive reception. Each time a woman fills a new role, there is no longer that hurdle to overcome and we achieve a "new normal".

In a 2002 issue of the *LOOKOUT* there was an article on International Women's Day that spoke volumes about the progress we've made and the legacy we are building:

> Women are doing amazing work, often quietly and efficiently, and continue to make major inroads. It is women in the middle of their careers, women who are in their 30s, 40s and 50s who have come into their own, who are leading the way, who have earned their way into positions of influence, who have paved and smoothed the once rocky road. Because of the doors these women have helped to swing wide, a new generation is marching through with the expectation those doors will remain open to them as equal partners within an organization that has experienced massive change in a very short time. For today's young women the 'can't do' idea is not in their vocabulary. This is a 'can do' generation who expects the opportunities to be available on an equal footing, not because they are women, but because they have earned those opportunities.[12]

So, how did I spend my summer vacations? I've had the time of my life developing my leadership legacy without deliberately setting out to do so. I've influenced and developed future leaders and I hope that I will be remembered as someone who not only opened doors, but encouraged people to go through them to achieve their greatest potential. Looking forward when I started my summer job, I hoped to achieve success in organizational or performance terms but now, looking back I hope that my efforts and my work will be seen and felt in a positive way by those with whom I worked or influenced directly or indirectly.

The CF has learned a great deal about women in the service through our active participation and as Canadian society has adjusted its views of women in leadership roles, so too has the Canadian military. We've come a long way and the CF has worked hard to create an environment that offers every possible opportunity to everyone who chooses the exciting and rewarding challenge of a military career – be it long-term or a "summer job".

1   *La Presse*, Jan 17, 1942, as cited in Dundas, B. *A History of Women in the Canadian Military.* (Montreal, QC: Art Global, 2000).

2   G.A. Yukl, *Leadership in Organizations: Custom Edition for LT 516, Royal Roads University.* (Upper Saddle River, New Jersey: Prentice-Hall, 2002).

3   G.A. Yukl, *Leadership in Organizations (5th edition).* (Upper Saddle, NJ: Prentice Hall, 2001), 193.

4   G.A. Yukl, *Leadership in Organizations (5th edition).*

5   G.A. Yukl, *Leadership in Organizations (5th edition)*, 192.

6   R.A. Hopwood, *The Laws of the Navy.* Originally published in the *Army and Navy Gazette.* (London, England: 23 July 1896).

7   R. Hughes, R. Ginnett, and G. Curphy, *Leadership: Enhancing the Lessons of Experience.* (Boston, MA: Richard D. Irwin, 1993).

8   M. McCrimmon, *What is Servant Leadership.* <http://www.leadersdirect.net>, accessed 19 August 2008.

9   Canada, Department of National Defence, *Leadership in the Canadian Forces: Conceptual Foundations.* (Kingston, ON: Canadian Defence Academy, Canadian Forces Leadership Institute, 2005).

10   J.M. Kouzes & B.Z. Posner, *The Leadership Challenge (3rd Ed.).* (San Francisco: Jossey-Bass, 2002), 13.

11   J.M. Kouzes & B.Z. Posner, B. Z. *The Leadership Challenge (3rd Ed.)*, 15.

12   Lookout Base Newspaper. *International Women's Day Conference.* (Esquimalt, BC: Maritime Forces Pacific Headquarters, March 2002).

CHAPTER 9

Blending In and Standing Out: Leading in a Sea of Gender Change

Chief Petty Officer 1ˢᵗ class Barbara Corbett

Chief Petty Officer 1ˢᵗ class (CPO1) Barbara Corbett, MMM, CD, joined the Canadian Forces in 1976 in Sydney, Nova Scotia as an Oceanographic Operator. She has served in a variety of locations, including Halifax and Shelburne, NS; US Naval Facility Argentia, Newfoundland; National Defence Headquarters in Ottawa; US Naval Facility, Whidbey Island, Washington and an exchange tour with the Royal Navy at HMS DRYAD, Portsmouth, England. One of her proudest moments occurred when she became a member of the Order of Military Merit. CPO1 Corbett is currently serving as the School Chief at the Canadian Forces Naval Operations School in Halifax. She is married to a retired Clearance Diver and has one son who recently joined the Navy as a Hull Technician.

I have been a Chief Petty Officer 1ˢᵗ class for the past ten years. The vast majority of my peers are male. Female Chief Petty Officers 1ˢᵗ class (CPO1s) and Chief Warrant Officers (CWOs) are less than one per cent of the total Regular Force, and approximately five per cent of all CPO1s and CWOs – there are 30 of us in a sea of over 66,000 Regular Force CF members and among close to 600 CPO1s and CWOs. To be successful, respected and accepted I had to adapt to working in a male dominated group. Frequently, that meant that I had to consider my reaction to potentially offensive jokes or comments, and openly object when people began meetings and e-mails with "Good Morning, Gents", etc. I stand up for myself without offending (most of the time) and have no difficulty in voicing my opinions when I feel it is important to do so. I am not a banner-waving feminist, but I do believe women have a place in all levels of command and are important contributors to the growth of a professional navy. I believe we can accomplish much by working within the system. That belief is one of the reasons I currently serve as the military co-chair for the Halifax Defence Women's Advisory Group and as member of the Executive on the Board of Directors for the Halifax & Region Military Family Resource Centre.

Much has been written over the years about leadership. It is a very large umbrella under which you can find such topics as motivation, recognition, discipline, and work-life balance. For me, it has always been very simple. Treat people the way you would want to be treated! I always try to use "please" and "thank-you" as a courtesy. Following my own philosophy to first ask, and then tell (order) has been very successful over the past thirty years. Treating your subordinates (and peers) with respect and decency, being up-front with your expectations and setting the guidelines very early in any situation forges a healthy work environment and eliminates potential personnel conflicts.

My leadership development started young. My parents instilled a solid foundation of ethical and moral behaviour. Military life and training has built upon those foundations. I don't consider myself an expert on the topic of leadership, but prefer to model behaviours I would like my subordinates to develop. The best leaders listen to and look after their personnel. I have seen supervisors take credit for the work of their subordinates without sharing the praise with their junior workers. In my opinion, individuals who use their subordinates to advance their own careers are not leaders and discredit their rank and uniform.

Education, training, my own mistakes and a variety of personal experiences have helped to shape my leadership style. No one person has the answer for every situation. I did not have a particular mentor, but chose to adopt strategies I observed from a variety of people I came into contact with through the course of my career. Conversely, I chose not to use techniques that I observed from others when I believed them to be unfair or questionable.

"Know your people and promote their welfare" is an old leadership mantra, but I believe it is effective and based on a fundamental truth. Being aware of your subordinates' personal/family circumstances, goals, strengths, and providing opportunities for them to improve their skill-sets lends credibility to any supervisor and helps build subordinates' level of trust and confidence in your leadership ability. Two important lessons I have gleaned over the years are (1) to start a new position a bit tough and (2) tailor your responses to individuals. It is much easier to relax as people get familiar with your leadership style then it is to recover ground lost in the beginning. Knowing how to address issues with your subordinates based on their particular personalities makes corrective action more effective. In 1987, while attending my Senior Leadership Course, one of my classmates told me "You aren't a good soldier unless you have been to jail!" Thankfully, we have progressed beyond that yardstick for measuring leadership.

Being fair is paramount. I remember a time, while supervising a section of about 15 people, I would allow the sport players time away from work to attend games or practices. The remainder of the people covered their duties. To be fair, when the "jocks" were at work, I would let the non-sport participants leave for a couple of hours to attend events or functions. This practice balanced the workload and eliminated any resentment of the "jocks".

My leadership style is different, because I am a woman, a wife and a mother. I don't think it is better or worse, just different. My personal views and experiences as a woman are not the same as my male counterparts. Being a woman, I believe I am more understanding of issues like childcare, family illness, family separation, etc., because I too had to deal with those same issues. Women tend to make decisions using both their heads and their hearts, while men mainly use their heads. I tend to be concerned about what subordinates are feeling and try to find an answer to the "why", while my male counterparts are more focused on the "who" and "what" questions. By asking the "why" you may get an understanding of the reasons for an action or behaviour. This additional insight may help determine the best course of action to address the issue.

I don't spend a lot of time thinking about being a role model, but it has become a part of my leadership role as I earned more rank, recognition and responsibility. What I have learned, and tried to practice over the years, is to recognize and seize opportunities to develop leadership. Step out of a comfort zone and tackle new challenges. We will not advance the role of women in the military by waiting for legislation to do it for us. We are our own best advocates for change. I have never settled for the status quo or believed that women cannot do something just because no woman has done it previously. As an Ordinary Seaman, during my first posting to the US Navy Station Argentia, Newfoundland, I wanted to be on the crew responsible for unloading supplies from the cargo ships that came each month from the US First, I was told I couldn't because I was a woman, then it was because I was a Canadian. Each time I was refused, for reasons that made no sense to me, I researched and presented facts to counter the excuse. There were other women, mostly Supply Techs, and one other Canadian unloading the ships. My supervisors finally got tired of my asking and let me go. Sometimes it takes constant questioning, dogged determination, and some support from other women to advance our cause. Every gain we have achieved over my thirty plus years has been worth the effort.

There are still positions that women have not held in the navy, and many women, including myself, have experienced being the "first" in different situations. I sincerely hope that my contributions as the first female career manager for three hard sea trades, the first female President of the Mess Committee for CFB Halifax, and the first female Naval Operations School Chief will make it easier for other women to break down any remaining barriers and continue to grow the role of women in the navy. I am a strong supporter of equal opportunity and believe that male and female viewpoints are necessary for balanced decision-making at all levels of leadership and command.

CHAPTER 10

The Testimony of a Senior Naval Representative for Canada at Naval Component Central Command, Manama, Bahrain[1]

Commander Barbara Carter

Commander (Cdr) Barbara Clerihue Carter, OMM, CD, BSc, MA, CA, joined in 1978 as a Logistics Officer in the Naval Reserve and in 1989 transferred to the Maritime Surface and Sub-Surface (MARS) occupation. She has served in a variety of capacities afloat and ashore, and is currently the Officer Commanding the Joint Personnel Support Unit (Pacific) and a Directing Staff at the Canadian Forces College for the distance Joint Command and Staff Program (JCSP).

Approximately one year prior to my deployment as the Senior Naval Representative (SNR) for Canada at Naval Component Central Command (NAVCENT) in Bahrain, I had placed my name on the international standby list for Maritime Forces Pacific (MARPAC). At the time, I was a Class B Reservist working as the Regional Manager Alternative Dispute Resolution (ADR) Services for the Pacific Region. In addition to placing my name on the MARPAC list, through the ADR organization I had indicated that I would be interested in applying for a deployed incremental position. Chris Ford, the Director General (DG) ADR was very interested in having one of his professional staff on deployment, as the Chief of Military Personnel (CMP) wanted to ensure that CMP personnel, which included those in the ADR organization, contributed to operational taskings. I had indicated my interest for a suggested incremental position (a political officer position for which I had applied) which became available early on. However, I was not initially picked up, I suspect in part because I was female, but also because I did not have a political science background. Time passed and the same job came up again. I believed that if they did not want me the first time, why would they want me this time? Regardless, I put my name on the list, once again expressing my interest in that position. This was in late September 2007, and there was a huge rush for me to agree so the tasking cell could decide whether to tag me. I agreed within four hours of notification that I was being considered (after a long-distance phone negotiation with my then-estranged husband regarding our co-parenting arrangements) and quick as a flash I heard nothing.

Call for Deployment

More time passed, and in mid-October 2007 I received a phone call from MARPAC, the J1 (Personnel and Training Headquarters) shop, asking if I could be on an airplane that night. "Going where?" I asked. The response: to Kingston for pre-deployment training. We cannot find anyone else and we have to get you PSTC (Peace Support Training Centre) qualified before you go. I had to ask where I was going and the answer was, to Bahrain. This was a surprise for me because I figured if I was to go anywhere it would be to Afghanistan.

I did not know anything about Bahrain and I had family responsibilities that week that had to be managed. I indicated in that phone call with J1 that it was difficult for me to go on such short notice, and asked if there were any other PSTC courses that I could attend. I was told no, there not any other courses available – if I was to deploy to Bahrain in January I absolutely had to be on a plane that night. I said I would think about it for a couple of hours and renegotiate family responsibilities with my ex-husband. After I hung up I did a bit of research and found out there were actually more courses. However, one thing led to another and things did not come together quickly enough that week to get me on one of them, and as far as MARPAC was concerned if I didn't make that training session they would find someone else for Bahrain. So I thought the matter was dead.

A week later, Commander (Cdr) Yves Bastien, a former Canadian SNR in Bahrain, sent me an e-mail saying that he had heard that I was going to Bahrain, and offered to share his own experience. I called DGADR ask them if they had seen the tasking message for Bahrain. They had not, but they had just received a tasking to Afghanistan for me on a standing rotation. At that point, I realized I was identified for two different jobs, in two different places, by two different tasking authorities. Somehow a decision had to be made regarding which job was the most appropriate in my case. DGADR weighed in indicating that it would be valuable to have one of the ADR regional managers in Bahrain for six months, primarily because the pre-deployment training time was less, and I would be absent from his workplace for a shorter period of time than if I had to carry out full Roto training. After what I am certain was much heated discussion and bargaining in Ottawa, because realistically Afghanistan was a manning priority, the final decision was Bahrain.

In the end, I was selected for this deployment because MARLANT (Maritime Forces Atlantic) was not able to fill the position. MARPAC was not able to fill the position (with anyone other than me). When the search was extended to the Naval Reserve (NAV RES) my name kept being the only one that came up. I agreed to take the job even though there were some folks in senior naval leadership positions who felt I did not have the requisite skills, competencies, and operational experience to be successful in the position, and that it would be inappropriate for me to go. I knew that because they told me so in direct and certain terms!

Training

In terms of briefings and training, it becomes complex when one person is deployed to a small mission. The posted job description was out of date and the terminology was not correct. No one knew much about the requirements of the position in Bahrain and there was not much available on the CEFCOM (Canadian Expeditionary Force Command) website. Pre-deployment was a bit of a challenge. With no specific guidance, I used the checklist for deployment, and arranged all of the training myself. I completed my fire-fighting refresher with the Coast Guard, my CBRN (Chemical, Biological, Radiological and Nuclear) training with 443 Squadron, my weapons qualification with 39 Brigade, and I took my defensive driving course along with the lawyers who were going to Sudan. I arbitrarily decided that in a worst-case scenario I would end up on short notice deployment to Afghanistan inside the wire, so that's what I trained for.

Travelling to Bahrain

I flew to Manama, Bahrain. The first flight of the trip was what I refer to as, "terror in the skies." The airplane experienced a mechanical incident causing it to fall thousands of feet out of the sky, ending with an emergency landing in Calgary. I seriously thought I was going to die, and was quite pleased that – on the bright side – all my financial affairs were in order and my children had had the chance to say goodbye to me and hear how much I loved them before I went. Talk about heightened sense of awareness coming into theatre! When I finally arrived in Bahrain, I relieved Commander (Cdr) Dan Stovel who had been there from July 2007 to January 2008.

The turnover was somewhat multi-phased. There is a very complex "in routine", consisting of the administration portion of the turnover, which also includes accommodation and living arrangements. The Canadian SNR has an apartment, car, phone and office, all of which are turned over to the next SNR. One of the turnover items was the "official" recipe for Moose Milk! Then there is the challenge of understanding the battle rhythms of the coalition headquarters as well as the actual duties of both SNR and the Canadians as staff officer. The Canadians are generally "double-hatted" with a headquarter staff position; on arrival I was learning the staff position of Deputy Director Future Operations (DFOPS). It was not the job I wound up doing, but that was the job that I was prepared for during the turnover.

The original headquarters job was DFOPS working within the coalition framework. What I actually ended up doing after a few weeks, mostly because there was a gap, but also because I had the requisite skill set and interest for it, was theatre security co-operation (TSC). The activities were acknowledged as an enabler to overall operations, but the position holding that portfolio had not been filled on a full-time basis. Although I also did not do it full-time, I was the first director – first CMF (Combined Maritime Forces) director – for TSC. As a new position, much of the framework and vision had to be created; however, in summary, the TSC job involved planning for six to eight months out the training and other work that we want to do with regional nations to enhance coalition interoperability. Ultimately, if regional nations would formally like to join the coalition, that is great, but as a minimum, we needed to know how to work in the region with the Omanis and the Yemenis, etc. and their maritime forces. TSC makes those connections by doing the work in coalition, whether it is operations or exercises or training, so that we become familiar with each other and how we work with the ultimate aim of being more effective when we operate together or intersect as partners in the maritime environment..

When the TSC position opened on the CMF staff, it was not intended as a Canadian staff position. The TSC duties were part of ACOS plans (Assistant Chief of Staff Plans). When I came into theatre, CDR (Commander) Mick Turner from Australia was the ACOS plans. He was trying to draft the first OP TSC message and it was not going well. The DFOPS position was not very challenging at the time, so I agreed to look at the OP TSC message. After review, I suggested a different framework – actually, I suggested going back to the fundamentals of determining what we, as a coalition, hoped to accomplish by engaging in TSC activities. After a few cups of tea, a discussion around the white board and some sticky notes, we had a new vision and framework hashed out. The ACOS asked me to write it up, which I did as a briefing paper to capture all of the information. After reviewing it, the ACOS and I went to see the then Commander of CMF (who was Vice Admiral Kevin Cosgriff, United States Navy) and his Deputy (Commodore Keith Winstanley, Royal Navy (RN)) who liked the focus on coalition interoperability and the next thing I knew, I was appointed as the Director of TSC and placed in the Plans section. Like most things in the coalition, it happened overnight. There was no staffing, no proposal for establishment change – if there was a need it just happened. Initially I held on to the DFOPS position, the SNR duties, the IT duties of the webmaster for CENTRIXS (Combined Enterprise Regional Information Exchange System), and became the Director TSC. When new staff arrived from New Zealand, I turned over the DFOPS and webmaster positions to the New Zealanders, and kept the TSC position. As I was now in the Plans world, I also continued to participate as a staff planner for select operations, as well as being the Canadian SNR.

An Average Day

The average day in headquarters for the planning cell was 12 to 14 hours. The headquarters battle rhythm included working Sunday through Thursday, with a working Friday every other week. Planning revolved around briefings; TSC is involved in just about everything and I was also pitching in as a planner, so as the TSC Director I attended just about every briefing. There were NAVCENT TSC meetings, planning meetings, coalition coordination boards, and coalition assessment boards. Each day was filled with at least two, if not more, briefings. The non-meeting work was addressed from about 1700 to 2000, so anything that needed to be staffed, routine communications such as e-mails, connection with Canada – taking time zone into account (eight hours in the winter, seven in the summer), etc., happened during that after-hours time frame.

I spent a lot of time with the operational analysts and the INT (intelligence) guys because of the various operations I was involved in the planning for, and some time working with the current operations planning cycle to be prepared for short notice changes depending on the operation. Those people were key contacts for me in my planning role. I also did a lot of networking with the representative from the regional nations because the TSC focus is co-operation with regional nations. Ultimately, I worked with everybody in the coalition headquarters. The Chief of Staff (COS) noted in my leaving interview that I was "the face of the coalition" because everyone knew me, and I talked to everyone. It might be particular to Canadians, but I did a significant amount of connecting with everyone to gather information so that I could do my various jobs.

Being a woman in the coalition

I was the first female SNR of any country, within the coalition. There had been an ACOS ONA (operational net assessment) for the coalition two ACOS previous; a female British Commander. She was actually a Canadian, Liz Hale, who went to the UK and joined the Royal Navy. She had been there on staff, but there were certainly not a lot of women in the coalition, and certainly no others who were officers. The reaction from the regional navies toward me, as a woman, was mixed. When I came, I was told that the Saudi Arabian staff were not sure what to think or do, and at the time, they were in the office next door to me. When my name came through as the SNR designate for 2008, my predecessor, Cdr Dan Stovel, sent an e-mail around to the other SNRs indicating that I was coming, and included "she's a 71" in the message. As a result, everyone thought I was 71 years old as opposed to MARS 71! In any case, I was told that the Saudi Arabian SNR came to Cdr Stovel to confirm that the Canadian SNR replacement was a woman. When it was confirmed there was a pause, followed by "she can do your job?" Cdr Stovel told him that I was coming and I was the same military occupation as him [Cdr Stovel], so it was assumed that I could do the job. Another pause – "But she's a woman". Confirmation – "Yes, she's a woman", and he left. That exchange characterized my relationship with the Saudi Arabian SNR – he was cautiously optimistic regarding my contribution.

Other reactions with the coalition ranged from "you're the greatest thing since sliced bread, I totally trust your opinion" to those who, like the Saudi, were cautiously optimistic but not really interested in working with me. In my experience, with some of the countries – Qatar, UAE (United Arab Emirates), Saudi Arabia – often it was best to work through a proxy. As a result, I often used the German SNR, the Korean SNR, or the Australian SNR to get information, invite them to do things, or to pass on tasking information. If it was not coming from me, it was easier for them to accept.

My experience with the Saudi Arabian SNR led me to the proxy solution. Through their original conversations with the ACOS, the Saudi Arabian SNR indicated that they were very interested in the TSC and wanted to be part of it. They wanted their staff officers to be part of the team and work on TSC. However, when I first approached the Saudi SNR to confirm that one of their officers would be working with me, I was told that the King had not approved it so they would not be involved. When I told the ACOS that they had changed their minds, the ACOS went to speak to them; they told the ACOS yes, we will have a staff officer work with you on TSC. Once again I approached the Saudi Arabian SNR to confirm attendance at a working group meeting and he seemed to have changed his mind again. At this point, I was about three months into my tour and had not confronted anything quite like this, so I was not sure, but had begun to wonder, if the hesitation to participate was because I was a woman. That is when I tried using proxies and I got much, much more success than before. The situation was somewhat ironic because I was actually enrolled in a program for intercultural studies before I left, and I was fairly good with anticipating a variety of cultural barriers, but I was totally oblivious to arguably the biggest barrier, my gender!

At the other end of the scale, I was able to work very well on a peer related basis with other SNRs, including the Jordanian and the Yemeni SNRs. The Pakistani SNR was not so much confused with my role in the job but was confused that I was divorcing my husband and I was deployed. He had some problems understanding why nobody would take care of me. In terms of the US, the Canadian or NATO plus group – working with our more traditional partners – my gender was not an issue. Most of them never knew I was a reservist, but when they found out they were quite surprised because I was not quite what they expected.

Turnovers

At some point, someone estimated that 10 per cent of the headquarters staff of the NAVCENT and CMF headquarters turns over each month. Most of the coalition officers, with some exceptions, remain for four or six months. On the US NAVCENT side, changes can occur in as short a time as one month when Reserves come in to do their reserve duty, to up to 18 months. Turnovers take place within a week, and then somebody is gone and it all starts all over again. A standardized system of record keeping, file structures, repositories of information; written documentation does not really exist, so you are constantly reinventing the wheel or backing up a few steps before you can move forward.

Within CMF there are some positions that people just come into because their nation has been permanently allocated a position. Examples of this would be the ACOS positions; they are standing positions. It was envisioned that the Canadian would always go into the position of Director TSC, but that could and I think did change under the new Command regime. Within CMF, all the other position incumbents are selected based on strength and personality. When you have a coalition it is similar to a potluck dinner. If you don't assign main dishes and desserts to people, sometimes you wind up with 18 pies and no main course. That is very much how the coalition emerges because not everyone arrives with the appropriate skill set for the job your anticipate they will fill so you have do the best you can with what you have. Some people have a very task-oriented perspective, and others are there for a four to six month vacation. It really depends on who's in the seat, how hard they want to work and how much they want to commit to working within the coalition.

In general terms, getting anything done in a combined headquarters with combined forces and US forces is challenging because of all the security issues. Also, there are times when important information is shared only in informal ways to allow you to do your work. If you do not have networks and connections, that won't happen and you can find yourself trying to work in a vacuum. As in many positions, success can become personality based.

Operations

Many of the operations focused on piracy-deterrence operations. At the time, United Nations Security Council Resolution 1816 provided the political will, if not an adequate framework, "to do something" about piracy. We were also dealing with migrant smuggling operations to address the frequent provision of transportation services from Somalia to Yemen, frequently characterized by abuse and neglect of passengers, including passengers who were beaten and thrown overboard before they got to the Yemeni coast. We discovered that some of our initiatives regarding anti-migrant smuggling operations were probably making the situation worse, so we tried to look at what could be done to at least ensure the safe delivery of passengers to Yemen, thus allowing them to enter the refugee process and move forward. Our efforts in this regard included gaining intelligence such as patterns of life, understanding the difference between routine smuggling and smuggling with probable terrorist links, and information that facilitated the interception of cargoes of interest.

The interception by **HMCS CHARLOTTETOWN** of a drug smuggler in the Gulf is an example of the type of operation that we influenced. In this particular case, it was the first big drug bust – first purveyor of fine narcotic products – that was intercepted in a long time. The CHARLOTTETOWN interception was the first of a series of successful anti-narcotic operations that evolved over the following few months.

Local Population Relations

As headquarters personnel, we did not have much involvement with the Bahrain civilian population. Our work hours keep us in this small slice of "middle America", the Naval Support Activity (NSA) base Bahrain. In fact, when you come in through the gates to the military base it is as if you have left the Middle East and entered the US. Bahrain is quite a cosmopolitan country. There are many ex-pats, and a lot of European influence. The working languages are English and Arabic. An invitation into a Bahrainis home is a very special thing. Even the Bahraini SNR had only one function during my deployment and I was on leave at the time. As a result of this overall separation from life outside the gates, I did not have an opportunity to learn a lot about the Bahraini life and what it's really like. However, we lived on the economy, shopped in grocery stores and purchased what we needed locally. In that sense, it was similar to living in suburbia – just like home except the clothes and the language are different.

Looking back to when I started the position, I didn't really know what to expect. The Canadian SNR before Cdr Dan Stovel was Cdr Paul McNeill, who worked on several special projects related to mine countermeasures over on the NAVCENT side. When Cdr Dan Stovel came in, he worked with CENTRIXS and future operations. When I came in I initially wound up doing just future operations and then changed roles appreciably. The two previous, and the current, SNRs, Cdr Yves Bastien, Cdr Paul McNeill, and Cdr Dan Stovel, were really my only sources of information about the SNR job, and they described three different jobs. Cdr McNeill said the job is what you make of it, and advised me to go and do whatever seemed relevant. Although I did not know what I was getting into, it is my third headquarters job so I had some expectations regarding work in a headquarters. In that sense, I was comfortable going in even though I had been working outside of headquarter positions for some time.

In anticipation of my deployment, I was really excited and looking forward to the experience of working in a US-led headquarters in one of the hottest theatres of maritime operation today. I believed I was going to learn so much, but did not realize until after I arrived in theatre how much I had to offer. I began to notice that Canadians are exceptionally well grounded in staff work, operational planning, and diplomacy skills. We understand the language and terminology used by the UK and the US. We have a history and possibly a cultural predisposition to being inter-culturally au fait and being comfortable working in different environments. We know we are a minor power, and understand that we have to ask the right questions and figure out how we can best contribute. As Canadians, I believe we are well suited to work in a coalition headquarters by training and by disposition.

Serving as a Reservist

I kept my "dirty secret" about being a reservist quiet for a long while, telling only a few people because I sensed it would not help my situation much; on top of my own self-doubt and the doubts expressed about me by others, I didn't think I needed that particular stigma. Before I left Canada, I did not feel that I was competent enough for the job because so many in Canada told me as much – it would be really difficult, a really steep learning curve, and it would take me a long time to figure things out, and I did not have the right qualifications or operational background. So when I got into theatre, when asked about my background, I highlighted my Directing Staff (DS) work at the CF College and said I was someone who had not been to sea in a while. That seemed to sit well with others. Many of the other officers there were in a similar situation and, respecting the "potluck principle", performance was the true test of worth in the coalition.

I never really fully came out of the closet as a reservist. The ACOS and the Italian SNR knew that I was reservist, mostly because they were my closest friends there. Initially, the Italian was shocked, and I remember he said to me "you can't be a reservist because you are all about the job"! I thought that was an interesting comment because no one had been so open about their attitude towards reservists to me in such along time. I guess it's our Canadian "politically correct" nature. As a result, I did not tell anyone else, and I certainly never told anyone that I did not feel confident coming into the position.

Here's the thing, "Barb's Theory" based on my experience as a DS for the Joint Command and Staff Program: I believe that people have different skill sets at different levels of granularity, and I know that I am not a good tactician. I also acknowledge that I don't have a deep tactical background, but conceptually I understand things very well and have the ability to contribute at an operational level because I understand all the concepts and how they fit together, and how it congeals into the overall conduct of the operation. Ultimately that's what planning at the operational level is all about, understanding the links, connections and interrelationships of the various warfare specialties and the near- or non-military aspects of an operation like media, diplomacy, policing, negotiation…the list could go on. From that, the operational art lies in merging that knowledge to craft a plan that is comprehensive and meets the objectives.

My personality, plus the training and this expertise, pulled me through. I do not believe that my lack and depth of operational experience had much of a bearing on the work that I did in the headquarters – which was really about conceptualizing an operation with the end state we were working towards to accomplish the mission. There was no need to know how many RAMs something could shoot or where the arcs of fire were or how the wind would impact the operation. You did not need that kind of knowledge to do the job that I did.

Expectations

I came into theatre somewhat concerned that I was not up to standard. Not only because I was a woman, but because of the concern that had been expressed by some Canadian navy leadership regarding my experience level and the fact that I was a reservist. I had not realized how high up the concern had gone until my outcall with Commodore (Cmdre) Winstanley, the Deputy Commander CMF. It is hard to work for someone who's seven time zones away from you and I was not sure exactly how my work would be reflected in my mission **PER** (personnel evaluation report). I had requested an input letter from Cmdre Winstanley outlining what I did, with a copy to MARPAC to convey appreciation for allowing me to deploy, and describing what I did during the deployment. In the outcall he related a conversation he had with the Canadian who was the Commander of Combined Task Force (CTF) 150 at the time. In the opinion of the Commander of CTF 150, it was pretty high risk for Canada and the CF to send me on the deployment. Cmdre Winstanley told me that he had never had any concerns about my ability to do any work that was sent my way, and that he had expressed that confidence to the Canadian Commander of CTF 150.[2] Also, Vice-Admiral (VAdm) Cosgriff, the departing Commander CMF (triple-hatted as Commander Fifth Fleet and Commander NAVCENT) came up to me at his change of command and told me that I had done a good job. VAdm Gortney, who replaced VAdm Cosgriff, came up to me one day in the passageway and said "I know talent when I see it. Would you stay around?" His Executive Assistant (EA) at one point said it was a "waste of your talents" when I told the staff I was returning to in Canada. When I did my outcall, the Chief of Staff CMF, Capt d'Angelo, had a citation certificate for me. He apologized that the citation had to be presented to me privately, for small "p" political reasons, rather than a public presentation. In his words, I was the face of the coalition, and everyone in the coalition knew that if they wanted an answer to find me and they would get it. He also said that I had gotten the attention of VAdm Gortney within the first week he was in command, and that was something special. So I know that I did fine. I did a good job.

The information above was synthesized from an oral history recording that I did with the Maritime Staff Historian the same day that I was leaving theatre. Reading through the transcript a year and a half later was a bit like travelling down memory lane. My immediate reaction on reading was to reminisce about the special time that was, not just for me but also for the coalition staff. There was a synergy among us that, I believe, was unique to the time and place. In subsequent e-mail exchanges and visits with many of the people I refer to (Winstanley, Turner, Cosgriff and others not mentioned in the transcript) that is a theme that is often talked about amongst ourselves.

For me it was a real turning point in my life. I was dealing long-distance with all the pain and administration that a divorce creates, including separation from my children for the duration of the deployment, while trying to reinvent myself as an operational MARS officer. I really wanted, needed, to do the latter to prove the naysayers wrong about my capabilities. It was an external challenge for me, and at the time I desperately wanted to be seen as cut from the same cloth as my peers, maybe because my identity as a naval officer was all I had left among the ruins of my personal life. Ultimately, I do not think I succeeded in emerging from the ashes like a phoenix in the MARS world, but I realize now it does not matter. I learned something new and profound in Bahrain about my leadership that has taken me over a year to understand.

A new "Barb's Theory": as humans, we are all unique. Sometimes the commonalities are easy to see, and if they are that sets conditions for a person's actions, knowledge and talents to be recognized and understood. The fewer similarities there are, the more difficult it is to adequately grasp the depth of talent that a person has. So because I do not have the temperament many other MARS officers do, or so I have been told, and because I do not have a recognizable MARS employment path, it is quite difficult to compare my talents and abilities to others. That makes it impossible for me to achieve the external recognition I was looking for. Personally, I think I would be an amazing flag officer, but the reality is ranking or comparing me against my peers is impossible because of these differences. I could be the most brilliant strategist, leader and operational thinker out there as reflected in my personnel file, but I will never be recognized for that because the work I choose is definitely not mainstream. Therefore, that means my talents remain largely uncelebrated, and promotion near impossible.

What I have come to understand because of my deployment to Bahrain is that I punch far above my weight class in many respects. I have an extremely broad range of knowledge, and few can do my work. I specialize in creating order out of chaos. I choose, and am entrusted with, doing the unknown or the impossible in the CF whether embedding collaboration in a culture that thrives on chain of command, standing up a new unit or a new regional structure, re-conceptualizing non-kinetic operations, or crafting a theatre security cooperation plan from a void. I have no fear of the unknown and think out of the box because I was never really in one! I am drawn to solve complex problems like moth to flame. That sort of work rarely garners promotion or other accolades (and therefore no one wants it) but it is work that leaves a legacy. How many people ever have the opportunity to do that? When I'm gone there will be no building named after me, and no photograph of me on the wall of former commanders, but each and every day someone in the CF will be working within a system I had the privilege to shape. My "stain" on the fabric of the Navy, as it were.

I have always been a private person: an outgoing introvert working in an extrovert's world; and success for me has generally been measured against a sliding internal measure stick I carry deep within me. Understanding very clearly now that I am a "connector" (à la Malcolm Gladwell), a visionary and a legacy creator, I measure my own success by the degree of success that others achieve – on their terms, with their talents recognized for what they are, and with their access to opportunities unfettered. When others succeed they become part of my legacy, and I would like to think this is my gift to the navy.

Some of my peers who have outpaced me in rank refer to Hopwood's lines in the Laws of the Navy "On the strength of one link in the cable, Dependeth the might of the chain" when they speak of leadership and role in team. My view is different: I see team leadership in the metaphor of rope. Individually the hemp strands comprising a length of rope are weak, but when these strands of varying length and thickness are bound together, the rope they create is strong. I am like a strand of hemp in that rope; my tenure limited in duration and visibility but the rope, the team, will carry on without me: stronger because I was there. I know that clearly now, and it was the synergy of the team in Bahrain that helped me learn that.

Barb – Esquimalt – January 2010

---

1   Editors' note: This chapter has been adapted by the author from an interview conducted by Dr. Gimblett, CWM Oral History Project, 20080712-358. Interview conducted with the author in Manama, Bahrain, 12 July 2008, original transcription by Lony Cole Lange. George Metcalf Archival Collection, Canadian War Museum.

2   Combined Task Force 150 was responsible for coalition maritime security operations in the region spanning from the Gulf of Oman through the Arabian Sea to the Horn of Africa and into the Red Sea.

CHAPTER 11

Placing a Fix on the Chart: Finding Your Leadership Edge, Regardless of Gender

Lieutenant-Commander Leanne Crowe

Lieutenant-Commander (LCdr) Leanne Crowe, CD, joined the Naval Reserve in 1983 at HMCS YORK in Toronto under the federal government Summer Youth Employment Program (SYEP). She remained in the primary Reserve for five years and worked as a Diesel Mechanic, attaining the rank of Master Seaman. During this period, she spent winter months working at YORK and summer months travelling to the east or west coast to sail on Gate Vessels. As a Reservist, she completed the Ship's Team Diver Course in 1986, and became part of the diving team at YORK. In 1989, she joined the Regular Force as a MARS (Maritime Surface and Sub-surface) officer. LCdr Crowe obtained her Bridge Watchkeeping qualification in 1991 on board HMCS NIPIGON. Through her performance on the two week pre-selection Clearance Diving Officer Preliminary course in early 1992, she was selected to attend the rigorous year long Clearance Diving Officer Course. She completed that course in 1993 and took up a position at Fleet Diving Unit (Atlantic) (FDU(A)) in Halifax. In the next few years, she held positions as Officer in Charge of Yard Diving Tender (YDT) 12 and Deck Officer of HMCS IROQUOIS and PROVIDER. In 2000, LCdr Crowe successfully completed the Operations Room Officer (ORO) Course, and went on to hold positions as Operations Officer in HMCS ALGONQUIN and Combat Officer in HMCS PROTECTEUR, which included deployment to the Persian Gulf during OPERATION APOLLO (War on Terrorism) in 2002. She returned to the diving community as the Executive Officer of Fleet Diving Unit (Pacific) near Victoria. Before coming to Halifax as Commanding Officer of FDU(A), she was the Officer Commanding the Experimental Diving and Undersea Group at Defence Research and Development (DRDC) Toronto for three years. She is currently at the CF Maritime Warfare Centre as the Mine Warfare Tactics Officer. LCdr Crowe completed her Bachelor of Arts degree with the University of Manitoba in 2008, and keeps busy with numerous activities, sports, and her peppy Portuguese Waterdog named DeWolf.

I have served for over 25 years in the Canadian navy, initially as a Reservist at HMCS YORK in Toronto, and now as a Regular Force MARS (Maritime Surface and Sub-Surface) officer. The majority of my military career has been spent fulfilling leadership roles. In addition to choosing a military profession, which in and of itself is a non-traditional career for women, I consistently chose paths within the navy that were often uncharted territory for women. I served at sea as a Diesel Mechanic, completed a Ship's Team Diver course, transferred to the

Regular Force as a MARS officer, and then pursued the sub-occupation specialty of Clearance Diving.

I have sometimes asked myself whether being a woman makes me a different leader than my male peers. Do I bring a different perspective to the table? Do I problem-solve the same way? Would a man make the same decision if in my shoes? I believe the way I lead is sometimes different from my peers, and sometimes quite similar. Are the differences because I am a woman? Perhaps, but maybe it is because I am a different person, with different experiences and expectations.

If gender affects leadership, is the result more or less pronounced within a historically male dominated environment? As with most, if not all military institutions, our navy was created by men and has historically been led by men; therefore its values and norms have an expected masculine centricity. It is the profession of arms after all. One expects a military force to be physically powerful, task-oriented, and superior in strength to its enemies, or potential enemies. As part of the Canadian Forces (CF), our modern navy reflects the norms and values of Canadian society. We live in a liberal, democratic society that has determined that men and women can, and should serve and fight side by side to protect Canadian values. This has not, in my opinion, emasculated us as a country or force, although years ago this may have been an expected outcome. Our war-fighting and peacekeeping history, along with our current performance in high-intensity conflict, paints a very positive and professional picture of our men and women in uniform, and in particular its leadership. Social evolution in our country is ongoing. I suspect the longer we see female leadership as the norm rather than the exception, the less the perception of gender disparity.

Before one can look at potential gender differences in leadership, there is first the question of whether there are differing thought processes and problem-solving approaches between men and women. I have had many experiences in my military career where I felt there might be a difference between "male and female thinking". I remember a particular event as a Reserve Diesel Mechanic that has made me pause for thought on occasion. It was during a fall Great Lakes/east coast deployment in a small naval reserve patrol craft. The salt water cooling pump on one of the two main engines started to leak on our way into Saint John, New Brunswick. As a result of the leak, the engine was overheating, and salt water was rapidly filling the bilge. We had an engineering crew of seven (five men, two women). We all had a look at the pump, and seemed to reach an accord that the leak was in the pump housing. The plan was to repair it on arrival in Saint John. As it was Friday (and being good sailors), the general consensus was that it should be fixed as expeditiously as possible. The pump and housing were removed from the engine for inspection, and it was at this point that divergent courses of action emerged.

My female counterpart and I felt that replacing the housing gasket might resolve the problem (the gasket looked worn). We also knew that fabricating and installing a new gasket might take at most an hour. The Chief Engine Room Artificer (CERA) remembered that he had an identical pump and housing, which he had "rabbited" from somewhere and was storing in tiller flat. It took him a half hour to find the spare pump and another half hour to install it. The other woman and I observed, as there was not enough room for all of us to get in on the job, and we were not that keen on the overall rectification plan. The spare, but not new, pump was installed with the old gasket, so when the engine was "flashed up", the pump still leaked. It also did not work. The pump impeller had seized from sitting in damp storage over such a long period of time. For the next 4.5 hours the five men rendered workable the "new" pump. My female colleague and I utilized this time to cut a new gasket and subtly suggested that since we had put forth the effort to make a new gasket, we might as well install it on the new pump. When all was said and done, the leak was repaired and by dinnertime we were free to go ashore.

What did I learn from this? I had identified the problem as a leaking pump, and had decided that fixing the leak was the requisite task. My female colleague came to the same conclusion. The CERA determined that the problem was a leaking pump, and decided that replacing the pump was the requisite task. Perhaps he was trying to rationalize why he hoarded and stored so many spare parts in tiller flat. Once it was determined that the pump did not work the new challenge of fixing something that is broken, became his new focus. Did we arrive at different possible courses of action because of our gender or because we are different people? Probably it was because we are different people. This experience may not have profoundly influenced my leadership perspective, or my future strategy to lead men and women, but it did reaffirm in my mind that we do not all think alike.

Does gender affect leadership? I believe that our experiences shape us as leaders and therefore if men and women have different experiences as a result of their gender, it is conceivable that they would develop different leadership approaches. Certainly my military experience has influenced my military leadership style. If that experience was different because I am a woman, then it only makes sense that my approach may differ from a man's.

Team-building is an important part of leadership, particularly in the military context. I have always been a team player, and feel that team-building results from strong leadership. When I went through basic officer training, I had a particularly "hard-core" officer as part of my Directing Staff (DS). He was army, infantry, Ranger qualified, and had very clear ideas about women in combat roles in the CF. I perplexed him, and he admitted as much near the end of the course. I was really having fun. The weather was horrible (coldest winter in Chilliwack since the 1920s), and I was physically and mentally challenged more than ever before in my life. There were lots of other officer candidates in my platoon who were not enjoying it. I utilized a lot of humour to inspire and motivate them. I also demonstrated an unyielding work ethic that quickly caught on once mission success resulted. The good Captain could not break my spirit, and since it had such a positive effect on the rest of the group, I think he realized that maybe "some women" could be leaders of men (and women). In retrospect, I do not believe I was doing anything different from what successful leaders do, regardless of gender.

As a MARS officer, leadership roles come early; initially, as Divisional Officers for combat operators, and then as Bridge Watchkeepers (BWKs). BWKs are granted "Charge" of the ship, and the responsibility for the safety of the ship and all personnel on board. Much of the training and employment is at sea, utilizing a combination of formal on the job training (OJT), and mentorship from senior officers and Commanding Officers. I feel the most profound impact on a MARS officer is the mentorship provided by their Commanding Officer (CO). After all, the goal of MARS officers is to one day command at sea themselves. I was once told by a more senior colleague that I would observe many leadership styles and competencies in my COs. I must, he advised, take the good or positive elements and place them in my right pocket and place the negative elements in my left pocket. As I evolve as a leader, I must draw from the right pocket, but must never open the left pocket. I must; however, never forget what is in there. It all sounded very philosophical at the time.

I have had a variety of COs in my career, many of whom have been extremely positive influences; however, my left pocket is certainly not empty. I had a CO once who lacked patience when it came to training junior MARS officers to manoeuvre the ship. He had a pair of red and green gloves that were to be worn by officers who would confuse port from starboard. Although, I think he felt that it was a good learning tool; for those required to wear them, it was humiliating. I had another CO who would visit his BWKs during quiet watches in the night and just talk with them one on one, impart wisdom, or quiz them on various aspects of their role. This approach was well received, facilitated learning, and fostered confidence in trainees.

Mentorship is a responsibility of leaders at all levels. We grow as leaders if we "hoist in" lessons en route and then pass them on to our subordinates. I have learned that good mentorship (right pocket) involves mutual respect, and that effective learning is only achieved in a positive, encouraging environment. These are good leadership principles regardless of whether one is male or female, and I don't feel their application is gender-based.

At the time I was undergoing MARS training, the senior leadership on board ships had very little experience leading mixed gender units. There were growing pains of course, but overall the experience was positive. I found that in terms of professional expectations, men and women for the most part were treated equally. On divisional matters; administrative, disciplinary, or personal, women were often treated a bit more delicately by their male supervisors who had not yet developed the necessary skill sets to handle some of these situations.

It was sometimes difficult for male supervisors to strike the correct balance between compassion and discipline, for example. Worrying that a female sailor would break down and cry (as was sometimes the case) if they were disciplined, or counselled, they would sometimes avoid or "pass off" disciplinary or corrective action. Unfortunately, a decision made to avoid an uncomfortable situation can be detrimental to the institutional requirement to maintain discipline and morale. The fact that it might be viewed by this sailor's peers as preferential treatment would also hamper team-building. If treatment and therefore experiences of female sailors, and potential future leaders, are different from their male counterparts, than it follows that their leadership style may differ as well. Fortunately, we have come a long way. Supervisors experienced with mixed gender units and a new generation (or two) of norms have led to little disparity on how men and women are treated in our navy.

As a junior leader, did I do anything differently than my male colleagues? My experience as a junior MARS officer was probably not much different from many of my peers. As a woman, and junior officer, I was not particularly comfortable counselling Petty Officers on personal matters; indebtedness for example. This might be a man, who was the same age as my father, who was on his third divorce, and who had spent more time at sea than I had been alive. What advice could I possibly give him? What made it easier was the fact that policy was pretty clear on many of these issues, and that there was help available to the individual from professionals ashore. Once I understood my role was not to be a social worker, financial advisor, or friend, but was to guide them, life became a lot easier.

My male peers had the same apprehensions; whether it was getting help for a subordinate with an addiction, or dealing with an individual going through the dissolution of a relationship, we were all pretty naïve. Regardless of gender, I think we learned the same lessons.

In my experience, military personnel will follow a leader for three main reasons; they are legally required, they believe the leader is professionally competent, and they have some notion that this is the "guy they want to follow into battle". What this statement refers to is inspiration. People want to be inspired. In fact, in some people's opinions, professional competency could be overlooked somewhat if an individual possesses this intangible characteristic.

This is one area, where I feel gender might affect leadership. I have never heard a female military leader being described as inspirational. Yet, it is not uncommon to hear comments of this nature about men at various leadership levels, whether it is General Hillier as Chief of Defence Staff (CDS) who many feel had exceptional vision, or some of the Clearance Divers in my own unit who others remarked had inspired them. It seems to me that women are not generally seen as having this quality in the eyes of their followers. Why is this? Perhaps it is because not enough time has passed for a critical mass of women to have executed military leadership and therefore create this possibility. In my mind, and I believe in the minds of many women in the CF, this is our reality. Evolution is not an expeditious process. As a result, professional competency for us becomes paramount to success as military leaders.

When I joined the Clearance Diving branch, many people worried about how I was going to be "accepted". Perhaps I was blissfully ignorant, but I wasn't worried about that at all. I knew I was a good diver, and was competent underwater (critical factors in my decision). I was also confident that I was a strong leader and team builder and that these qualities had served me well in the past. Working in the generally cold, underwater environment is very physically demanding. Additionally, the nature of the work can be mentally and emotionally challenging. Since I enjoy being pushed to my limits in these ways, the branch was a natural fit for me. There is no doubt that I have never been, nor ever will be as physically strong as my male peers – that is biology. I have made sure that I have kept myself as physically able as possible, and have utilized my greatest tool, my brain, to offset any gaps. I would expect any leader to optimize their strengths.

I have heard anecdotally, that female rock climbers are more technically proficient than males, in order to make up for a lower centre of gravity and less upper body strength. This is probably true for any job that women perform that requires physical strength, and diving is no exception. In the underwater, neutral buoyancy world, there is often nothing to support the diver to provide the leverage required for some work. I remember receiving strange looks as I straddled a sonar dome upside down, utilizing my legs to hold me in place while I removed the numerous nuts from the fairing band. My supervisor also wondered why I used significantly less air than my male counterparts when performing tasks like this. I would say it was because I had smaller lungs. Although, this is true, it had more to do with me calmly and easily performing the task once I was secured to the dome, while my male peers tried to aggressively haul on the wrench suspended in water almost to the point of passing out.

So what did I learn from this, and similar experiences? Perhaps it is that different strategies can achieve the same outcome, or is it that people tend to develop strategies to overcome weaknesses but not strengths. I feel I placed a lot of emphasis on my professional abilities throughout my career. In my mind, this was the primary factor by which my leadership ability would be judged.

As I have had the very good fortune of commanding one of the Fleet Diving Units, any fears of how I would be accepted in the branch have long disappeared. I am the first, and still unfortunately, the only female Clearance Diving officer in the CF. I am always trying to recruit young MARS officers into this exciting and challenging sub-occupation specialty. What I find interesting, is that the young men do not seem surprised that a woman commanded this unit, but the young women are. I actually had one young woman come to me and say, she did not know that she could ever be in command of a unit like this. Since she was a military college graduate, I found her revelation shocking, as I assume our military institutions foster a sense of potential and possibility in all our young leaders. Perhaps this was an isolated case. The naval institution has certainly evolved; however, proving oneself to be as good as a man is a societal "hang-up" that women cannot easily shake. Regardless, I set her straight, and I think she walked away with a better feeling about her chosen profession.

I have said that I believe experience shapes the leader in many ways, including their individual style and the strategies they use. I would suggest that since gender can influence experience, then it must form part of the leader's perspective, but does not necessarily affect leadership. If one used common gender stereotypes female leaders would all be more communal and nurturing than their more aggressive male counterparts. Is a good military leader necessarily one or the other of these, or is a combination preferable? Can a woman only be a successful military leader if she leads like a man? Just as there is no universal definition of leadership, there is not any one perfect style, nor should there be.

The following six attributes have guided my personal strategy of leadership. Firstly, a leader must have vision. A leader needs to be looking to the future, as there needs to be a destination to which they are leading their charges. Secondly, a leader needs to be professionally competent. Thirdly, a leader must inspire. This can often be done simply by leading by example. It also helps when the leader believes in the mission and fosters a positive outlook. Fourthly, a leader must be honest. There will be times when the leader does not know the solution, and must seek advice prior to making a decision. This creates trust within the organization that is vital to team cohesion and effectiveness. Fifthly, a leader must demonstrate ethical courage, by always doing "the right thing". Finally, a leader must be consistent. Lack of consistency, will render all other attributes meaningless.

Although there are many other important leadership traits, these six have allowed me to successfully lead operational military teams. When I look at these qualities, nothing stands out in my mind as being intrinsically male or female. Is it a perfect solution? No. Have I made mistakes? Yes. All of my collective experiences and the lessons I have learned over my lifetime have made me the person and leader I am.

I have been a pioneer in many ways in my military career. Early on I was often asked to comment on what it felt like to be a woman in a non-traditional role. I never really knew how to answer that question and generally shied away from public attention. I could not see what purpose my input would serve, or what being made an example of would accomplish. When 25 years later, a young woman cannot conceive that she has the potential to reach the highest leadership level within the CF, it puts this in perspective. Does gender affect leadership? Perhaps it does, perhaps it does not. I'm still not sure how to answer the question about what it feels like to be a woman in a non-traditional role. What I do know is that I no longer shy away from opportunities to inspire young people. After all, it is my responsibility as a leader, regardless of gender.

CHAPTER 12

The Experience of a Naval Reserve Officer during Operation Argus in Afghanistan[1]

Commander Marta Mulkins

Commander (Cdr) Marta Mulkins, CD, has been a member of the Naval Reserve since 1985. She has served as a Maritime Surface officer in various units across the country and as a ship's officer in several classes of ships. Taking time while in university and through occasional leaves of absence from her civilian career as a landscape architect, she served in sea-going positions of increasing responsibility which culminated in July 2003 with her assumption of command of HMCS KINGSTON. After two years in command she worked at National Defence Headquarters and in 2006 deployed to Kabul, Afghanistan for a six-month tour in with the Canadian Forces' "Strategic Advisory Team – Afghanistan". Upon her return to Canada she returned to her civilian career; she was promoted to her current rank in January 2008.

Introduction

This chapter is based largely on an interview I had conducted with the Canadian War Museum's oral history programme not long after having returned from Afghanistan. As I read through it again in preparation for writing, it brought Kabul back so much that I could almost feel the dust. Despite having had about six months back at home to readjust to my regular life, the account I gave revealed that I was still deeply concerned about the progress in that country, as in fact I remain today.

The work in the Strategic Advisory Team (SAT) was a challenge of a lifetime, drawing not only on the military training and ethos that all of us had learned and lived over the years, but also demanding we search our collective life experiences to adapt to very non-military environments, develop trust and collaboration with different cultures and, at all times, to roll with whatever happened next.

I have not yet been able to return to Kabul – but still hope to be able to one day. In the meantime the lessons I learned there remain fresh and are a constant motivation.

Events leading up to selection for Afghanistan

I was a Naval Reserve member, working at the Chief of Maritime Staff (CMS). I had been working in Strategic Communications for a couple of months when I received an e-mail from a former colleague of mine who was working in the J-3 International Staffing Cell. She informed me that there was an operation that was now soliciting for positions; Operation (OP) ARGUS, the first rotation (ROTO 0). She asked if I knew anybody who would perhaps be available for it. In her duties for staffing, she really tried to make sure that everybody had an equal opportunity to be a part of operations like this. So along with soliciting the Militia and Air Force reserve, she had also sent out the message to a few people in the Navy reserve. I told her that if there was anybody I could think of I would be happy to pass it on. I didn't think of myself at all, initially. But over the course of that week, in fact, I had been looking at the web site on the Defence Information Network (DIN) about the military's activities in Afghanistan. Over the course of the following week I decided that maybe I should think about doing it. So I responded to her and asked for more information about it.

The SAT was planned as a group of about a dozen people deployed for a year to Kabul. A part of the team would be there for the full year and the other part of the team would be there for six month positions. By the time I heard about the team it had already partly been formed but was still looking to fill up the extra billets. They were currently in Kingston finishing the Peace Support Training Centre (PSTC) training and would be in Ottawa the following week. So I had a very quick interview with the staffing boss. At the time, the staffing boss thought that I would be a good candidate. My own boss in the CMS staff referred me for a quick interview with the head of the team, an army colonel. And so I was allowed to join the training on spec if a position were to open up. My boss at the naval Strategic Communications cell that I was working in thought that it was a great opportunity. But he would, of course, pursue it from his end with the CMS – to see if I would actually be allowed to take it. It all happened very quickly, the interview was successful and so I joined the training in Ottawa. The Chief of Staff (COS) decided that I could not go for the first six months but he promised me that if a billet was still required for the second six months, which was the (half) ROTO starting in February, then I would be allowed to go.

Operation ARGUS

OP ARGUS was a completely separate operation from the other engagements that we had in Afghanistan at the time, and that we have there now. It was designed as a small advisory team to render strategic planning assistance to the government of Afghanistan. It was an unconventional military operation, and the genesis of it lay in the very particular personal relationship that our Chief of Defence Staff, General Hillier, had with the President of Afghanistan, President Karzai. This was a result of the period of time that General Hillier was the head of the International Security Assistance Force (ISAF), and based in the strategic planning assistance he rendered to the interim Afghan government at the time. They had recognized that the small, fragile government of Afghanistan, in flux at that time, lacked strategic planning capability. President Karzai said, "Look, you know, I'm still not seeing enough strategic advisory assistance." So the General said, "Fine. I'll take it back to my government and we'll see what we can put together for you." And Colonel Mike Capstick, now retired, was chosen to lead the team.

The team was called the Strategic Advisory Team, Afghanistan, or SAT-A. The intent was that it would be a relatively small group that would render strategic planning assistance to the Afghan government on a bilateral basis. Team members were not to be subject matter experts in economic development or infrastructure or policy development or whatever – but rather, the skills we would bring to the table were our ability to listen to, understand and analyse what the government wanted, and then be able to, with them, develop plans that would accomplish those goals. We were providing mentorship to their planners. To put it directly, the Canadian Forces (CF) Operational Planning Process (OPP) was translated into policy development instead of military operations development.

The team was envisioned as the expression of Canada's then "3D approach" (defence, diplomacy, development) to international engagement to the government at the time. That meant that development, i.e. the Canadian International Development Agency (CIDA), Diplomacy and Defence, would be working together. CIDA provided an expert in development and in mentoring new governments and how to develop plans. Foreign Affairs did not send a team to work with us directly, but the activities that we did while in Afghanistan kept in close communications with Foreign Affairs, through the Embassy in Kabul.

Job Description

One might ask how we military folks would prepare ourselves for this non-military mission, above and beyond the normal pre-deployment refresher training and stint at the PSTC. We received briefs from Foreign Affairs experts, military personnel who had been involved in General Hillier's original strategic planning group in ISAF and, I think, we all "read in" as much as we could. With my background in the Naval Reserve and as a civilian landscape architect, I don't know what would have made me feel truly prepared; on the other hand, my range of experience gave me some confidence that I could adapt. At the end of the day, planning is planning, whether you are tasked with a fisheries patrol off the south coast of Newfoundland or, as a landscape architect, helping clients figure out the functional programme for a site. Everything is running projects; planning and executing that plan. Once we allowed ourselves not to be overwhelmed by the unknowns, it all came down to the ability to identify goals, identify a plan for how you're going to achieve those goals and then in turn to execute that plan.

My position in the SAT was as a member of one of the two teams that were sent to work in the different government departments. I initially was a part of the team that was sent to work in the Afghanistan National Development Strategy (ANDS) working group, which was a team of people who were helping to develop the oversight document and national strategy which was meant to coordinate all aid and development activities in the country.

My team consisted of three people. There was a commander or lieutenant-colonel-rank leader and two lieutenant-commander/major-level employees, the workers; my commander was a naval officer who had had a great deal of experience in operations and in personnel management.

Our task was to assist the working group in developing the ANDS document. The framework had been established but it now was necessary to develop the actual goals and target levels that would allow any given ministry to measure and report development in their areas of responsibility. That was a pretty challenging process because it required a lot of consultation with various ministries to identify what their goals were, how to set their performance targets, and how we would measure that success. In some cases, some ministries were quite strong and had good procedures in place while others were less organised or capable. This also required collaboration with international organisations and we all came to know the "UN community" quite well: the United Nations Assistance Mission in Afghanistan (UNAMA) and the United Nations Development Programme (UNDP) being the principal players.

The ANDS working group was located in a building called the Prime Minister's Compound, the "Sederat", a compound of buildings that were sort of old palaces. It was fascinating to interpret the history of that part of Kabul in the style of architecture and in the layout of the gardens – very beautiful stone work inside and out – enormous plane trees and masses of old exotic roses tumbling over arbours – and shell holes in the garden walls which had never been repaired. When I arrived in February, there were geraniums in pots wintering in the glass and stone front entrance vestibule. Everywhere was a sort of shabby elegance that spoke volumes and within its walls it was a little oasis of calm in a busy part of the capital.

We worked directly with a dozen Afghan colleagues, men and women. Some of them had had some western education and all spoke excellent English. For the most part they were young, thirty-something, highly motivated, forward thinking Afghans. We followed the Afghan work schedule (six-day workweek) and the entire compound assembled in the cafeteria every day for the office lunch provided to us all – one of the benefits of a government job. The excellent working relationships we all developed spilled out beyond the office; we often hosted our Afghan colleagues at our compound and would occasionally see each other out on the town. There were no other foreign assistants, per se, on a full time basis the way we were. There was certainly no foreign military. Occasionally, a representative from ISAF or from Coalition Joint Task Force (CJTF)-76 would come in on a liaison basis, because what we were doing informed the framework for the activities of provincial reconstruction teams as well. And, in fact, some members of my team did travel out and brief the Provincial Reconstruction Team (PRT) conferences on ANDS to give them an idea of how they might do organise their PRT development activities in line with the broader picture.

I was in the ANDS for about two and half months and then was tasked with a new project: I was tasked to explore whatever assistance we could render to the COS to the President, who wanted to modernise the Office of the President. Initially, we had meetings with him to explore what role we might possibly play. We made a proposal to him that was accepted. I was then dedicated full time to assisting the COS in his restructuring plan. I worked closely with an Afghan colleague who had extensive experience working with non-governmental organisations and who was highly respected in the Afghan government.

The COS had worked in the western world and had a very specific perspective on how the Office had to function; his biggest challenge was in working against some of the cultural norms, as can be imagined. My status as a foreign military officer could have been misconstrued and I kept a rather low profile; when I worked at the Palace I always worked in civilian dress. I was very conscious of the fact that I was the only woman there aside from the female security guards and sometimes wondered, when walking through the courtyard to my little office in an annex behind the Palace, who might be watching with disapproval. But the people with whom I dealt most directly were of modern outlook and, in any case, exceedingly polite. I never had a problem feeling marginalised or that my presence was inappropriate, either in the ANDS or in the Palace. Of course, it is always important that one behaves in a way that is polite and respectful. You don't want to push the envelope too much.

From the SAT-A perspective, the potential risk to the team of getting embroiled in Afghan politics was very much on our minds when we were discussing at the beginning whether it was an appropriate place for us to engage. But as it proceeded we decided that it was worthwhile because it was an opportunity to really assist a man who was very sincere in what he wanted to accomplish. Of course there were intrigues swirling through the Palace and it was to our advantage at times to be seen as little as possible – but I'm told that after we had left the work carried on and that the foundation we had laid in that short period was later built upon further by non-government organizations (NGOs).

Life in Kabul

The city is pretty breathtaking. Nothing really prepares you for landing on the tarmac at Kabul International Airport and seeing the mountains and the sky and the character of the landscape. Everything was new and interesting. Throughout my tour, I watched Kabul change from a dreary, muddy, winter-bound place to a sunny city of dusty streets and walled gardens full of roses and fruit trees.

There obviously is risk in Kabul, but it's not like going out on patrol in Kandahar where you know you are the target. In Kabul it's very different: it's much more random for improvised explosive devices (IEDs) but much more specific for political and psychological hits – attacks aimed at making Afghans and internationals feel more vulnerable and for making the western news. We would frequently be warned about the vehicle-borne improvised explosive device (VBIED) threats in the city. There were all sorts of risk, really. Rockets would still occasionally be lobbed into the city, although it was much less frequent than it had been a few years before, from what I understand.

We lived in the Wazir Akhbar Khan neighbourhood which is where many of the foreigners, embassies and international organisation residences are located in Kabul. I think it probably was developed in the 1950s and 1960s, judging by the style of architecture that I saw. The wealthier Kabulis live in that neighbourhood as well, and it's pretty well guarded because of that. A lot of the streets are controlled with barriers at the front and back, with guards who will let you in if they know you belong there. There was a lot of police presence in that area as well, just because there are so many targets in the area. That said, we would walk up and down certain streets to specific destinations and embassies during the working day. We got to know the guards fairly well.

In terms of our own comfort level, I think the best way to put the experience is that we were constantly at a higher level of stress. If we were driving across the city, specifically on the routes that were known to be the high-threat routes, i.e. where most of the suicide bombers would target military convoys or even sport utility vehicles (SUVs) that were clearly driven by foreigners, then obviously we would armour up and be prepared for anything. Driving was crazy – though I've heard that it is much better now – more traffic police and people actually obey them now. When we were there, there really were no rules in traffic, people driving the wrong way, no streetlights at night, merging lanes being a vehicle-scraping sport. We got used to that, but it's less easy to get used to the idea that one day you might be in the wrong place at the wrong time. Lots of incidents happened while we were there – and they continue today. As much as we felt that we had established very positive personal relationships with our Afghan colleagues and felt good about the work that we might be doing on any given day with them, you never knew what the people out on the streets where thinking.

There was also, to some degree, stress from the mission perspective of where it was appropriate for the SAT to engage (or to disengage, as the case could be), when we would ask the question "could this backfire?" I think at the end of the day, really, we all just focused on trying to deliver a good product.

Kabul 100

Canadians were dispersed throughout the city in a number of places. There were the National Support Element representatives, the clerks, vehicle technicians and the like, who were located in Camp Souter, which was the British base. There were also representatives in ISAF headquarters, serving staff functions. There were liaison positions with the Americans, with CJTF-76, who served different functions. And, in fact, the CMS Public Affairs Officer, who was my boss in Strategic Communications in Ottawa, was deployed to Kabul at the same time that I was. He was working with the Americans just up the street in their camp, Camp Eggers. Every now and again he would come and visit us at our house just to have a little escape from camp life. The Embassy was good at hosting us all together for holidays like Canada Day, or when Canadian dignitaries were visiting.

Redeployment Home

Over a course of a month, we went home in separate little groups, and I was in the last group. There were three others and I have to say it was awfully weird in the last few days when we were the last four and all the new team was in. They were understandably rather wary. Our goal in those last few days was, to help them adjust a little, telling them it was actually not a bad place to live (all things considered) once they could understand what was around them. From what I later heard, they adjusted quite well. We were all finishing off projects and conducting turnovers with the new team. In the last couple of weeks I visited two eastern PRTs by helicopter, escorting some senior Afghan government bureaucrats to conduct some consultation. In the end, leaving seemed to happen very abruptly. We went from 60 to zero.

When we left, we actually flew home civilian airline as it was difficult to organise any military transport once the bulk of the Canadian operation was down in Kandahar. We all flew out on one of the Afghan airlines, KAMAIR, into Dubai and then Luftansa/Air Canada the rest of the way home. We had a few hours to kill in Dubai and so one of my colleagues from the ANDS team and I hit the town and had, of all things, a sushi dinner, before coming back to the airport and embarking on the long leg home.

So, we arrived home, went through customs, met our families in the airports and that was it. We basically – and this really speaks to the fact that we were a very small team – didn't fit within the larger structure. We onesies and twosies checked in at the office just to let everybody know we were home and then we all proceeded on our post-deployment leave. And I, as a reservist, at the conclusion of my post-deployment leave, went back to my former job at the CMS just to do the formalities of checking out because I was returning to my civilian job. I spent the last week at the CMS, returned my kit, did the paper work and then started back at Public Works the following week. That was it.

Readjusting

When asked what it was like to readjust in the interview, it was pretty clear that, just as our whole experience of Afghanistan and Afghans was quite different than that of those in other parts of the country, readjustment was possibly different too. Mine was certainly pretty smooth. I didn't experience any Post Traumatic Stress Disorder (PTSD) or any other difficulties with readjusting once I returned home. I did notice that everything was much more relaxing, of course. But there are always little things after powerful experiences, violent or otherwise, which remain with you. I still recall that just before the interview I had just been walking with my husband in my Ottawa neighbourhood and there were two explosions. Believe me – I froze– we used to hear explosions, not infrequently, in Kabul; gunfire, rockets – one of the rockets exploded just two hundred meters from our compound one night. It took me a very "aware" moment to figure out that what I had heard was workers clearing the ice in the river at the little power dam. We laughed about it. I say this humbly, because so many are coming back from Kandahar with serious issues.

In the conclusion of the interview, I was asked something along the lines of what impact the experience had had on me, but it was likely still too immediate an experience and in some ways, raw. What I did know was that I had learned a lot and that it had really opened my outlook on how Canada engages in the world.

Not to say that I had a completely different view before, but there is nothing like being in the thick of things to start to analyse the question of values versus interests.

While not a typical military operation, I learned a great deal about the joint environment from my teammates, and our day-to-day interaction with all number of other Canadians (Department of Foreign Affairs and International Trade, CIDA), internationals and non-governmental organisations was a front-row seat for Global Politics 101. My recent experience not long before OP ARGUS in command of one of Her Majesty's Canadian Ships undoubtedly had given me a certain confidence and initiative in problem solving, working with my team or Afghan colleagues. The extensive analytical and planning experience from my civilian career was important too, and some might also enjoy the possibility that my experience working in a federal government department in Canada may have allowed me to feel not too-far out of my depth while wading through Kabuli bureaucracy – such is the added value that members of the Reserve can bring to the military team! And not to be trite, but sometimes it seems one of the most effective elements of leadership in an environment like that is simply, as a woman, presence. To be seen to fit in, to speak with confidence, to act effectively and even to walk with purpose can make a difference in certain contexts. I'm sure my two other female team mates felt the same way.

Ultimately, the CF prepare us with superb leadership training, but it is up to us to use our life experience to adapt and to lead as the new challenge demands – nothing less is expected of us. Upon my return, I was regaling a senior naval officer with tales from the deployment and he asked me what the "secret of success" was for naval officers in making their way through a completely non-naval environment. I decided that a contributing factor must be our solid training as junior officers in being attentive and considerate hosts at ships' cocktail parties during foreign port visits!

I recall in answering the final questions of the interview that I struggled a little to express the "next steps" that would come out of my recent experience. Then as now, I thought we had such a great opportunity as a country and believed what we're doing is so important. It's not to say we shouldn't keep questioning and re-examining how we're doing it, but I think it is very much worthwhile. Coming up now on four years after the deployment, the experience has definitely left a lasting influence. I would go back to Afghanistan. It would be hard to say no. I care very much about what happens in that country. I know what hard working people the Afghans are, what a tough time they've had, and where they could have been by now if the changes in the seventies hadn't started to go the way they did. I think they have hope.

We have such huge expectations as aid givers; the scores of countries that are donating aid. The thirty-some countries that have military presence there all have their own ideas about what's right for Afghanistan. But, really, only Afghanistan can truly make it happen because they'll either believe it themselves and make sure that it happens, or not. I think we really have to temper our expectations. It's going to be very, very tough to rebuild an economy, never mind anything else, but I think they have a chance. Only time will allow the true measure of the value of Canada's engagement, but I for one feel honoured to have played some role in it.

---

1   Editors' note: This chapter has been adapted by the author from an interview conducted by Dr. Gimblett, CWM Oral History Project, 20070226-31D 7 Mulkins. Location of the interview: Ottawa, Ontario. Transcribed by M. Assaff. George Metcalf Archival Collection, Canadian War Museum. The transcription of this interview was first published in *The Salty Dips*, Vol 9. (Ottawa: Naval Officers' Association of Canada, Ottawa Branch, 2008), 325-348. The publication of this interview was generously granted by the The Salty Dips Committee of the Ottawa Branch of the Naval Officers Association of Canada.

CHAPTER 13

On Track By Leadmark

Commander Sarah McMillan and Commander Michelaine Lahaie

Commander (Cdr) Sarah McMillan, CD, attended Collège militaire royal de St-Jean prior to completing an Honours Degree in Applied Military Psychology at Royal Roads Military College in Victoria, BC in 1995. She successfully completed Maritime Surface (MARS) training in June 1997 before accepting an occupational transfer. Cdr McMillan trained as a Personnel Selection Officer (PSO) in what was formerly known as the Formation Personnel Development Office (FPDO), in Halifax, and was subsequently selected in 1999 for post-graduate training at Saint Mary's University (SMU), earning a Master of Science in Applied Psychology in 2001. Following graduation from SMU, Cdr McMillan was appointed to a Lecturer position within the Department of Military Psychology and Leadership at Canada's Royal Military College (RMC). She was assigned teaching responsibilities, in both official languages in the following subjects: Military Leadership, Professionalism and Ethics, Organizational Behaviour, Combat Psychology and Human Resource Management. In 2003, she was promoted academically to Assistant Professor. In 2004, Cdr McMillan was appointed to the position of Group PSO (GPSO) at CFB Borden. In her capacity as the senior officer in charge of personnel selection for Canadian Forces Support Training Group (CFSTG), she was responsible for all matters pertaining to in-service selection and the provision of Second Career Assistance Network (SCAN) services. Cdr McMillan also taught the material for Officer Professional Military Education (OPMEs) 402 (Military Professionalism Leadership and Ethics), in addition to her normal duties for RMC, and while posted in Borden. She returned to Halifax in June 2006 and assumed the position of Formation Personnel Selection Officer at the Formation Personnel Selection Office. Upon promotion to Cdr she was posted to the National Capital Region to the Director Military Personnel Operational Research and Analysis as the Operational Effectiveness and Leadership (OEL) Team Leader. Cdr McMillan is a part-time student (Ph.D. Industrial/Organizational Psychology) at Saint Mary's University (Halifax) and the proud mother of Lauren (6) and Grace (4).

Cdr Michelaine Lahaie, CD, joined the Canadian Forces in 1987 under the Regular Officer Training Plan. She graduated from Collège militaire royal de St-Jean in 1992 with a Bachelor of Arts in Military and Strategic Studies. Upon completion of her MARS officer training in Esquimalt, she was posted to Halifax to HMCS PRESERVER, where she completed her Bridge Watchkeeping Certificate and her Certificate of Competency Level 2 qualification, deploying twice in support of OPERATION SHARPGUARD. In 1996, she was posted to NCSM VILLE DE QUÉBEC as the Anti-Submarine Warfare Officer. Her first shore posting was in summer 1998 as the Deputy Scheduling Officer at Maritime Forces Atlantic Headquarters. She completed the year-long Operations Room Officer Course in 2001 and was subsequently posted to HMCS MONTREAL as the Operations Officer. During her time in MONTREAL, the ship deployed as the flagship for OPERATION APOLLO. Upon return from the Arabian Sea, she was promoted to Lieutenant-Commander (LCdr) and posted into the role of Ship's Combat Officer. In January 2004, she was posted to Canadian Forces Naval Operations School (CFNOS) as the Command Control Information Systems Department Head. After a short tour at CFNOS, she was posted to the Royal Military College of Canada as a division commander. On completion of her tour at RMC, she was posted to Ottawa, completing nine months as the MARS Occupation Manager and then taking over as the MARS LCdr Career Manager. Promoted to her current rank in May 2009, she is currently employed at the Director Maritime Personnel as the officer responsible for HR policies on the Maritime Staff. Cdr Lahaie is married to Lieutenant-Colonel Gary Hardwick and in her spare time, she enjoys running, reading and travel.

There is a United States (US) Navy WWI poster that one can purchase through the Smithsonian Institute that states rather brazenly "Gee, I wish I were a man. I'd join the Navy!" At the bottom, the poster proclaims "Be a man and do it!" The picture on the poster is of an attractive brunette, wearing a traditional American Sailor's uniform. Clearly, the poster was designed as a means of cajoling men into joining – after all, if a woman is prepared to enlist in the navy, every man should not only want to join, but should be very capable of succeeding. For many young women, the promise of an exciting career has been the navy's great draw. For some of us, the opportunity to blaze a trail was too good to pass up; for others, the promise of "join the Navy, see the world" was the hook. No matter the reason for "signing up", each of the women, like any man, who has chosen to make the navy a career, has a tale to tell.

At the dawn of the Canadian Naval Centennial, it is quite the revelation to look back upon the last twenty years in the Canadian navy from a woman's perspective. It is interesting to see how far we truly have come in our quest to "Be a man and do it". The days of the gender sensitivity training are well astern of us and it is quite clear that, in today's navy, a sailor is a sailor is a sailor, regardless of gender, race or religion. In many ways, the introduction of women into our ships has paved the way for many other individuals to succeed in the navy, in effect leading the way for diversity. So, where did we start and where are we now? What are some of the unique challenges that women have experienced on the road to operational equity? Was all the turmoil really worth it in the end? Do we as women lead sailors differently? This article will explore some of these issues, particularly where leadership is concerned. It will hopefully acknowledge the successes and highlight some of the areas where improvement may still be needed.

The military has traditionally been perceived as very masculine.[1] This environment is still dominated by males,[2] the navy is no exception. In 1989, the Canadian Human Rights Tribunal ordered the Canadian Forces to fully integrate women into combat roles, including those in surface warships (with the exception of submarines due to a perceived Bona Fide Occupational Requirement (BFOR)). In 1990, recruiting opened up, and for many women, service on board Her Majesty's Canadian Ships suddenly became a viable career option. With this change came a slew of official policies many of which were accompanied by some non-official common practices. For the men who had grown up in a single-gendered navy, the change would prove to be challenging at times and it was made all the more difficult by pre-conceived notions, biases and, sometimes, by the refusal to accept that the decision had been made. The decision to exclude females from submarines was subsequently overturned following a report by Bradley in 2001.[3]

From a personal perspective, the second author (Commander Michelaine Lahaie) joined HMCS SASKATCHEWAN as a Maritime Surface Officer (MARS) IV trainee in the summer of 1993. Up until that time, SASKATCHEWAN, like some of the other steamers,[4] had only had a few female MARS II trainees join for a very short duration. The commanding officer of the ship of the day fought vehemently against having three women join for what would essentially be four months of intense training. He lost that battle and the women arrived at the end of April 1994. Change is never easy, immediate reactions to the fact that things are going to be different often instills fear.[5] Prior to the arrival of women, the crew in SASKATCHEWAN was subjected to long lectures on gender sensitivity. They were told that they could no longer prowl the flats naked (as they often would to travel to the heads and washplaces) and that use of profanity on board was banned as the young lady officers would not be able to deal with hearing such language. Walking across the brow the first day was daunting for everyone, the women had no idea what it was going to be like, and it became pretty apparent that there was some nervousness and some general resentment amongst the crew. Fortunately, the decision had been made to berth all MARS IV trainees together in 2 Mess, the bunks on the starboard side. A curtain was hung to provide necessary privacy and the heads and washplaces were shared with not only the other trainees, but also with the Leading Seamen (LS) and below boatswains (Bos'ns) and Naval Weapons Technicians. There were some bumps in the road, but eventually, all worked out well. Through tenaciousness and the support of the other trainees, the women managed to integrate into the crew as much as any trainee can become a part of the crew. In the end, all the gender sensitivity training was completely unnecessary. The leadership of the time had failed to recognize that the women who chose the navy had chosen it expecting it to be a male-dominated environment. No one was seeking to change the navy; women were merely seeking equal opportunity. If the "rules of the game" are made clear to them, women should still succeed as leaders when entering previously all-male institutions.[6] Certainly, respect and common decency were expected, but there was no expectation of special treatment, whether "the rules" were made clear, is another question. Often it was the senior leadership and course instructors who resented the presence of women and not the women's male colleagues; for these men, working alongside women was the norm, not the exception.

With the removal of restrictions on the employment of women in surface ships, two things occurred. First, the doors were opened wide in recruiting and quotas were established. As a result, many women who perhaps would not have chosen the navy as a career option found themselves being recruited into the navy. This eventually led to other issues as a large number of them attempted to leave the navy for the pure reason that they had never wanted to be in the navy in the first place or simply did not account for the higher levels of stress that required extra effort and coping to live as a token population in an environment where male predispositions (i.e., physical and social) are favoured.[7]

At the same time, the navy instituted a critical mass policy. Essentially, certain ships were designated as Mixed Gender Units, much like certain ships were designated as French Language Units or as Bilingual Units. Women could only be posted to one of the Mixed Gender Units. At first glance, this seemed like a very good idea. Mixed Gender Units would have what was viewed as an optimal critical mass of 20 per cent of the crew being women. For example, with a crew of 240, that would mean about 48 women. The ships selected to be Mixed Gender Units were selected based upon berthing arrangements. HMCS CORMORANT and supply ships were easily modified to accommodate women and so, they were among the first to be designated as Mixed Gender Units. Unfortunately, for a number of the operator occupations, this was not a positive move. The women going to these ships were not getting the same quality of operational experience as their peers who were serving in Steamers and the 280s[8] of the day. This situation was ultimately rectified by the addition of HMCS NIPIGON and HMCS ANNAPOLIS. With the introduction of the HALIFAX class,[9] HMCS MONTREAL and NCSM VILLE DE QUÉBEC were declared as Mixed Gender Units on the East Coast while HMCS VANCOUVER and HMCS OTTAWA were declared Mixed Gender Units on the West Coast. Eventually, HMCS IROQUOIS was also added into the mix. Opportunities for women to progress improved with a broader range of platforms available for posting. However, the critical 20 per cent mass was not achievable given that the rate of attrition for women was more than twice that of men in naval operational/technical occupations.[10] Clearly, the career management issues associated with Mixed Gender Units soon became untenable. In 2000, the navy decided to do away with the Mixed Gender construct and opened up all ships for women to serve. This was followed in 2001 by the removal of the restrictions against women serving in submarines.[11] All the doors were truly open.

From the very outset, there were issues with the employment of women on board ships. The senior men of the day had grown up in a culture where everyone was the same – the navy was essentially a very homogenous environment. Junior sailors were expected to adapt to navy life and it was believed that the women who arrived on board would do much the same thing. Unfortunately, women's issues were in no short supply as the navy was not given a great deal of time to adapt the environment for the arrival of women. The ships were old and had not been designed to accommodate a mixed gender crew. As a result, some of the most basic things had not been considered, like heads and wash places, or the placement of washers and dryers onboard (sometimes in the females head's or even in their actual cabins in the now defunct Minesweepers). Of most concern, however, was the inability of the divisional system to adapt (of note, Hinton & White found that women who released from the CF, were still struggling with major gender barriers stemming from their, at that time, recent acceptance into restricted sea occupations).[12] On board many of the mixed gender ships, ad hoc divisional systems developed whereby women dealt with what were perceived as women's issues. Many of the senior men were fearful of harassment complaints and so, chose to completely divest themselves of their leadership responsibilities vis-à-vis their women sailors. Anecdotally, this often led to a breakdown in the chain of command and perceived inequities as junior sailors were often bringing their problems direct to the officers. Eventually, there was a realization that the divisional system needed to take charge of the situation. The women were completely integrated and the chain of command adapted and reassumed its original role. There can be no doubt that there were growing pains. About 10 years into the process of integrating women, the navy showed its ability to be flexible when it became clear that it needed to take a proactive approach in managing its newest additions.

It is well known that traditional military leadership models have been male-oriented;[13] such frameworks have presented many challenges for women in military settings and the Canadian navy is no different in this regard. From the very arrival of women on board, it was anecdotally noted that women tend to lead differently than their male counterparts. For the navy, this was perhaps the greatest adjustment as naval leadership has traditionally been known for its transactional leadership style. Women leaders tend to be more transformational, more open to new ideas and more willing to alter their course of action after they have made a decision.[14] Not surprising, this was a huge adjustment; add to this the fact that women tend to be viewed as less effective than their male counterparts in male dominated fields[15] and it was clear that it would be a challenge for women to succeed in the navy.

Little scientific research exists that examines leadership styles of women in a naval environment. Research conducted by NASA may provide some perspective on how, objectively speaking, female leadership differs from male leadership styles in an operational and isolated environment. Further, crews work in close proximity to one another in isolation from civilization for long periods of time allowing for loose extrapolations. Leon found that while men's leadership styles tend to be characterized by high levels of competitiveness and minimal sharing of personal concerns among crew members, women tend to be concerned with not only their crew's personal concerns, but are also simultaneously focused on task orientation and mentoring others.[16] These findings are consistent with the literature;[17] despite these differences, Leon found that where mixed crews were concerned, women assumed the role of peacemaker defusing conflict, crew members found it easier to express their feelings and it was felt that the mission, overall, was calmer.[18] These are interesting findings and anecdotally speaking, do parallel experiences of sailors in the Canadian navy. Some men even disclosed that they preferred sailing with women as personal hygiene of the sailors as a general rule, improved substantially from the days where they sailed with only men. Further, they have commented that the ship's routine often ran smoother as well.

Some may be reading this article and wonder if women are treated any differently from their male colleagues. Given that Elacqua, Beehr, Hansen and Webster found women perceived that they were treated differently to their male counterparts and that their male colleagues did not share the same perceptions – this is a fair question that requires more exploration in this specific context.[19] Nevertheless, it is known that sex role stereotypes and behaviours congruent with such stereotypes have been shown to influence perceptions of competence in military environments.[20] Even in cases where men and women do not differ on objective measures of military performance, albeit in US training institutions, women were perceived to possess more feminine attributes that negatively impact that military performance.[21] While we know that stereotypes affect performance evaluations; they can also affect access to training opportunities and ultimately opportunities for promotion.[22] Only when women gain credible operational experience (certainly in the combat arms, including the navy), and concurrently progress through the ranks can they be properly equipped to assume senior leadership positions.[23]

Growing a senior naval officer or non-commissioned member (NCM) takes time; preparing a female naval officer should take time as well (including time for maternity and parental leave should she so choose); accordingly, time will tell if the integration of women into the navy has been successful given that women have been allowed in the surface fleet for only 20 years. Holden and Tanner demonstrated that across the CF, the rate of progress of women into the senior ranks is not generally comparable to their male counterparts;[24] statistics on the career progression rates of female MARS Officers are not available. Consistent with this, the Canadian navy, has produced one Regular and one Reserve Force Commanding Officer of an HMC Ship and one Coxswain. Currently, 12 per cent of the navy is comprised of women (15.9 per cent Officers and 10.2 per cent NCMs).[25] Considering this along with the high attrition rates as compared to their male counterparts, only time will tell if integration has been successful and how the navy as an institution will define it. In the meantime, it might be timely for the navy, and perhaps even the CF to revisit its definitions of what constitutes leadership given the marked differences in the genders' respective leadership styles.[26] Loughin and Arnold postulate that transformational leadership (we know that women tend to be transformational leaders) is essential at higher levels to set the vision for their subordinates.[27] Senior leaders, in the meantime need to communicate a compelling vision of a future that includes women in all senior leadership roles while motivating their followers to support this goal.

There can be no doubt that the navy of 2010 differs significantly from the navy of 1910 – indeed, some of our forefathers would roll over in their graves to see women serving in ships and submarines. However, there is also no doubt that one of the milestones of the past 100 years is the integration of women into the fleet. Although the road to integration has been bumpy at times, the fact remains that the women who choose the navy choose it because of the unique employment opportunities. Isn't it truly wonderful that you no longer have to be a man to join the navy?

---

1   W. Arkins & L.R. Dobrofsky, "Military socialization and masculinity," *Journal of Social Issues* 34 (1978): 151-168.

2   C. Loughlin & K.A. Arnold, "Seeking the Best: Leadership Lessons from the Military," *Human Resource Management* 46 (1, 2007): 147-167.

3   B.L. Bradley, *Mixed Gender Crewing of VICTORIA-Class Submarines*, Maritime Staff Research Report 99-1. (Ottawa: NDHQ, Maritime Staff, 1999).

4   "Steamers" was the colloquial term for Canada's steam driven destroyers. These ships were difficult to integrate due to large mess deck (crew quarters) size. These vessels have now all been decommissioned and were replaced by the HALIFAX-class.

5   Loughlin & Arnold, "Seeking the Best: Leadership Lessons from the Military".

6   R.W. Rice, J.D. Yoder, J. Adams, R.F. Priest, & H.T. Prince, "Leadership Ratings for Male and Female Military Cadets," *Sex Roles* 10 (1984): 885-901.

7   R.L. Kent & S.E. Moss, "Effects of Sex and Gender Role on Leader Emergence," *Academy of Management Journal* 37 (1994): 1335-1346.

8   The 280s (IROQUOIS-class) are Canada's command platforms. Crew size ranges from mid to high 200s depending on shipboard mission. A mix of small and large mess decks made gender integration possible in these ships, as in the supply ships (PROTECTEUR-class).

9   The HALIFAX-class were easier to integrate due to smaller crew quarters. Heads and washplaces were also added/changed to accommodate women. The 280s (IROQUOIS-class) are Canada's command platforms. Crew size ranges from mid to high 200s depending on shipboard mission. A mix of small and large mess decks made gender integration possible in these ships, as in the supply ships (PROTECTEUR-class).

10   *Minister's Advisory Board on Canadian Forces Gender Integration and Employment Equity*. 2000 Annual Report. (Ottawa, ON: Department of National Defence).

11   Lieutenant-Commander Lynn Bradley with Lieutenant-Commander Debbie Pestell, "Experiences with Mixed Gender Submarine Crews," Chapter 20 in this volume.

12   H.L. Hinton & R.E. White, *Why they leave: An analysis of Interviews of Released Naval Personnel*, (Ottawa, ON: National Defence, Director Human Resources Research and Evaluation, Sponsor Research Report 00-16, 2000).

13   L.A. Boyce & A.M. Herd, "The Relationship Between Gender Role Stereotypes and Requisite Military Leadership Characteristics," *Sex Roles* 49, 7/8 (October 2003): 365-378.

14   C. Loughlin & K.A. Arnold, "Seeking the Best: Leadership Lessons from the Military."

15   Boyce & Herd, 2003; F.J. Yammarino et al., "Women and Transformational and Contingent Reward Leadership: A Multiple-Levels-of-Analysis Perspective," *Academy of Management Journal* 40 (1997): 205-222.

16   G.R. Leon, "Men and Women in Space Aviation", *Space and Environmental Medicine* Vol. 76, No. 6s (2005): B84-88.

17   M.N. Ruderman et al., "Benefits of Multiple Roles for managerial Women," *Academy of Management Journal* 45: 2 (2002): 369-386.

18   Leon, "Men and Women in Space Aviation."

19   T.C. Elacqua et al., "Manager's Beliefs about the Glass Ceiling: Interpersonal and Organizational Factors," *Psychology of Women Quarterly* 33 (2009): 285-294.

20   A.E. Eagly, S.J. Karau & M.G. Makhijani, "Gender and the effectiveness of leaders: A meta-analysis," *Psychological Bulletin* 117 (1995):125-145.

21   J. Boldry, W. Wood, & D.A. Kashy, "Gender Stereotypes and Evaluation of Men and Women in Military training," *Journal of Social Issues* 57 (2001): 689-705.

22   Loughlin & Arnold, "Seeking the Best: Leadership Lessons from the Military."

23   Loughlin & Arnold, "Seeking the Best: Leadership Lessons from the Military."

24   N.J. Holden & L.M. Tanner, *An Examination of Current Gender Integration Policies And Practices in TTCP Nations*, The Technical Cooperation Program TTCP/HUM/01/03 (September 2001): 55.

25   Nicola J. Holden & Karen D. Davis, "Chapter 4: Harassment in the Military: Cross-National Comparisons," in *Challenge and Change in the Military: Gender and Diversity Issues*, edited by Franklin C. Pinch et al., Vol. 3 (Kingston: Canadian Defence Academy Press, 2007), 97-121.

26   Notwithstanding, the importance of transformational leadership was introduced into CF leadership doctrine in 2005. See *Leadership in the Canadian Forces: Conceptual Foundations*. (Kingston, ON: Canadian Defence Academy – Canadian Forces Leadership Institute, 2005), 67-71.

27   Loughlin & Arnold, "Seeking the Best: Leadership Lessons from the Military."

CHAPTER 14

My Evolving Role as a Leader and as a Woman: A Personal Story

Petty Officer 1*st* class Alena Mondelli

Petty Officer 1*st* class (PO1) Alena Mondelli, CD, MA, joined the Canadian Forces on 1 November, 1991. She is a Naval Communicator and served on board Her Majesty's Canadian Ships ANNAPOLIS, PROVIDER, THUNDER, ALGONQUIN, HURON, PROTECTEUR, REGINA and, VANCOUVER. She has been posted ashore to Naval Radio Station (NRS) Aldergrove, Canadian Forces Language and Recruit School (CFLRS) St-Jean, and Canadian Forces Fleet School (CFFS) Esquimalt.

How often have we sat around and listened to the experiences of others and have somehow been influenced by their stories? I have many memories of sitting with my fellow sailors, listening to their stories and learning from their experiences. Although, I sometimes had to relive the lesson on my own to fully grasp the learning involved. Storytelling is that powerful medium to assist us in our ability to enable others through our own personal endeavours. To approach my perception of leadership, the role of women in leadership and my contribution to leadership in the navy, I will share some of my story through the lens of being a woman employed in a hard sea trade within the Canadian navy.

Perception of Leadership

I believe that it is safe to say that my leadership has evolved throughout the years. If my leadership has evolved then I can assume that others around me have also evolved within their own leadership roles. We might not all agree with each other's leadership practices, but we acknowledge that we are all learning together and even from each other.

When I first joined the Canadian navy as a Naval Radio Operator in 1991, I was 18 and had no idea what I was getting into. I had just graduated high school and needed to do something with my life. Funny enough, when I was around 10 years old I had dreamed of learning how to play the clarinet and joining the army to be in the band. I never learned how to play the clarinet and my aspirations were forgotten by high school. However, it was a conversation with a friend that re-kindled the spark and three months later I was in Cornwallis. I joined the navy instead of the army, and the closest thing to learning the clarinet was using a Morse code key and typewriter. In those days, I had no concept of the Canadian Forces (CF) or the navy or even leadership.

From early on in my career I have been placed in positions of leadership. The early years have somewhat faded from memory, but there are specific memories I have where I was placed in positions of responsibility. Back then I did not consider myself a leader. In the beginning of the third week of basic training, I had overheard my master corporal tell the second-week squad senior that, "it was time to shake-up Mondelli." I was horrified with this knowledge and could not figure out why I was chosen to wear the dreaded sleeve of responsibility. In time I had learned to realize why, but it took three more weeks of basic training, and an interview with the platoon sergeant, for me to understand. He told me I had maturity that was beyond my 18 years of age. Looking back, this sergeant was defining for me that maturity, in his eyes, was a characteristic of being a leader. I could effectively take charge of those around me if I acted older than I was. I was gaining a perception that a good leader had to be older in nature.

Two years later I was sailing back from Operation FORWARD ACTION. I was an Ordinary Seaman and my POTEL (Petty Officer of Telecommunications)[1] had placed me as the Senior Hand of a Corporal Signal Operator, who was an army individual that had volunteered for the trip, and an able seaman. I questioned my PO's decision because I was the junior person on the watch and he told me that he felt I had the confidence and job-knowledge to take charge of these two individuals and to run the watch efficiently and effectively. Leadership was beginning to take shape in my mind as someone who displayed maturity, confidence and was knowledgeable. Something else that was occurring, but I was not yet aware of it at the time, was that the PO was beginning to mentor me by placing me in a position above my rank level in order to develop me. This was the start of a mentoring relationship that continues to this day.[2]

I quickly progressed through the ranks and was beginning to have an awareness of what leadership actually was and what it meant to be a good leader. I was not able to define it or tell others what exactly it was, but I knew what it was for me and it involved more than just maturity and confidence. I knew I was a hard worker, fair in how I treated those around me, and always willing to learn and pass on my job knowledge and skills.

In 1997, I went on my Junior Leadership Course. I was looking forward to finally learning about leadership. I remember completing the course very frustrated as I disagreed with several of the leadership philosophies being taught – especially the use of fear as a leadership tool. Fear was in abundance and was the motivating factor in a power relationship used by the instructors on the students to influence how we behaved and carried ourselves while on the course. I know now that back then the leadership paradigm was rules-based and it was conflicting with my own developing leadership philosophy. I also began to see "how not to be" when it came to leadership. I knew there were those around me who were authoritarians and used fear, abuse, and humiliation to lead and had created atmospheres of toxicity. There were also those who were so laissez-fair about their leadership some of their subordinates released from the navy in frustration. I did not want to lead like those folks. I was leading with an awareness of "how not to be" as I did not have any other name for it. I had formed the basis of my leadership philosophy; I just did not know what to call it.

Another interesting phenomenon was occurring during the process of learning about my leadership role and philosophy. I was basing my self-worth on the assessment of my leadership ability. I knew I was a good leader because my assessments and course reports told me so. My superiors consistently told me so. My ego was continuously being fed positive input without actually digesting what I was doing that made me a good leader. I was good because I was told I was good and began to base my identity on this. This naturally created conflict between my developing leadership philosophy and my ego, eventually resulting in several years of self-doubt and a lack of confidence. I was also beginning to recognize that my leadership philosophy was different than that of my mentor. I saw that he led using fear as a motivator and was an authoritarian. I would hear him tell stories of how he became successful by bullying the situation to his advantage and was proud that he damaged relationships in the process. The difference made me question my leadership beliefs and values. How could I respect a senior leader and call him my mentor when his actions contradicted what I believed?[3] This awareness had devastated me and left me with a sense of being alone and somewhat of an individual.

My turning point was when I was at the Petty Officer 2nd class (PO2) rank. I had just completed a difficult posting on board ship. I felt I was completely surrounded by "how not to be". I was exhausted, frustrated, and beaten down. The armour that I had created over the years to protect my ego was rusted and chipped away, leaving me vulnerable and raw. I left the ship not only disappointed with myself, but also with the navy. I had to find a reason to stay in for the next six years in order to fulfill my 20-year contract. If I could not find it, I was going to release. I had gone from an Able Seaman wanting to someday be the Canadian Forces Chief, to a PO2 believing I would not progress any further in rank or trade. I began taking education to prepare myself for the reality of releasing from the navy. I was accepted into a university program and began a journey of learning, self-awareness, change, and personal transformation.

Education is a powerful tool. I learned many things, but in particular I learned that I have a values-base that guides me in my decision-making process. It is my values, my awareness, and my personal experience that determine my leadership role in how I lead, not the external factors of where I work or the expectations of supervisors. I also discovered that the CF has a core set of values that forms the basis of military professionalism. I realized that my values coincided with that of military ethos and the navy. More importantly, I realized my leadership philosophy of "how not to be" was consistent with values-based leadership and coincided with the CF Effectiveness Framework. I had discovered this on my own through my study and research as *Duty with Honour* and the *Leadership in the Canadian Forces* publications were just beginning to surface. The information was available, but was yet to be disseminated in a language that most of us could relate to. Whether teaching in front of a class, supervising manoeuvring on the bridge, or managing my section onboard a ship, I now have a name for my leadership philosophy and make every effort to lead with a values-based framework utilizing a multitude of influential behaviours in order to achieve mission success. It is not easy but it is effective.

Perception of Women

When I first joined the navy, I did not consider myself a woman joining the navy, but a person joining the navy. There were nine other women with me in my platoon of 90 during basic training and when I made my way to Esquimalt for my basic trades training, there was no shortage of women at Nelles Block.[4] Even the sailing in the early years had me working in sections where all the Leading Seamen and below were women except for the odd male. That was the nature of most combat hard sea trades back then. The Master Seaman and above were the males and the Leading Seaman and below were predominantly females. In those days I had received the usual comments[5] from the males about the size of my breasts, my body shape, and women not belonging on ships, however I never really perceived myself as a woman sailing on a ship, but as a sailor doing her job. Even though I knew the comments to be derogatory, unethical, and wrong, I did not have issue with them and ignored them most of the time. I was socialized to assume that they were a part of culture and society as a whole as the comments I received then were similar in nature to what I heard in high school.

It was not until I was a Leading Seaman and posted to a smaller vessel with a crew of approximately 30 did I begin to become aware of, and acknowledge, a separation of sailor and gender. I was the only female on board, and the first female non-commissioned member (NCM) posted to this class of ship, and my thought process was that of being a sailor. However, those around me, regardless of rank, perceived me as a woman first, and then a sailor and crewmember only once I had proven myself a hard worker and trustworthy. Some never saw me as anything more than a woman. I remember one night in particular when I was on duty and standing Quartermaster at the brow. We were in a foreign port and there were several ships nested together. It was late at night and some sailors had made their way up to the brow and wanted to go ashore. One sailor was so intoxicated that he could barely walk. I told his shipmate that he could not go ashore and that he should put him to bed. They left the brow area and had a discussion in which I clearly heard, "She's a woman, and I don't have to listen to her." I looked right at this sailor's shipmate and told him that I was a Quartermaster on a HMC Ship and he will go to bed, if not I was calling the Duty Coxswain (Cox'n). This threat seemed to work after some more arguing between the two of them. What was more interesting was that several days later this person, with an audience of my shipmates, apologized to me.[6]

I had come to the realization that my gender was not an issue to me, but it was to those around me, including the spouses of my fellow shipmates. One time I had answered the ship's external phone and it was a spouse asking for a fellow sailor. While on the phone this sailor had stated, "oh she's just a reserve and temporary". This sailor had to lie to his wife in having her believe that I was not Regular

Force and thus not a permanent member of the ship's company. It made sense now why my name, Alena, was masculinised to Al. If I was Al, I was perceived as a sailor and male. If I was Alena, I was female and a threat. There were many introductions with military spouses where they would exclaim, "Oh, Al is a girl", and then walk away from me.

By the late 1990s my trade had amalgamated to Naval Communicator (Nav Comm). There were several women who had achieved the rank of Master Seaman. They were the first women to do so in our trade, even pre-amalgamation. I quickly joined their ranks. I also quickly came face-to-face with the reality of jealousy from my male counterparts and the rumours that can be spread because of that jealousy. I did not let this stop me though; I learned to create a thick psychological armour that, for a while, would protect my ego. I still lead with my leadership philosophy and continued to develop it throughout. I also began to experience the weight of the expectations my superiors had of my achievements. Comments like, "you'll be the first female chief" and "you'll be a female Cox'n someday" were being said to me by many folks, including my mentor. Nav Comm is a hard sea trade,[7] and hard sea trades did not admit women until the late 1980s. It was important for some folks to see women move up the ranks and have their own identity associated with those women. It was very common to hear, "As her supervisor, I got her advanced promoted".

I did not have any female role models to emulate. High-ranking female NCMs on board ships were usually support trades, not hard sea trades, and I could not find a common ground with them. Female officers in the navy are told from early on that they lead the naval NCM and to not fraternize with them.[8] They themselves are involved in their own means of survival in what it means to be a female sailor in the Officer Corps. All I had was a very small female peer group who were either the same rank as me or one rank lower. We were going through the same things and so we would console each other and discuss what it meant to break the glass ceiling of the Chief and POs (Petty Officers) mess only to find another more solid ceiling. It had felt like the higher up in rank I was going, the less accepting the naval culture was of female sailors. It was an overwhelmingly discouraging reality and one that was exhausting me. Interestingly enough, by this time in my career, I was sailing on a ship that traditionally had an older aged culture in the Chief and POs' mess.

Several years later, I sailed on a different class ship that had a much younger mess population and the experience was much different. The experience was positive, inclusive, and enjoyable. I was comfortable with being a woman, a senior NCO, and a sailor. Although by this time I had also learned how to be all three without denying one over the other. Earlier in my career, I felt that in order to survive in the navy I had to give up my femininity and deny a very important part of myself in how I led and worked. With education and awareness, I recognized the importance my personal values played in how I perceived myself as a woman in a traditionally male occupation. I had to acknowledge within myself that there is a difference and to lead with that newfound awareness

My Contribution to Leadership in the Canadian Navy.

Just by being a woman in the Canadian navy, I have contributed to its success. Although I am one person, my contributions, as small as they are, unite with those contributions from men and women around me, to propel then navy forward. I am a transformative leader and change agent, as well as a mentor.

To be a transformative leader, one must have an awareness of the transformation in order to fully understand what it is and to learn from it to move forward with the new way of thinking. An element of the current CF Transformation is the paradigm shift from a rules-based to a values-based leadership philosophy. I ensure that when I lead, it is with an awareness of CF values as well as my own. I will not compromise on my beliefs. I recognize that we are faced with decisions everyday that will place weight on one value over another, but that is the nature of values based leadership. Leading goes hand in hand with analysing the risks associated with the decision making process involved with mission success. Learning from analysing the risks coupled with lessons learned from previous decisions is what transforms a situation into something more effective the next time it comes around. I lead in how I believe I want to be treated. I ensure that those around me are aware and a part of the shifting paradigm from rules-based to values based leadership. I speak it in a language those around me understand and I make reference to our own leadership manuals to back up my views.

I also feel that being a transformative leader ties in with being a change agent as you are living the change you want to see. I firmly believe that by just being the first Regular Force female Nav Comm to reach the rank of PO2 and Petty Officer

1st class (PO1), and to become the first Regular Force female Senior Nav Comm on board a ship[9] on either coast, I have been a part of the change process. How I conduct myself in my leadership philosophy and ability will determine just how much change I can in fact effect. I contribute to leadership by being the change I wish to see and by shaping the change through transformation.

Mentoring is a valuable tool that as leaders, regardless of gender or rank, we can use to transform the CF into a values-based philosophy. One of our own Principles of Leadership is to mentor, educate and develop subordinates. When I am having conversations around mentoring, I like to change up the principle by discussing how we can mentor, educate and develop not only our subordinates, but each other as well. When I am leading I have awareness that my actions, behaviours and even decisions will be emulated and could possibly lead to the development of those around me. I recognize the importance in how establishing relationship, even through discussion, is a powerful mechanism for mentoring through transformative change.

Conclusion

In writing my story, so many other ideas began to surface. For example, what happened to the sense of community we had as women in the early days? Not only did we all go out as one group in a foreign port – even if we did not always get along, but we also socialized as that same group when we were in home port. That community seems to be gone now. Has the navy changed through retention and recruitment? Has my personal lens changed in how I now view community? Or has the naval culture as a whole shifted? It would be interesting to see a comparison of what community meant in 1991 compared to what we believe community is in 2010. But that is another essay.

Over the last 18 years, I have seen the evolution of leadership within the CF. I have witnessed the effects of leading within a dynamic system utilizing a holistic approach that encompasses all that it means to be a member of the CF: Military Ethos and the Warrior's Honour. However, it is a young system still and there is much growing and nurturing involved. Change takes time. Our culture still needs to play catch-up with our policy and doctrine. As a woman and a senior leader within my trade and the navy, I now find myself thinking of the challenges the young female sailors face and the challenges I face in leading them. I now feel a sense of responsibility to be present with my leadership and to use my experience, and story, to continue the momentum of change that is occurring within the navy. I lead as a sailor, making decisions based on what I hope are the right factors for the situation at the right time. I also acknowledge my accomplishments as a female sailor in a dynamic CF where leadership and gender roles are continuously evolving.

---

1   POTEL: This person was a PO1 and the section head of the Naval Radiomen section on board ship.

2   This person will be referred to as my mentor throughout this paper.

3   My mentor, over a period of quite a few years, has gone through his own personal transformation journey and now leads with values-based leadership.

4   The barrack block at CFB Esquimalt where junior sailors reside.

5   Comments such as: "Those are always nice to look at", "Your ass will expand when you get on board ship", and "It's your place as a woman to be at home for your fiancé and give him children".

6   I found out later that several of my shipmates had threatened this sailor into apologizing to me.

7   Created from two hard sea trades: Naval Radioman and Naval Signalman.

8   This was information that was shared by several MARS officer females that I had previously sailed with.

9   HMCS VANCOUVER.

CHAPTER 15

Toasting Positive Change and Progress... Every Day of the Week!

Lieutenant-Commander Nancy Setchell

Lieutenant-Commander (LCdr) Nancy Setchell (nee Nicholls), CD, BA, was raised in Midland, Ontario. She joined the Canadian Forces in 1995 and attended the Royal Military College, graduating in 1999 with a Bachelor of Arts (Honours) in English. On completion of her Maritime Surface and Subsurface (MARS) training, she sailed in the Pacific Fleet. She earned her Bridge Watchkeeping Certificate aboard HMCS OTTAWA and completed her Naval Officer Professional Qualification in 2001. In 2002, she deployed with HMCS OTTAWA for Operation APOLLO. She then earned her qualification as a ship's Navigating Officer, and navigated HMCS OTTAWA. She instructed the Fleet Navigating Officers' course at the Naval Officer Training Centre Venture from 2004 to 2006. In 2007, she completed the Operations Room Officer course and was posted to HMCS TORONTO as the Weapons Officer. In 2009, she joined Maritime Forces Atlantic Headquarters and worked in Military Personnel Management. LCdr Setchell lives in Dartmouth with her husband, Scott, and daughter, Nora.

Canada's navy has evolved greatly since its creation in 1910, and has reached significant and unforeseen milestones. One of the most noteworthy evolutions is that women have equal access to every position in the Navy at sea and ashore. This tremendous fact is a tribute to a change in attitude and a general acceptance of the equality of women by Canada and the Canadian Forces (CF). The transformation has not been without difficulties and we are not yet in a position to proclaim that we have achieved perfection, but the overall achievement in the past 100 years is dramatic. With such a significant change in naval culture, it comes as no surprise that our traditions have transformed. It is very important that they have evolved since traditions form a large part of every navy's culture and encourage a special camaraderie. In Canada, we celebrate a proud history steeped in stories of heroism and of a navy that solidified our country's position on the world stage. However, traditions can be a double-edged sword. With a nod to our naval history, our traditions are observed both to honour those who came before us and also to celebrate that which makes us unique. In short, we need traditions in our navy to define and observe our distinct culture, but we are in dangerous waters when we focus on the past, ignoring the present or the future.

Our navy must occasionally re-visit that which defines our culture to make certain it is reflective of our reality. Just as our ships have evolved from steam engines to gas turbines, our culture must evolve and change to stay current and appropriate. It is important that women have the right to pursue any career in our navy; what is equally important is that women are fulfilling roles and that the navy believes in the equality of women. This change has already been deemed a success and, indeed, women are advancing in the navy. I have personally seen a dramatic change since joining the fleet ten years ago.

However, of great concern is the failed transformation in one particular tradition. Ten years ago, the naval toasts were amended to reflect the navy's developing demographics. The participation of women in the navy today represents a significant change since the early part of the 19th century when naval toasts were first practiced in Canada. Unfortunately, it is still common at mess dinners to use the old toasts, a practice that blatantly alienates women.

As a Naval Cadet under training at the Naval Officer Training Centre *Venture*, my class was deemed a novelty, as it was one of the first that was 50 per cent women. Early on, I had a good indication that the navy was changing; from one year to the next, a tradition transformed before my eyes. Junior officers quickly memorize naval toasts in the event they are called on to make the toast at a mess dinner. I learned the "old" naval toasts in 1997 as follows:

Monday: Our ships at sea

Tuesday: Our men

Wednesday: Ourselves

Thursday: A bloody war or a sickly season

Friday: A willing foe and sea room

Saturday: Wives and sweethearts

(with the reply: May they never meet)

Sunday: Absent friends

While the old toasts represent a part of our history, they also embody a now defunct all-male demographic of a navy that toasted a "Bloody war or a sickly season" to favour promotion and a "willing foe." In 1997, the Naval Board recognised that the toasts were outdated and no longer reflected the reality of the navy and the values of Canadians.[1] After much deliberation, two toasts were altered slightly (Monday and Tuesday) and three were changed altogether (Thursday, Friday, and Saturday). The new toasts are:

Monday: Our ships

Tuesday: Our sailors

Wednesday: Ourselves

Thursday: Our navy

Friday: Our nation

Saturday: Our families

Sunday: Absent friends

In 1998, we learned the "new" toasts, and I believed the changes were due. I felt included. However, the change seemed to be met with disappointment, and anger. How dare we change a naval tradition? This resistance ignored that we had already broken with several traditions by changing policies and allowing women at sea. For the first time it occurred to me that maybe women were not entirely accepted in the navy culture and were, in fact, to blame for changing the important tradition of toasts. While it may have seemed emasculating not to toast war for the sake of promotion, extramarital affairs and men, the old toasts exclude parts of our navy, my navy. Perhaps the outrage was merely a latent expression of the anger towards what had been an arguably larger change in the navy. Only once the old toasts are a footnote in our history rather than a common practice can we consider our navy to have changed.

The toasts were re-written to strike a balance between naval traditions and Canada's vision of its navy. While the Canadian Forces are charged with defending Canada's values, interests and sovereignty at home and abroad,[2] we are not a nation that seeks a willing foe in order to further our riches. Likewise, our country embraces and celebrates equality, and it is time that the navy does so as well or we will risk losing our relevance as a symbol of our country. The navy must hold the same values and interests as Canada's in order to have credibility within Canada and abroad.

Today, the old toasts are rightly included in initial training. While it is important to mention them as a history lesson, we need to draw the line there. Unfortunately, those charged with making the toasts at mess dinners are often encouraged to use the old toast. I challenge our leadership to call on the youngest attendees at mess dinners to use the "new" toasts. These toasts best reflect who we are as a navy and what Canada expects of us. Any use of the old toasts marginalises the progress women have made in the navy and alienates them.

I realise that in reading this essay, traditionalists may scoff at what seems to be a small point; however, in supporting the old toasts and ignoring the new ones, I believe we are making a dangerous error. We are encouraging the celebration of a time in the navy when women were not allowed at sea, when a bloody war and sickly season were required for promotion, (rather than merit and ability), and we sought a willing foe in search of glory and gold to line the Captain's pockets. Today's Canadian navy should reflect the will of the citizens it represents. If we are truly going to embrace change, we need to celebrate our progress and ensure it does not regress. Continuing to use the old toasts will deny the progress we have so clearly made in the equality of women. We must celebrate the participation of all Canadians in our navy. It's time to get on with transforming our traditions and accepting the changes in our navy so that we can effectively move into the future.

---

1   Department of National Defence and Canadian Forces, *The Maple Leaf* 2 (8, 1999).

2   Department of National Defence and Canadian Forces, *About DND/CF*, <http://www.forces. gc.ca/site/about-notresujet/index-eng.asp>, accessed 30 November 2009.

CHAPTER 16

Yesterday, Today, and Tomorrow

Sub-Lieutenant Louise Walton

Sub-Lieutenant (SLt) Louise Ann Marie Walton, CD, BA, joined the Naval Reserve in a 1996 as a Diesel Mechanic (now called Marine Engineering Systems Operator). After university and many years at sea, she left the Reserves as a Petty Officer 1st class (PO1) Main Propulsion Supervisor and took a commission in the Regular Force navy in 2009.

I was encouraged by the Canadian Forces Leadership Institute's interest in the topic of "Transforming Traditions: Women, Leadership and the Canadian Navy." I feel that the topic is of great importance and particularly timely in nature. The biggest concern and risk, I believe, for a serving CF member when expressing her opinion on such a controversial topic is that it may be misconstrued or worse, that she be accused of airing the dirty laundry in public. What comes to mind are the spring 1998 *McLean's* articles on harassment in the navy whose inflammatory tone undermined the serious subject matter. I appreciate now that the 1990s was a period of great change for the navy and, like all change, had its own obstacles to overcome. This does not, however, erase my memory of the antagonism raised by those articles and my concern that it could be reignited. However, those risks are outweighed by the importance of communicating the thoughts and experiences of serving members so that continued improvements in gender integration in the CF can be made. The way I understand things is that the military's legitimacy is based on its conformity with society's values and its direction from government. It then stands to rest that the military's composition should ideally reflect this same society.

Early Gender Integration in the Canadian Navy and the Naval Centennial

Gender equality in the Canadian Forces, more specifically the navy, has made significant advances since the 1987 Canadian Human Rights Commission challenge, which opened all hard sea trades to women.[1] Recruiting and Public

129

Affairs constantly remind us and the public that women have cracked the last male bastions in the CF. It is true that within the navy women have achieved positions as Commanding and Executive officers, Coxswains, divers, engineers, and submariners.[2] What is not so widely acknowledged is that these successes remain largely the exception; not the rule. Roughly 13 to 15 per cent of the navy overall is female but those numbers drastically decline as you look higher in rank and position of authority.[3] While many of the traditional gender stereotypes held by the general public are no longer formally perpetuated in the CF, there remains an element of resistance to change.[4] Although there are clear enforced policies designed to prohibit discrimination and promote merit based success, there is much that can and should be done internally to promote women in leadership and achieve further gender equality. The formal restrictions have been lifted but what informal barriers remain? It is logical that female representation in positions of authority will leg behind the overall representation in the navy due to the length of time it takes to train and earn promotions. It is now 2009,[5] and they remain under-represented in the Chiefs' and Petty Officers' mess and the Wardroom. Rules and regulations are now in black and white and are more easily addressed and measured than in the past, but it is going to take a combination of resources and attitude to effectively impact the current gender and related leadership imbalances. As both an organization and as individuals we must acknowledge those who paved the way, maximize our leadership potential today, and help the next generation who will be following in our footsteps.

In order to reach true gender equality and promote women in leadership, it is essential that every aspect of the past be acknowledged. The navy may be celebrating its centennial in 2010 but it has only been twenty years since hard sea trades were opened to women and only fourteen years since gays and lesbians were allowed to serve openly.[6] As a senior non-commissioned officer (NCO) and Main Propulsion Supervisor, I thought I had a good grasp on naval history and women in the navy. It was not until I went to university that I became aware of the less glamorous history of gender integration in the CF and the navy. With the way the CF portrays the changes, one would think that on its own volition it decided to lift all gender related employment restrictions. In reality it took cases such as Lieutenant (retired) Michelle Douglas and the treatment she endured before she resigned from the military and sued the CF for discrimination.[7] Also, the circumstances leading up to the 1989 Human Rights Tribunal had a significant influence on the legislation that ordered the CF to carry out full integration.[8] I've taken the Sexual Harassment and Racism Prevention Program (SHARP), Primary and Intermediate Leadership Qualification courses, Naval Environmental Leadership Training, and the Coxswain course, but I do not recall ever being taught more than the standard policy line regarding gender integration in the CF. You can be sure that many heated discussions on the topic have taken place in messes throughout the fleet, and still do. What bothers me more is not so much the CF's past struggles towards gender integration, but that I had to find out about it from civilians. I wonder if more effort is being put into Public Relations than concrete efforts to achieve real gender equality within the navy at all levels. I've worn my uniform on the university campus while manning the recruiting booth and fielded many pointed questions of which a recurring theme was women in the military. Why then was there a nagging thought in the back of my mind that by propagating the standard lines that I was not being completely forthright? Was I selling an incomplete reality?

The Past

I joined the Naval Reserves in 1996 as a Diesel Mechanic (now called Marine Engineering Systems Operator) and started training on the west coast Maritime Coastal Defence Vessels in 1998, right after high school graduation. Looking back, my earlier naïveté still amazes me. I had joined for the usual reasons: money, travel, to meet new people, and belong to an honourable institution. A couple of my first Chief Engineers were women who joined as soon as the hard sea trades became open to them. Through perseverance and stubbornness they progressed. From them and my other shipmates I received a quick education in what life had been like not that long ago. Attitudes toward women were consistent with those held in civilian male-dominant occupations at the time. It was common for pornography to be played in the messes. "Pig of the Port" competitions took place: essentially, in foreign port, male sailors would try to bring back to the ship the least attractive woman they could meet. Also, an early question posed by a seasoned sailor that remains etched in my memory was "which one are you?" The idea was that women only joined the navy to be a man, get a man, or forget a man. I remember feeling both relieved that my experience was going to be different and appreciative that it was through the efforts of others that this was so.

The majority of the men I first met and worked with in the CF were decent hard working people who demonstrated a genuine concern and interest in my training and well-being. I believe that I received, from my supervisors, a comparable level of training and attention as my fellow male trainees. When there was trouble ashore my male shipmates quickly adopted a "big brother" attitude and put the offending individual in their place; and for that I'm appreciative. This could be seen as being a bit patriarchal, but the point is that they were being good shipmates and looking out for a winger. At that time in my life and career I was too young and not confident enough to always know how to stand up for myself in that kind of setting. It is important to remember that the navy was the first place that many of my generation of sailors faced such specific gender-based challenges. Our typical profile was the recent high school graduate, perhaps a little university, with minimum workforce experience, which was generally more mainstream in nature. Both new male and female sailors found themselves in an operational organization with the unique pressures and expectations of responding and adjusting to new realities. I think it's safe to say that gender-relation focused tensions were strained a bit more in the CF than what the general public faced.

It wasn't until I joined the Chiefs and Petty Officers mess that I fully grasped the challenges that the female sailors in leadership before me had faced. The higher in rank women reach, the fewer female peers they have and thus a smaller support network. It was felt that there was less tolerance for failure by women than by men. Male failure was seen as an exception, female failure as typical. It was either because there were fewer women and the impact was more noticeable or there was just a general resistance to change. It was as if women had been reluctantly let into the boys club so they'd better not go messing things up.

Resistance to Equality

It has been noted that the hostility experienced based on gender was generally proportionate to rank/qualification level.[9] Female Reservists have the additional obstacle of being considered lesser sailors because of their Reserve status, even despite situations that have them on class C service with similar terms of service (TOS) as the Regular Force. As a Petty Officer 2nd class (PO2), not that long ago I witnessed a Regular Force male Chief Petty Officer 2nd class (CPO2) aggressively verbally assault another CPO2 in front of her subordinates and peers. It was clear to all that he felt he could do this because of her gender and the fact that she was a

Reservist. As a PO2 visiting a dockyard support office I had a similar experience. The office supervisor, a Regular Force male CPO2, stood up and came around from his desk so that he could physically tower over me while he laced into me about Reservists. This was in front of his male office staff who couldn't look me in the eye when I left. Another compounding factor is age. Reservists progress faster in rank than the average Regular Force member. You aren't always taken seriously because of age even when you have all the formal qualifications to legitimize your point. To me this raises various complex core issues about trust. When you combine gender, unit, and age, one is bound to face occasional resistance. I do think that it is important to emphasize that, while incidents like these are fewer and further between, they did happen and they influence the leadership of women in today's navy. We are who we are because of where we've been, what we've done, and the choices we've made. To not openly discuss the past with all its warts is to not fully acknowledge how we've become who we are; it undermines the ability to maximize future potential. This applies equally to individuals and to the group. Within the naval context one could consider the Mainguy Commission a successful example of this.[10]

Lessons learned

Sometimes we are our own worst enemy. In the past, many women, myself included, bought into the idea that women must be twice as good as men to be thought half as good.[11] I'll admit that in the beginning I was guilty of expecting more from my female subordinates for two reasons; first, I wanted there to be no question of their abilities, and second, I did not want to be accused of favouritism. It took me a while to realize that this approach was only reinforcing the very attitudes I disagreed with and impeded gender integration. Two standards help no one. It breeds resentment and disrespect all around. There is one standard and it is imperative that it be upheld. Not to do so undermines the whole principle of success by merit.

Changes yet to be made

Gender integration in the navy has come a long way over the past ten years. The up and coming generations do not have to deal with many of the obstacles previously faced by women in hard sea trades. In my mind, two main issues still require progress. First is the attitude towards certain health issues. It is more acceptable for a male to be sent to a rehabilitation centre for alcohol abuse than a female to a social worker for eating disorders. I believe that this is a holdover of more traditional ideas of gender-related weaknesses. Which one costs more monetarily or socially? I expect that continuing education and understanding will alleviate this problem.

The biggest issue that, if corrected, would see the most immediate results, is affordable childcare. I believe there is a direct relation between career progression and childcare availability. Long gone are the days of single income households. Not only do the spouses of most sailors work, but more commonly that spouse is also in the military. Registered childcare is expensive and hard to find (on the west coast). What often happens is that one of the parents, usually the mother, takes a shore position. Single parents don't have much choice but to go ashore. To a Reservist, this means a 15 per cent drop in pay from class C to B, plus loss of sea duty allowance. For someone in a hard sea trade this also has an impact on their qualification progression. For a Petty Officer or Master Seaman to remuster from a hard sea trade to a shore-based NCM trade would mean the loss of significant rank and pay. Many choose this option in order to be home more and/or save money on childcare. While I personally know multiple military couples who have resorted to hiring live-in nannies, this is not a viable option for junior military members. The fallout from this remustering trend is that even fewer females make it to senior NCO and officer positions. On-base childcare or more openings at Military Family Resource Centre daycares would greatly reduce the stress on parents returning to work after maternity/paternity leave.

The Future

I believe that mentorship is the vehicle by which real gender equality in the navy will be achieved. There are a number of formal CF Mentoring Programs made available to its members. We must resist that reflex, which is all too common in the navy, of "eating our own". It is possible to be empathic and compassionate without jeopardizing standards or appearing weak. My advice to all: Look at the next generation following behind and identify someone worth mentoring, even if they are unconscious of it. Take the extra time to check in on them, be a listening ear, and dish out some tough love. Encourage them to move beyond their comfort level; taking calculated risks, and pushing past discouragements. Applaud when they succeed and be supportive during disappointments. These seem like simple ideas but knowing you're not alone can empower you to try. It often only takes one person to make a defining impact on the course of someone's life.

As women in leadership roles we owe it to ourselves and the organization to maximize our own personal and collective leadership potential. Self-reflect and take an honest inventory of your strengths and weaknesses. Make the decision to address shortcomings. We need to encourage each other to pursue challenges; everything from professional development and new qualifications for fitness and health. Remember that people are always watching when you are in a leadership position so be sure to use it for good and set a positive example. Think of all the things that infuriated you as a junior sailor and try not to repeat them. Treat people how you expect and demand to be treated; be consistent and fair. If you make a mistake, admit it and correct it. Be the change you want to see.

---

1   Canadian Human Rights Commission. (1989). Tribunal Decision 3/89 Between: ISABELLE GAUTHIER, JOSEPH G. HOULDEN, MARIE-CLAUDE GAUTHIER, GEORGINA ANN BROWN Complainants and CANADIAN ARMED FORCES Respondent (Decision rendered on February 20, 1989).

2   "Unlimited Opportunities," Canadian Forces Recruiting, <http://www.forces.ca/html/womeninthecf_en.aspx>, accessed 9 January 2010.

3   Junguee Park, "A Profile of the Canadian Forces," *Perspectives July 2008*, Statistics Canada, Catalogue no 75-001-X.

4   When I use "gender" I mean the socially assigned traits assigned to the sexes. When discussing gender equality I mean the full scope of gender: male, female, gay, lesbian, bisexual, and trans-gendered.

5   SLt Louise Walton wrote her article in 2009, as a Petty Officer, prior to taking her commission with the Regular Force. Note from the editors.

6   Matthew Foster, "Sexual Orientation and the Armed Forces: An Analysis of the Canadian Context", Wilfrid Laurier University Political Science Department Graduate Seminar 4 December 2008.

7   Bruce Poulin, "The official integration of homosexuals in the CF," *Esprit de Corps*, June 2004 <http://findarticles.com/p/articles/mi_6972/is_7_11/ai_n28209334/>, accessed 9 January 2010.

8   Donna Winslow and Jason Dunn, "Women in the Canadian Forces: Between Legal and Social Integration." *Current Sociology*. Vol 50 (5, September, 2002): 641-667.

9   Claudia Kennedy (Lt.Gen., Ret U.S.), "Redefining the Warrior Mentality: Women in the Military," *Sisterhood is Forever: the Women's Anthology for a New Millennium*, Robin Morgan (ed.), (New York: Washington Square Press, 2003), 409-417.

10   Marc Milner, *Canada's Navy: the First Century*, (Toronto: University of Toronto Press, 1999), 193-194.

11   Erin Solaro, *Women in the Line of Fire*, (Emeryville, CA: Seal Press, 2006).

CHAPTER 17

Integration and Innovation in Our New Navy: A View from the Lower Deck

Leading Seaman Geneviève Jobin and Private Lorraine van Rensburg

Leading Seaman (LS) Geneviève Jobin of Baie-Comeau, Québec joined the Canadian Forces in January 2000 as a Naval Communicator. Although she completed a College Diploma in Audio Recording in 1997 at the Collège d'Alma, the appeal of traveling around the world and learning a second language were the main reasons that attracted her into the Canadian navy. She began her naval career on the east coast initially onboard the NCSM VILLE DE QUÉBEC in February 2001 and was subsequently posted onboard the HMCS ST. JOHN'S in March 2002 to participate in the campaign against terrorism in the Persian Gulf (Op APOLLO). She was posted ashore in June 2005 to the Regional Joint Operations Centre (RJOC) in Halifax and worked as an Information Manager Operator (IMO). She then did a voluntary occupation transfer to a Resources Management System Clerk in July 2008 in order to be more present for her three-year-old daughter. LS Jobin is currently an AVPOL Clerk with the Wing Comptroller at Base des Forces canadiennes (BFC) Bagotville.

Private (Pte) Lorraine van Rensburg, BSc, was born in Singapore and immigrated to Canada with her parents when she was four years old. She has a Bachelor of Science (Botany) from the University of Calgary, Alberta. Her previous professional experience includes working as medical laboratory assistant in Alberta, an English teacher in South Korea, and as a legal secretary for numerous law firms in British Columbia, Alberta and Nova Scotia over a span of ten years. Pte van Rensburg felt called to join the Canadian Forces and enrolled as a Resource Management Support Clerk (Air) in September 2007. She is hoping to make a positive difference in the country that has become home. Although she wears the air force uniform, she was posted – and remains posted – to the Client Services Orderly Room (CSOR) Dockyard at CFB Halifax upon completion of her QL3 course. This has given her the opportunity to see the navy, meet the personnel and experience many of its traditions.

Our Canadian navy is undergoing important transitions both in its fleet and in its personnel. Current situations demand constant adaptation while maintaining operational readiness. As changes occur in the structure of the Canadian naval fleet, changes also occur in the structure of naval personnel. In this time of transition, it is imperative to appreciate the leadership within our navy for what it has done to bring us to the present and what it will do to lead us into the future.

Undoubtedly, women compose a significant portion of this leadership within the Canadian navy.

In reference to her leadership role, Her Excellency the Right Honourable Michaëlle Jean, CC, CMM, COM, CD, Governor General and Commander-in-Chief of Canada has stated "It's not about me. It's about them."[1]

In many ways, leadership in the Canadian navy is exactly that: it's not about me, it's about the country we serve; it's not about me, it's about the sailors serving under me; it's not about me, it's about the mission. It's also not about merely coping with change; it's about making change happen.

Our naval leadership has and is undergoing a significant transformation as well, triggered most recently in 2005 under the command of our former Chief of Defence Staff (CDS), General Rick Hillier, who identified six principles to guide transformation and change.[2] Since then transformation has continued and part of that transformation is the development of an increasingly mixed gender navy. In the past we had women like Dr. Wendy Clay who was the first woman officer cadet in the Royal Canadian Navy; Lieutenant-Commander Marta Mulkins who was the first woman to serve as captain of a Canadian warship, HMCS KINGSTON in 2003; and Master Seaman Colleen Beattie who was the first woman in the Canadian Forces (CF) to qualify as a submariner in 2003.[3]

This paper will communicate views on diverse questions such as why women join the Canadian navy? How well do mixed gender crews work together? How is effective military leadership defined? How are military women perceived in foreign ports? And what are the recruiting and retention plans? Military and civilian sources are used to answer these questions because certain principles are applicable to people in any workplace environment. Leadmark states: "The character of the Canadian labour market is that of an ever-shrinking workforce pursued by increasingly competitive employers. Positioning the navy as 'an employer of choice for Canadians' will be absolutely critical to the ability to recruit and retain officers and sailors with the essential skills and competencies to handle the complexities of our new equipment, and to function effectively in the more complex security environment of the future".[4]

Indisputably, the CF must appreciate the past, current and future contributions of women leaders to hold the navy together as an effective military team and to be the forerunners in the process of perpetual adaptation to changing global situations. We must focus on appreciation, recruitment and retention. In addition, the critical questions remain: where is the Canadian navy heading now and how can we improve it?

Background

We came upon this writing project by mere circumstance. There are many more personnel more qualified to write a paper on this topic. Perhaps the driving force behind this project has been a personal curiosity to find out what has indeed changed over the years in the Canadian navy and how women fit into the scheme of things. For those reasons, this paper has been written in direct consultation with women who are currently serving in leadership roles in the Canadian navy. The writers wish to thank these members for willingly sharing their experiences. In an effort to focus on the issues at hand rather than individuals, we incorporated experiences or views expressed by the named personnel in addition to selected authors and our own perspectives regarding the various topics discussed. Foremost, a brief introduction of these members is indubitably essential.

Commander (Cdr) Catherine Corrigan, Logistics Officer, is currently the Formation Administration Officer (FAdmO) at Canadian Forces Base (CFB) Halifax, Nova Scotia. Cdr Corrigan holds a Bachelor of Commerce degree and a Masters in Defence Studies. She oversees Chaplaincy, Personnel Selection Services, Client Services, Hospitality Services and Personnel Support Programs. These include three Client Services Orderly Rooms, nine accommodation blocks, six messes, four galleys, three satellite food service locations and three gymnasiums. Cdr Corrigan has served 25 years in the military including five years of subsidized university education and five years on board Canadian warships.

Lieutenant (Navy) (Lt(N)) Heather Galbraith, Logistics Officer, is currently the Client Services Support Officer (CSSO) at CFB Halifax, Nova Scotia. Lt(N) Galbraith holds a Bachelor of Arts in History and English, a Master of Science in Kinesiology (Sport Science) and has completed some post-graduate studies. She oversees Administration and Finance for Maritime Forces Atlantic (MARLANT)/ Joint Task Force (Atlantic) (JTFA), including the management of 3 dynamic and large Client Services Orderly Rooms. Lt(N) Galbraith has served 14 years in the military.

Chief Petty Officer 1st class (CPO1) Barbara Corbett, Sonar Op, is a former Unit Chief of Trinity and is currently the first female Chief of the Fleet School, both at CFB Halifax, Nova Scotia. She is responsible for all matters relating to non-commissioned members and acts as an advisor to the Commanding Officer on all such matters. CPO1 Corbett was also the first female President of the Mess Committee (PMC) for CFB Halifax. She has served 32 years in the military.

Chief Petty Officer 2nd class (CPO2) Carole Chiasson, Cook, is currently the Cadre Sergeant-Major, Food Service Training Cadre at the Canadian Forces School of Logistics (CFSAL), CFB Borden, Ontario and is currently the highest ranking female Cook in the CF. She is the senior instructor for Food Service Training at CFSAL and as such controls the deportment and discipline within the cadre for both staff and students which includes providing counselling in a timely manner and following up on progress. She also instructs and functions as the Course Director for the Annual Qualification Level (QL) 7) Cook Managers Course. CPO2 Chiasson has served 29 years in the military.

These members have graciously provided us with their military backgrounds, their views on women in the military and what they would propose for the future of the Canadian navy. Collectively, they have served in postings all across Canada, the United States, England, the United Arab Emirates, Sri Lanka, Kandahar, The Netherlands, the Golan Heights and Syria. They have participated in numerous tours and deployments including OP APOLLO, OP SCULPTURE, Fleet Week, Fisheries Patrols, Golan Heights and supporting operations at a Forward Logistics Site.

How did we select these four women? We can admit that finding women that we could look up to as role models pertaining to leadership in the navy has been the easiest part of this project! Three of the leaders that we consulted for this paper were identified through our direct experience with them in our workplaces. It was also important to us to profile the leadership experiences of officers and non-commissioned members. As members of the Formation Administration team, we wanted to highlight the leadership experiences of the FAdmO, Commander (Cdr) Corrigan, and the CSSO, Lt(N) Galbraith. LS Jobin, formerly worked as a shift worker at Trinity from 2005 to 2008, where she came under the leadership of the Unit Chief, CPO1 Corbett. In the case of our fourth leader, a colleague recommended her step-mother, CPO2 Chiasson. Each of these four women kindly agreed to help us and was a great source of inspiration in the writing of this paper.

Why Did Women Join?

According to noted naval historian Marc Milner, 1980-1991 was the Renaissance period of our Canadian navy.[5] It was during this time when our naval fleet was rebuilt, the navy's new uniforms appeared and mixed gender crews were introduced. Milner states: "Through the 1980s the navy was rebuilt – both materially and morally."[6] He goes on to state that "Perhaps the most important change in the nature of naval service in the early 1980s was the introduction of mixed gender crews. In 1980 women were admitted into the military colleges for the first time, and it was only a matter of time before they appeared in operational units."[7] Another important offset to this came from the Canadian Human Rights Tribunal in February 1989 which compelled the formerly known "Canadian Armed Forces" to open all trades to women within the next 10 years excluding service on board submarines. Continued exclusion of women from submarine service was based on the lack of privacy in the old OBERON-class; however, the CF did finally open their watertight hatches to women during the acquisition of the VICTORIA-class. And lastly, the Standard for Harassment and Racism Prevention (SHARP) course, which was mandatory upon completion of Basic Military Qualification, promoted the process of integration not only for women but for visible minorities as well.

With the doors to military service open, progressive parents who wanted their daughters to gain an education were attracted to the chance to save substantial amounts of money that would have been spent on university tuition. Progressive young women who wanted to get a university degree saw the opportunity too. For example, the offer of subsidized education was a key factor in attracting Cdr Corrigan to the Canadian military.

CPO2 Chiasson saw the military as a source of stable employment, Lt(N) Galbraith joined because her twin sister was signing up with the navy, and CPO1 Corbett joined due to a schoolmate's influence. Coming from military families certainly did not seem to be a significant influencing factor, however some of these female members have now started their own families and their children are carrying on as military members.

Cdr Corrigan stressed that the women who were among the groups of "firsts" have achieved their goals because they were given the opportunity to do so, and when those opportunities came they proved themselves as sailors and CF members, not as women.

Why the Navy?

Clearly, many women who joined the military were eager to find new experiences and adventures. They wanted to be operational, and they were intrigued and challenged with what the CF offered them, even though the opportunities for women who are currently serving were somewhat limited when they joined, compared to the opportunities available to women joining today. It is equally apparent that women who decided to wear the navy uniform did it for both motivational and practical reasons. For example, when mixed gender crews were introduced aboard ships, some of the women that we spoke to were not attracted to the army, but were attracted to the operational tempo that was offered on board ships. Lt(N) Galbraith joined the navy because she enjoyed the nautical environment. Cdr Corrigan joined the military in a tri-service occupation and accepted the opportunity to sail when it was provided to her.

Mixed Gender Crews

When mixed gender crews were initially introduced into the Canadian navy, it was a time of cultural change for both men and women. Men had to adjust to a different environment aboard ship. According to Lt(N) Galbraith, some of these men accepted the change while others took on a paternal attitude towards the women who joined, and others left because they were not willing to accept change. Regardless, the Canadian navy has worked hard to integrate men and women. Most notably, "in 2000, the label 'mixed gender' was removed and all units are now considered mixed."[8] Further, as a result of recommendations stemming from a study directed in 1998 by the Chief of Maritime Staff, women were accepted into the submarine service in 2002.[9]

In Chapter 20, Lieutenant-Commanders Lynn Bradley and Debbie Pestell highlight the uniqueness of Canada in its practise of gender integration in respect to submarines: In 2001, when Canada began accepting women into submarine service, Norway and Denmark[10] were the only other NATO nations to have successfully integrated women into this role. Norway has allowed women to serve in submarines since the late 1980s, and in 1995 Solveig Krey of the Royal Norwegian Navy became the world's first female officer to command a submarine, HNoMS KOBBEN. Today several other NATO nations, including Poland and Spain, are considering the possibility of integrating women into submarine service."[11]

The concept of women serving in the navy is now more than a novelty; it is a reality and a necessity. Captain D. Michael Abrashoff, former Commander of USS BENFOLD, states: "Obviously, there are some jobs that women physically can't do, but those are relatively few – and, truth be told, many men can't do them either...We could not get the ships out of port if we didn't accept women."[12]

Effective Military Leadership

The formal definition of effective military leadership states that it is the "directing, motivating, and enabling others to accomplish the mission professionally and ethically, while developing or improving capabilities that contribute to mission success."[13] Effective military leadership is, therefore, gender neutral by definition. It is gender neutral in reality too, with both males and females facing the same challenges. There are many leadership strategies and one must know when to use the appropriate strategy. Men and women must adapt to stressful, battle-rhythm scenarios when authoritarian discipline is necessary but also be ready to alter their approach in non-operational settings when a more collaborative approach is appropriate. Military leaders must also adapt their approaches between military members and civilian members. Perception, experience and sound judgment all play important roles in the execution of effective military leadership.

While effective military leadership is gender neutral, leadership roles tend to be masculine. According to the *American Psychological Association,*

> (W)omen are slightly more likely to be "transformational" leaders, serving as role models, helping employees develop their skills, and motivating them to be dedicated and creative. That approach may actually be more effective in today's less hierarchical organizations. But not all workplaces are alike: The participatory style may backfire in traditional male settings such as the military or organized sports. Conversely, the command-and-

control style more typical of men may backfire in a social-service agency or retail outlet. ... At the same time, the analysis revealed that women were more effective leaders in female-dominated or female-oriented settings, and that men were more effective leaders in male-dominated or male-oriented settings. Thus working in a leadership role congruent with one's gender appears to make one more effective – or at least perceived as being more effective.[14]

In reality, men and women contribute different dynamics to the team. Women tend to talk things out, be less confrontational and be more of a moderating influence. Generally, women possess a natural skill set that allows a more collaborative approach to problem solving. Women are more comfortable expressing emotion and possess an intuitive perception which allows them to be more apt to identify problems than their male counterparts. Anthropologist Margaret Mead believes that, "Because of their age-long training in human relations – for that is what feminine intuition is – women have a special contribution to make to any group enterprise."[15]

According to journalist and former Executive Vice-President of the Cable News Network (CNN), Gail Evans, it is more common for women than men to personalize situations,

> ...Study after study has shown that women are more likely than men to make, and keep, close friends...there are hazards, however to having a relationship orientation. For instance, women often interpret basic information in personal terms. Say the boss is talking with you in the hall and seems taken by your ideas for restructuring your department. Suddenly he excuses himself. You suspect he's changed his mind and doesn't like your ideas after all. Actually, he had to go to the bathroom... I've watched women personalize the office to the point where they won't hire people they don't like – even if they are exactly right for the job.[16]

Considering that women are typically closer to their emotions; it is obvious that they bring that mindset into the workplace. They generally have a support network of close friends from whom they can draw encouragement and strength. We consider this support network and source of strength central to the successes that women achieve in all elements of the Canadian Forces especially during times of separation from family, training, deployments and foreign postings. Here is an example expressed by Major Jamie Speiser-Blanchet:

> Some key elements stood out as I learned to deal with life as a woman on a military deployment; while we are all arguably different, I found that I shared some unique traits with the other women I deployed with, even if they were of other occupations or units. These were primarily the need for communication and emotional expression, a strong sense of community and the sharing of common experiences. I was definitely more emotional than the men I worked with, meaning that I expressed my feelings (e.g. happiness, loneliness, frustration) differently, often by inadvertently wearing them on my sleeve.[17]

When it comes to dealing with subordinates, men and women must follow the rules and regulations in the system. Navy personnel are taught – just as all other CF members – leadership responsibilities and the structure, culture and doctrine which guides the responsibilities of leaders. In spite of this, CPO2 Chiasson stressed that more men are given the tasks of leading in dangerous situations, including those situations in which leaders might be required to put their own lives in danger to demonstrate care and consideration for their subordinates.

In some ways, the male standard is maintained, even in the navy. Women are considered equal in many ways; however, at the same time they are held to a particular standard that reflects beliefs and stereotypes about women and men. As noted by Evans, women are,

> ...judged by male standards...which means men can take certain actions freely that [women] cannot...Men can get away with tears because it's unexpected. Men believe powerful people don't cry. If they do, they must have an excellent reason...Women are expected to cry. And when we do, men think it's because we're giving in to a natural instinct or worse, they think we're using tears as a game prop, a tool to manipulate them into feeling guilt.[18]

As a result, women on board ship have to be cautious about conducting themselves in stereotypically female ways. The following story comes from Lt(N) Galbraith:

The ship was in the beginning stages of emergency stations and personnel were gathered to put on their fire-fighting gear: chemox[19] gear including mask, etc. The person in charge of this particular group was a woman who had worked hard and demonstrated her ability to get the job done. Everyone was rushing to beat the clock and complete the drill under the required time limit. Just before donning her mask, she pulled out a stick of bright red lipstick and proceeded to apply it to her lips. In a few seconds, at an instant when it was professionally inappropriate, this member managed to undermine all the hard work that she had done to gain respect of her subordinates, peers and supervisors.

Traditionally considered the weaker sex, women are still proving that they possess the inner strength and determination required to adapt to situations and successfully serve in traditional male leadership roles. As a result, an inadvertent action that supports perceptions based on stereotypes can disproportionately influence perceptions of their capability.

All this taken into account, resistance to women in most leadership positions and roles in the navy has more or less gone to the wayside. An exception to this general claim would be in those situations in which women are breaking new ground. Although women are essential and integrated contributors to our modern navy, there are still new opportunities where women find themselves leading the way and thus encountering old challenges in new domains. Perhaps this is most evident in senior naval leadership positions where women are still significantly outnumbered. We believe that the best method is for women to get on with the job, stay the course and prove that it can be done well, just as many have done in the past. While proving themselves, women may have to bear extra scrutiny, but most of them are willing to do that.

Women also continue to face challenges when operating outside of the strict context of Canadian society and the CF. In other parts of the world the roles and expectations of women are quite different from Canada. On some occasions according to Lt(N) Galbraith, this requires more creativity in getting the job done, for example obtaining the presence of a male shipmate when dealing for the ship' supplies while in Dubai. At other times, people in foreign ports are more amenable to women and perceive them to be less threatening.

While ashore in foreign ports, members have to remember that there is a wide array of cultural standards and practices. This applies especially to women. When CPO2 Chiasson was in Syria, for example, she discovered that women do not expose their legs. She indicates that she "...was dressed in shorts and was sneered at." The next time she visited Syria she wore a long skirt and instead received smiles and positive acknowledgement."

Recruit, Retain, Innovate and Lead into the Future

"Creativity is thinking up new things. Innovation is doing new things."[20] With current members leaving the navy in large numbers, new measures have to be taken soon to counteract this trend. The first question is: what is being done now? The next questions are: what and how can we change?

Recruiting and retention are top priorities for the CF.[21] However, this is also a difficult challenge. The Force Reduction Program (FRP) outlined in the 1994 Defence White Paper resulted in deep and permanent damage to the number of personnel in the Canadian military. All three elements of the CF are dealing with the effects of the FRP. "In 2008, the Canada First Defence Strategy provided the additional resources needed to expand the Forces to 100,000 (70,000 Regular Force and 30,000 Primary Reserve). Now, the CF is engaged in a vast and dynamic recruiting campaign with an aim to grow the Forces.[22] Recruiters reaching out to communities now consider demographics. Visible minorities are being targeted but they remain in small numbers in the CF and in the navy. Programs are being implemented to reach into high schools and expose people to the military early.

While the CF has generally met or exceeded its recruiting goals, keeping trained, qualified personnel has proven more difficult. Over the past three years, the rate of CF attrition has risen – from approximately seven per cent in March 2006 to eight per cent in March 2007, and to nine per cent in March 2008.[23] The numbers tell us that something is wrong with the current situation. What are the reasons? The CF understands that,

> When CF personnel leave early in their career, their reasons include the requirement to maintain high physical fitness standards, personal and family issues, and dissatisfaction with their chosen military occupation. In terms of late-career attrition, the CF is experiencing a surge in the

number of personnel who have become entitled to a military pension that is comparable to the increased numbers of "Baby Boomers" retiring from Canadian public and private sector jobs.[24]

In addition, voluntary attrition can result from dissatisfaction related to the stresses resulting from under manning situations. The current system in place in the navy "is designed on the concept of 'one sailor, one job'; there are no pools of extra people to draw upon to make up for shortages. These shortages increase the workload of those that stay in the navy."[25]

In other cases, members are forced to make values and lifestyle choices as they progress in their careers. Women in particular can find themselves challenged by family and lifestyle issues that become incompatible with military service.[26] In 2002, the CF reported to the Committee on Women in NATO Forces (CWINF),

> The CF is re-examining pregnancy policies in the field and aboard ships (i.e. employment limitations) and enhancement of maternity and parental benefits. Furthermore, the Services are conducting innovative studies on the high attrition rates of women and validation studies on physical standards comprising gender and age free measurement criteria to predict performance. A new physical training program, tailored to meet the needs of women, has been developed and is currently under review. Over the years, an understanding of the benefits of physical training for pre- and post-natal mothers has grown and a voluntary programme is under construction to assist expectant mothers to maintain physical tone during the pregnancy and regain physical condition prior to their return to work.[27]

By 2008, policy focus in the CF had shifted toward increasing flexibility in the applications of existing policies to provide employment options that are appealing to women and beneficial for CF recruitment and retention efforts. For example, when operational requirements permit, the intent is that existing policies on Leave Without Pay, compassionate postings, and parental leave can be applied in ways that allow women and men to transition smoothly in and out of the CF to fulfill family obligations, such as child and elder care without permanently leaving their career in the CF.[28]

Compared with many civilian employers, the CF offers its members a competitive pension plan, adequate leave time, education reimbursement program and applicable financial allowances to offset hardships caused by service requirements such as Family Care Assistance and Separation Expense. However, there is room for improvement.

Childcare in the CF should be more accommodating, for example, to take into account early daily start times for occupations such as Cooks who begin at 5:30 a.m., as well as shift-workers who have constantly changing schedules. The Military Family Resource Centre (MFRC) in Halifax offers childcare from 6:00 a.m. to 6:00 p.m. during week days, as well as emergency childcare but this service is only for temporary support. In LS Jobin's opinion, the MFRC is not fulfilling the fundamental need of giving access to good childcare during odd hours which is the reality for a lot of women in the military as they also have to work during weekends and overnights on irregular schedules. They have to take into consideration that a lot of military women have little family support surrounding them which is largely due to postings and more often than not, have an absent military spouse (i.e. on deployment, at sea, on duty). LS Jobin shares her experience:

> When I returned to work after taking nine months of maternity/parental leave my partner took care of our daughter for the next three months. I had been actively searching for an in-home daycare through postings or answering online classified ads ever since I was six months pregnant but got turned down by potential caregivers each time I explained my hectic schedule to them. I had registered our daughter at the MFRC Daycare as a back up so I would have childcare during week days at least if I couldn't find anything else because I knew I was not going to have any childcare support from my family or my step family as they all resided in Quebec and New Brunswick. My request to change to a day worker position had been turned down. Not too long before my partner was scheduled to go back to sea, a civilian co-worker at Trinity where I worked talked to me about the live-in caregiver program, which consisted of hiring temporarily a nanny from outside Canada. I quickly went on with the search of finding a caregiver online and after going through the complex process, I finally hired an aupair from the United States. Fortunately, our daughter liked her very much and I can say, it relieved a lot of my stress.

Based upon her research with military members who are also mothers, Kathie Petite asserts that,

> The Department of National Defence needs to conduct a systemic review of the experiences of women with regard to pregnancy and related leave while recognising that women's role as mothers may require accommodation in order to achieve equity. This necessitates an understanding that achieving gender equity sometimes involves unequal implementation of policy.[29]

As the CF continues to improve its leave without pay policies, members will be more willing to stay the course. For both men and women this is important in relation to young families and elder parents.

Much can be achieved with effective leadership. In our experience, many navy non-commissioned junior ranks are not aware that the CF believes that "leadership... may be exercised by anyone, regardless of organizational position".[30] All ranks should be encouraged to have a sense of ownership and opportunities to reach their full potential. "It's the troops in the trenches that are dealing with the day-to-day issues and the challenges of being in the business environment that are going to have the opportunities and the good ideas."[31]

It is always the leader who sets the stage for good or bad morale. Lt(N) Galbraith specified that approachability is essential; also know your people and use them to the best of their ability. We agree that these principles should be used between officers and non-commissioned members and between military and civilian workers. Also, leaders in command positions must be careful not to micromanage. A leader will never accomplish what he or she wants by ordering it done. According to Abrashoff, and we agree, "Real leadership must be done by example, not precept."[32]

Because of the traditional navy culture, there is still a gap between officers and non-commissioned members. There are spoken and unspoken barriers that need to be broken down to create a more cohesive and effective team on board ship. There might be three separate messes but there is only one crew. Therefore, preferential treatment between mess ranks should be minimized. CPO2 Chiasson emphasized that although not consistently practiced, the Hands (Junior Ranks) must always come first, not the Officers. Every crewmember should get the same privileges, and in the case that exceptions might be justified, open and transparent communication should be the standard – there are no secrets on ships – between the bulkheads everything somehow gets tattled.

For most ships personnel, there are many tedious tasks which, if better planned and executed would improve the morale of many sailors. For example, storing ship can be strenuous for all sailors, but some women who are of smaller build can have even greater difficulty because of the size and weight of supplies. LS Jobin acknowledges that she did have to get help from male shipmates on a few occasions when it was necessary to handle pieces of meat which were half her size. Differences in ability such as strength are inevitable among female and male crewmembers. A cooperative team approach to many tasks improves not only morale, but the overall effectiveness of the ship's operations.

Summary

In the past several decades, women have joined the navy and forged the way in many areas. In the years since, men have accepted it. Now, gender integration is commonly accepted in the Canadian navy. The first group of women to climb the ranks made the most of the opportunities that were made available to them. They underwent extra scrutiny and are now role models for other women. There are a number of reasons why women have joined the Canadian navy over the years; some joined for practical reasons and some joined seeking adventure. Women have also taken on leadership roles and will, without a doubt, continue to break new leadership ground. Even though they are typically still outnumbered in ships; it is important for them to feel that they are needed and appreciated.

Today's Canadian navy is represented by great women in leadership positions such as Cdr Corrigan, Lt(N) Galbraith, CPO1 Corbett and CPO2 Chiasson, to name a few. They demonstrate that it is indeed possible for a woman to pursue a career and be an effective leader in the military regardless of gender. Although still barely represented in most senior naval leadership positions, it is just a matter of time before more women share leadership at all levels. Regardless of potential obstacles along the way, we truly believe a woman can be whatever she wants to be if she sets her mind to it. There are still many new opportunities for women to take advantage of, and those of us following their lead are grateful for their willingness to persist, perform and pave the way. After all, our sailors are the best ones to promote that a career in the Canadian navy can be fulfilling and rewarding

Leadership is gender neutral; however, leadership roles are still masculine. Although there are leadership principles and guidelines that apply to all members of the military, there are still characteristics that are judged differently because of traditional gender stereotypes. Women must adjust to these masculine roles and lead accordingly. According to CPO1 Corbett, women who lead "...must be firm and fair. Be more concerned with doing the right thing vice being liked or popular. Accept that one cannot satisfy everyone and pick their battles wisely."

Fair Winds and Following Seas!!

---

1   Dr. Karen Shue, "6 Positive Guidelines from Michaëlle Jean, Canada's Governor General." <http://positivepolitics.wordpress.com/2008/01/16/6-positive-guidelines-from-michaelle-jean-canadas-governer-general/>, accessed 29 January 2009.

2   The six principles: Canadian Forces Identity; Command Centric Imperative; Authorities, Responsibilities, and Accountabilities; Operational Focus; Mission Command; and An Integrated Regular, Reserve and Civilian CF. The latter specifies the need to ensure the best utilization of appropriate skills and experience at every level, a challenge that renders the contributions of women essential.

3   Dawn E. Monroe, (2004) "Famous Canadian Women's Famous Firsts – Military Leaders." <http://famouscanadianwomen.com/famous%20firsts/military%20leaders.htm>, accessed 29 January 2009.

4   Canada (2002) *Leadmark: The Navy's Strategy for 2020*. (Ottawa: Department of National Defence), <http://www.navy.dnd.ca/leadmark/doc/part4_e.asp>, accessed 1 December 2009.

5   Marc Milner, *Canada's Navy The First Century* (Toronto: University of Toronto Press Incorporated, 1999), 281.

6   Marc Milner, *Canada's Navy The First Century*, 281.

7   Marc Milner, *Canada's Navy The First Century*, 286.

8   NATO International Military Staff (2002) "NATO/IMS: Committee on Women in the NATO Forces: Canada."< http://www.nato.int/ims/2001/win/canada.htm>, accessed 16 March 2009.

9   Lieutenant-Commander Lynn Bradley and Lieutenant-Commander Debbie Pestell, "Experiences with Mixed Gender Submarine Crews", see Chapter 20 in this volume (report on a study that was first conducted by LCdr Lynn Bradley, *Mixed Gender Crewing of VICTORIA-Class Submarines* (Ottawa, ON: Department of National Defence, Maritime Staff Research Report, 1999). Ottawa: NDHQ, Maritime Staff). then updated and presented at a NATO symposium in October 2009 (Human Factors and Medicine Panel (HFM) 158) in Antalya, Turkey by LCdr Debbie Pestell..

10   Denmark no longer has a submarine service, Bradley and Pestell, "Experiences with Mixed Gender Submarine Crews."

11   Bradley and Pestell, "Experiences with Mixed Gender Submarine Crews", 5-6.

12   Captain Michael D.Abrashoff, *It's Your Ship*. (New York, Business Plus Hachette Book Group USA, 2002), 181.

13   Canada. *Leadership in the Canadian Forces: Doctrine*. (Kingston, ON: Department of National Defence, Canadian Forces Leadership Institute, 2005) <http://www.cda-acd.forces.gc.ca/cfli-ilfc/lea/doctrine/toc-eng.asp>, accessed 1 December 2009.

14   American Psychological Association, *When the Boss is a Woman*. (Washington: PsychNET, 2006) <http://www.psychologymatters.org/womanboss.html> , accessed 1 December 2009.

15   Gail Evans, *Play Like a Man Win Like a Woman*. (New York: Broadway Books, 2000), 173.

16   Gail Evans, *Play Like a Man Win Like a Woman*, 26-27.

17   Major Jamie Speiser-Blanchet, "There's No Hell Like Tac Hel!" in Karen D. Davis (ed.) *Women and Leadership in the Canadian Forces: Perspectives & Experience*. (Kingston, ON: Canadian Defence Academy Press, 2007), 54.

18   Angela Febbraro, "Gender and Leadership in the Canadian Forces Combat Arms: Perspectives of Women Leaders" in Karen D. Davis (ed.) *Women and Leadership in the Canadian Forces: Perspectives & Experience* (Kingston, ON: Defence Canadian Defence Academy Press, 2007), 120-121.

19   Chemical oxygen.

20   Andy Holloway, Andy, "Are You the Next Great Canadian Innovator?" *Canadian Business*. (March 2009): 40.

21   Canada. Backgrounder Recruiting and Retention in the Canadian Forces. (Ottawa: Department of National Defence, 2009) <http://www.forces.gc.ca/site/news-nouvelles/news-nouvelles-eng.asp?cat=3>, accessed 1 December 2009.

22   Canada, Backgrounder Recruiting and Retention in the Canadian Forces, 2.

23   Canada, Backgrounder Recruiting and Retention in the Canadian Forces, 2.

24   Canada, Backgrounder Recruiting and Retention in the Canadian Forces, 3.

25   "Backgrounder: The Management of Naval Personnel." March 2008 Issue. Dalhousie University Centre for Foreign Policy Studies. <http://naval.review.cfps.dal.ca/pdf/Personnel_Management.pdf>, accessed 22 March 2009.

26   See, for example, discussion of impact of family, organization, and values on retention/ attrition of women in the CF in K.D. Davis (2001) *The Future of Women in the Canadian Forces: Defining the Strategic Human Resource Challenge*. (Ottawa, ON: Department of National Defence, Directorate of Strategic Human Resource Coordination).

27   NATO International Military Staff , "NATO/IMS: Committee on Women in the NATO Forces: Canada.

28   Canada (2008) Canadian Forces 2008 National Report to Committee for Women in NATO Forces, (Ottawa, ON: Department of National Defence, Directorate of Human Rights and Diversity).

29   Petite, Kathie (2008) *Tinker, tailor! Soldier, sailor! Mother?: Making sense of the competing institutions of motherhood and the military*, Unpublished thesis submitted in partial fulfillment of the requiements for the degree of Master of Arts in Family Studies and Gerontology, (Halifax, NS: Mount Saint Vincent University), 138.

30   Canada. *Leadership in the Canadian Forces: Doctrine*.

31   Andy Holloway, "Off the rails." *Canadian Business*. (March 2009): 30.

32   Captain D. Michael Abrashoff, *It's Your Ship*, 32.

CHAPTER 18

Exploring Gender and Identity through the Experience of Women in the Canadian Navy at the Dawn of the 21st Century: A Study of Ten Testimonies

Lieutenant (Navy) Stéphanie Bélanger

Lieutenant (Navy) (Lt(N)) Stéphanie Bélanger, PhD, is an assistant professor in the Department of French Studies at the Royal Military College of Canada. She enrolled in the Naval Reserve as a logistics officer in 2004. She has published numerous papers on the representation of the warrior and is the author of the recently published book, *Guerre, sacrifices et persécutions* on the representation of warriors and the just war theory (Paris: Éditions L'Harmattan, 2010).

Six years ago, I was staring at the window, in the midst of finalizing a paper exploring some dimensions of the representation of ancient warriors. My attention was caught by a man and a woman running side by side, both wearing some gray sweatshirts. It occurred to me that they were both military, both much more knowledgeable than I was on warriors and soldering and the like. As I was observing the woman, I noticed she was not much bigger than I was, although she looked much healthier. A few days later, I started running too. Within a year, I was jogging in the same gray PT gear.[1] I was enrolled in the Naval Reserve, curious to see how I would manage to grow in what I then considered to be a male and anglophone environment. Even though quite challenging, the experience has been enriching. I am now focusing my research on soldiering identity, incidentally, on the way females perceive themselves as warriors, and I am presenting my findings in English. I knew back then, and I reaffirm it every day, that the transformations I was going through (and still counting), although quite drastic, could not be unique. The Canadian Forces (CF) changed me the same way they changed my sisters in arms, they modulated my own relationship with my core identity. How did they achieve this? Is there a typical way to feel transformed, how do we become a female soldier, and more specifically, a female sailor? Does the institution make us become mere "sailors", or "female sailors"?

More precisely, in this paper, I will analyze the way women perceive their own integration based on their experience in the Canadian navy. In this case, the target group is composed of women holding leadership positions aboard a warship or in a theatre of war, and their perceptions will be assessed through the analysis of the testimony of their experience as naval officers, in the Regular Forces or in the Reserves, whether they participated to war in support role or in combat arms, and whether they were or not aboard war ship. This chapter intends to articulate theoretical concepts on gender integration based on the testimonies of ten female officers (from Lieutenant (Navy) to Commander) still serving in the Canadian navy, that I had the honour of interviewing during the past year.[2] These personal sources will be reinforced by similar interviews taken by different sources.

As I will focus my analysis on interviews I conducted in Spring 2009, I will also be referring to some testimonies that already exist in print. Some interviews have already been conducted in the context of the Canadian Naval Museum Oral History Project and were generously provided by the Navy Command Historian, Richard Gimblett, and the Canadian War Museum Historian, Andrew Burtch. Some others have already been published by the Canadian Forces Leadership Institute (CFLI), mainly the book *Women and Leadership in the Canadian Forces*.[3] This source includes testimonies of officers (males and females) and non-commissioned members from all elements (land, air and sea), which will allow some cross-referencing with woman of different war experience. Much of the research on CF female identity focuses on the combat arms, and mainly, the green element. Nothing in the testimonies I gathered seems to contradict their conclusions: it does not seem, at first glance, that the way a female member of the Canadian navy perceives her own identity as a sailor differs from the way female members of the air and land elements perceive their identities, at least not in the parameters studied in this chapter. As the CF as an institution seem to have standardized across the organization the way to impose its ideology, sailors, air force crews and soldiers seem to have common ways of reacting to the structural forces they are subjected to. If there were some differences, it is not the purpose of this chapter to identify them.

Background

Gender studies stress the importance of the relationship between the cultural background and self-identity. Within the CF, this relationship seems to be obliterated by the omnipresence and omnipotence of the chain of command, through which all authorities, rules, decisions, and concepts that fall under the broader term of "regulations", are passed, imposed, top down. Regulations tend to shape an individual's identity: in the vast majority of work places, through a set of rules, by their way of imposing daily activities and outlook, institutions provide their employees with guidelines for their behavior as a group, a collectivity: "Institutions operate primarily by affecting person's prospective bets about the collective environment and collective activity."[4] Many argue that the armed forces in general are stricter, more authoritative, more structured and more masculine than any other institution.[5] In the CF in particular, these guidelines do not leave much space for an equitable relationship between the organizational culture and the individual identity, as they are being imposed top down.

Moreover, such a "relationship" can be seen as a betrayal of the most prized adage: "Soldier First", that is, the state before the individual. In other words, the CF member is trained to give away his or her personal needs for the greater good, that is, not only for the collectivity to which he or she belongs, but foremost for the organization under the regulations by which he or she abides, and, *a fortiori*, for the population it protects. The so called "relationship" between the institution and its members tends, therefore, to be one-sided. It seems that "Soldier First" is the essence of the organization itself; it is the first expression that comes to the lips of CF members when they are asked to talk about their singular job, it is the way in which they define themselves. At least, this is the way it looks at first sight. Even though CF members automatically make reference to this motto when asked questions about their work, they often question it in their everyday activities, but not necessarily in an organized fashion. Of course, the point is neither to expose the inefficiency of CF's practices in the spreading out of an ideology nor to pretend that CF members all suffer from their personnel sacrifices for the greater good. The point is to develop a thorough explanation of the way in which military members, and more specifically, females in the Canadian navy, live their everyday commitments in the CF: how do they see themselves as a "soldier/sailor"? According to literature,[6] it seems that not only do female CF members find it hard to sacrifice their personal needs for the organization, and in this regard they don't really differ from their male counterparts[7] (Goldstein, 2001), but it seems that they also find it hard to be further challenged by the idea of becoming a "soldier/sailor", with all the gender connotation it can involve.[8]

This ambiguous relationship between female members and the concept of soldier can be understood as a direct consequence of the adoption of the Employment Equity Act, which permitted women to have the same job opportunities as males in the CF.[9] The Employment Equity Act of 1986 has been in effect in the CF since 2002, and ensures "equality in the workplace so that no person shall be denied employment opportunities or benefits for reasons unrelated to ability".[10] As stipulated in a Canadian Defence website, the CF "exemplify many values that unite Canadians" (such as helping Canadians and people from abroad and participating in peacekeeping and peace reinforcement missions).[11] But this exemplification can only be achieved by the acceptance of all sectors of the nations that reflect Canada's demographic diversity. For instance, all recruitment and HR related issues in the CF, such as quotas to be followed by recruiters, redresses of grievances, courses on Harassment Awareness or Dispute Resolutions, among others, serve this same purpose: equity. The way in which CF's organization implements its practices influences not only the structure itself by increasing the number of women, (as well as the number of aboriginals and immigrants, although these two other target groups will not be specifically analyzed here), but also by transforming some standards such as dress, washrooms, dorms, CF EXPRES[12] requirements, and by the establishment of some services such as the Dispute Resolution Center (2001)[13] and the permanent Directorate of the Quality of Life (2001).[14] Despite all these internal transformations that aim at easing (in favour of fairness) the relationship between all employees and the institution, the study of testimonies tends to show that many women still argue that equity is a target that is yet to be achieved; female members tend to proclaim that in the CF, the male way of doing these jobs is the rule, the standard. And most of the female naval members I interviewed concur with these findings. Where the organization tends to deny the difference, the question, for the serving female members, does not seem to be "is there a double standard", meaning, is there a difference between a male and a female sailor, but "how do I relate myself to that double standard"?

As the story of their leadership experience in the Canadian navy tends to demonstrate, whether it is seen as a motivating challenge or a demotivating factor, the way the female members I interviewed perceive themselves as a "sailor" is very similar to the way female CF members in general perceive themselves as "soldiers", and as such, this relationship between what they are and what they are trained to become becomes the cornerstone in the study of the aftermaths of the application of the Employment Equity Act. How do the CF construct an image of the gender, how do their members perceive this image? Is this perception itself a CF construct? More precisely, I wish to examine, through the analysis of the testimonies of women holding leadership positions in the Canadian navy, how the institution to which they belong shapes their perception of who they are, as women evolving in a so-called "masculine organization"[15] that is trying, without, maybe, the anticipated success, to impose "gender-neutral" regulations.[16]

"Soldier First" from top to bottom

Even though the current theatre of war in Afghanistan is mainly army-based, it directly concerns many naval members, as the sea element plays a crucial role both operationally and logistically, mainly through intelligence and supplies. Further, many Naval Reservists who choose (because in the Reserve, participation in a theatre of war is voluntary) to participate to this theatre of war are deployed "in green", in a land environment. Further, what affects soldiers ashore affects also sailors, ashore or at sea, by the virtue of the fact they are, to the same degree, members of the same organization, submitted to similar training and experience, and affected by a same common faith: signing a contract with the CF is, basically, accepting a job that encompasses a high risk of dying in a theatre of war.

And when it comes to dying in a theatre of war, there is no questioning from any of the officials of where the CF stands right now: women are equal to men, which is being reinforced, in official discourses, by the fact that women die in combat or during missions just like men. At the death of the late Corporal Karine Blais (armoured), the 117th CF member in Afghanistan, who also happened to be the second female CF member to loose her life in this mission (after Captain Nichola Goddard, also armoured, 17 May 2006), Lieutenant-Colonel (LCol) Jocelyn Paul, Commander, Task Force, Kandahar, said to the press: "Those women are showing a lot of courage. They are standing shoulder to shoulder with all the men on the battlefield" (12 April 2009).[17] Less than one year before, general Rick Hillier, Chief of Defence staff and keynote addressee at the 23rd Annual Seminar of the Conference of Defence Associations Institute (2007), related the brilliant career of the late Captain Nichola Goddard, and talked about the great achievements of "sons and daughters of our country".[18] The official discourse stresses the equality between men and women, who work together for the greater good.

I was literally collecting this information on how the official discourse treats female losses, when I received an e-mail, addressed to the Royal Military College of Canada's (RMC) master e-mail list, dated 24 April 2009, sent at 9:57 a.m. A third female CF member, Major Michelle Mendes (Intelligence officer), who was known at RMC as 22007 Officer Cadet Michelle Knight, Class of 2001, BA Honours History, died in Afghanistan. The statement by the Minister of National Defence on the Death of Major Michelle Mendes was just released that morning;[19] that same morning I was doing some investigation on that specific subject (it was the first time that reality was catching up with my researches...). Both written discourses quoted the universal condolence message which is, of course, very much neutral, and even more so that the circumstances surrounding her death were not combat-related and had not yet been revealed to the public: "our thoughts and prayers go out to the entire Mendes and Knight families and all those who have been personally touched by this tragic loss" (RMC Commandant); "I would like to offer my sincere condolences to the family, friends and colleagues of Major Michelle Mendes, who died yesterday in Afghanistan. Our thoughts and prayers are with them during this difficult time" (Minister of National Defence).

It is specifically this vision of neutrality that is sought by the CF, an approach that focuses on "the performance, abilities and potential of individuals, regardless of gender,"[20] and, as illustrated by these three examples, regardless of rank and trade. To pay no heed to the formal discourse, one might ask how ready is the Canadian population (let alone its female serving members) to see a women soldier plunging her children into mourning. If it is not raised by the official discourse, this problem is nevertheless addressed by serving female members when they share their experience. For instance, at the 2009 Women Leading in Defence conference, entitled Challenge the Past, Embrace the Future (Ottawa, 3 March 2009, led by the CFLI), during a period of questions, one of the attendees stood up, saying: "I have an infant and I am leaving, three months from now for a pre-deployment training. How will I do this?" The question was first followed by a silence, then by a debate, ranging from "this is what you signed for" to "there are now great support programs for your family" to "do not let the CF break your family". Of course, I asked the question, in a subtle way, to the female naval officers I was interviewing: "How do you balance work and life, considering the nature of your work?" "I would prefer not going to war", said a Maritime Surface and Sub-Surface (MARS) officer I interviewed, "because I am a mother of young ones, and it would not seem right", which does not prevent her from being an excellent Staff Officer ready to serve her country "where ever the government will ask me to go," she insisted, proud of her career achievements. Just like her, among my interviews, all the ones who happened to also be mothers chose not to leave for dangerous missions, nor for too long postings, without the family, except once the children were "old enough" (typically early in the teenage years), regardless of the consequences for their career. And for all of them, the sacrifice for their career was worth it, especially because they found other opportunities for development (especially reservists). The question of the risk of death seems to be mitigated by the insistence on the diversity of experiences within the CF.

And the experiences are described as very exciting: most of the interviewees in this project saw their participation as important because they needed to testify to the great experience they lived. All of my participants had moments, during the interviews, where it felt they were doing a recruitment speech. Some had to fight for their place within the CF, and some insisted more than others on this specific aspect, but all gained a career, a life, that they were proud of and that they needed to share. Obviously, the recourse to testimony is an important component of understanding the relationship to sailing, and, ultimately, to soldering. CF members testify about a lived experience, an experience that is considered as sensational, singular, historical, or simply important to them: "To write a testimony is a political statement to be recognized by the nation, but also a statement of truth and dignity, a statement of social existence and of visibility in public space."[21] As stated by one of the participants, a Logistics Naval Officer: "It is important that women hear from other women, particularly the positive aspects of this career. It is an excellent career, why should women not have the opportunity?"

Advantages of being a Woman

This attitude, this feeling of pride in one's accomplishments, is spread throughout the interviews to a point that women, when speaking about their experience as CF members, will almost automatically talk about the fact that they are women, in an attempt to convince their audience that the experience of being part of the CF is a great opportunity and that feminine attributes play a positive role in this regard:

I don't think we're the same as men. I don't think that we lead in the same way in general as men. [...] I do think that many women offer different things to the combat arms than men [...] I think they're maybe a little more understanding to certain personal issues, just kind of our nurturing side kind of comes out [...].[22]

Following the example of this member, many will argue that it is not right to totally change one's personality, that it is important to accept femininity, and will insist on how positive and rewarding it is to be feminine (to a certain extent): "There is a gender difference, it requires a little more effort to impose oneself, but once this is done, it opens more doors: more fraternity in conversations, people remember me because I was the only woman at the table", said a Naval Cooperation and Guidance for Shipping (NCAGS)[23] officer, as she was talking of her experience aboard warship in 2004. In the same way, another NCAGS officer who served in Afghanistan (in green...) said "Being an officer superseded the fact that I was a woman. And in fact, being a woman was an even bigger advantage."

Women in general appear to be more sensitive than men to the quality of their relationship with their peers,[24] and women in the CF are not an exception. Being a woman opened the doors to some unofficial conversations with quite official personalities, who would happen to reveal themselves to them just because they were talking to a woman. But before they get to the point where they inspire confidence and respect, female CF members must go through the steps of being a "sailor", which refers more generically to the so called non-gendered soldier promulgated by the CF. So if, in the one hand, they appreciate some specific circumstances they lived because they were women, they nevertheless insist on the fact, on the other hand, that they got to this point because they proved themselves ethically and physically: "For me, physical fitness had an incredible impact. My physical fitness inspired respect around me, and the fact that I was attending the gym on a daily basis reinforced my authority", said an NCAGS officer I interviewed after her experience at a theatre of war.

These success stories may make one wonder "To what extent are masculinity and maleness implicitly built into the very notion of soldiering?"[25] For the most part, the women I interviewed felt that, once they understood the concept of masculinity, once they had proven themselves capable of achieving the masculine standards (CF EXPRES, etc.), they could then impose themselves as being women. This process, this duality, made them two people, really, a soldier (the supposedly non-gendered one promulgated by the CF) and a woman. These two personalities gave them two experiences of the world, and they took advantage of both experiences. "It is like knowing two languages, two cultures, two ways of thinking", explained the NCAGS officer I interviewed after her experience on board warship. They know two "genders" that cohabit in them and help them cooperate with their colleagues, both genders taken into account. And in that sense, yes, the non -gendered sailor (let alone the non-gendered soldier) has a little bit of a male-ish flavour, at least to some women.

Hiding feminine attributes

For these women, this double identity was handled with some flexibility; for others, it involved an internal battle. Many women seem to have two wars to fight, the war out there, and the war within. Not only do they have to face the enemy, but they also have to struggle within, with their own brothers and sisters of arms.

When they are not trying to defend themselves, to excuse the fact they are women, many female military members will bluntly insist on how important it is not to emphasize their feminine attributes: "A woman leader who acts in a very feminine way is probably not perceived as effective as someone who wasn't acting that way I guess. Just because it's not the place here, you know what I mean, it's just not an accepted norm I guess."[26] As evidenced by this testimony, it is important to downplay or conceal any feminine attitudinal attributes as much as possible, in order to gain the esteem of subordinates.

Similarly, this other member will reject feminine physical attributes and favour a neutral approach to the image that a member perpetuates:

> You do in some senses need to behave in a masculine way in order to be perceived to be an effective soldier. [...] I don't think it's positive to be too feminine, quote unquote. I mean, you can't spend hours doing make-up or anything like that. [...] You do have to have a certain degree of [...] non-sexuality about you.[27]

The imperative tone she uses stresses the importance it has for her: you "do need to" behave like males, you "can't" wear makeup, you "do have to have" a neutral image. It seems that for some of the CF female members, you have to hold back your feminine attributes and attitudes to be more accepted.

This holding back implies that a woman is hiding behind this apparently gender neutral soldier, a soldier that is not a woman, a soldier that is different from what they identify with, as females. This concept is thoroughly described in an autoethnographical study conducted by Nancy Taber,[28] a scholar and former military member who uses her academic knowledge to analyze her personal life: "I was socialized into the masculine military construct, where it was essential that I think and act like a male in order to be accepted and valued as an organizational member. [...] Men were the norm; women the exception."[29] There is no doubt in her mind that there is no such a thing as a full "integration" of women in the CF; rather, there is "assimilation", where women try to become like men.

A naval logistics officer I interviewed, who also participated (as a reservist) in a theatre of war, recalled how she was, back then: "...dressed in green, with the C7, just like the other guys". And she goes on explaining how the "guys" she was working with knew her as another person. The people who knew her then knew another part of herself, a second identity, a person who was dressed in green like them. And this identity still lives inside of her, she still relates to it: "I still feel bound to this identity, it never escaped me."

We are not women, but CF members

Yet, some other women will not see this identity as a second nature that lives within themselves and to which they relate; they will completely adhere to this new person that the CF constructed when they trained them. Some of the women I interviewed rather insisted on the fact that they never perceived themselves as being different from men. A MARS officer asked me during an interview: "Does it make a difference to be a woman in the navy?" She then answered to her own question: "In an exercise I went to, it was around the year 2000, it took 3 to 4 weeks before I realized that I was the only girl in the wardroom. This realization came after 4 weeks, so it did not make a difference after all". What this officer expresses, here, is that they were all sailors first. Is it because she did "whatever she could to be seen as a soldier, just like the other men"?[30] It is not so clear. It seems rather that she was really herself and that she was accepted as such by the group, to a point that they did not mind, or perhaps did not even see, her difference.

Many said, when asked to compare the CF structure with other countries' armed forces, that they would not change for any other army in the world. For instance, a NCAGS officer told me her experience during an international exercise, where she played the role of a commanding officer. Although she did acknowledge that some other countries were not happy to see women in leadership role, this experience nevertheless reinforced her position: there was "one expectation, one norm", meaning that the others, following the example of the CF members, had to get over her difference and concentrate on the task.

In the same way, another of my interviewees explained that for the most part, she did not find that being a woman was an issue: "I was just another MARS officer, another officer on the ship, and this is the way I want to be seen". Another MARS officer explained to me that it is the number of rings on the shoulder that imposes authority: "There is no gender distinction; we are all Naval Reserve members, the problems that affect women affect men as well. [...] I don't think of myself as a woman, but as a member of the Naval Reserve."

Conclusion

Whether they cooperate with both the CF standard and their own female personality, whether they hide the fact that they are a woman or whether they don't see themselves as a woman but as a member of the CF, at the end, they all say the same thing: they strive for gender neutrality. When bluntly asked how they perceive the way the CF constructs gender, they all answer the same thing: there is not such a thing as a construction of a gender, it is "soldier first", assuming that the soldiers, and with them, the sailors, are genderless.

Nevertheless, as soon as they testify, women talk of the fact that they are women and position themselves either as female CF member, females playing the role of a masculine CF member or, simply, a genderless CF member. Their testimony, before being an acknowledgment of what they lived in specific missions or during combat related exercise, is a testimony of what they lived as a women in those tasks. Not only do they live the challenges of being part of the CF, of being warriors, but also of being female warriors, females at war or on a warship. CF made tremendous efforts in attenuating, modulating this tension between men and women in their organization by insisting on the concept of "Soldier First". This is why, despite their different ways of approaching their femininity within the military, most women will say that the CF does not construct any gender concept, that they have a genderless concept of the soldier. It is only when asked to talk a little longer and in more detail about their experience that some contradictions or mere subtleties arise. The spectrum of possible reactions or interpretation of women's self position is wide, ranging from taking advantage of having female attributes to hiding these attributes to not seeing any gender specific attributes. The vast majority stand at the far end of it: they do not see significant difference between themselves and their male counterparts and believe it is reciprocal. The way the CF has integrated women since the Employment Equity Act really has a profound impact on the way female CF members perceive themselves as serving members, after all.

It seems that the ten testimonies I studied on female naval officers are a microcosm of what is observed in the CF, as an organization, and of what is observed in the Canadian society in general. Organizations evolve in a highly competitive and changing environment. As the society in which they evolve is being transformed, organizations are subject to changes in the very core of their organizational structure. In that sense, many argue that apart from the passage from Cold War to asymmetric war theories in the turning of the 21st Century, the most dramatic change that occurred in the CF is related to the integration of women at all level of services, in all trades, combat as well as non-combat.[31] War was once described with masculine attributes, while feminine attributes were used to describe negative behaviour of some warriors or to make reference to a negative dimension to the experience. With the new approaches to war that involve peacekeeping and asymmetric strategies, masculine attributes are still used to describe war, and "it appears that the negative relation of femininity to war holds, regardless of what the feminine might mean".[32] Not so much anymore, I would like to argue. Considering the very limited sampling, my results are far too modest to illustrate such a drastic change in mentalities. Nevertheless, I really hope that more and more testimonies will be collected in the years to come, highlighting the experiences of women serving in the Canadian navy, and that they will participate in orienting the researches and perceptions in that new direction undertaken by the navy – its transformed traditions.

1   Physical training kit issued by the CF: grey hooded sweatshirt and jogging pants.

2   This research project was founded by the Royal Military College of Canada and approved by the Ethics Board (13 Feb 2009, REB #2009-03 FRENCH).

3   Karen D. Davis (ed.), *Women and Leadership in the Canadian Forces*, (Kingston, ON: Canadian Defence Academy Press, 2008).

4   R. Jepperson, "Institutions, institutional effects, and institutionalism" in W. W. Powell and P. J. Dimaggio, *The new institutionalism in organizational analysis*, (Chicago, University of Chicago Press, 1991), 147.

5   Annica Kronsell, "Gendered Pratices in Institutions of Hegemonic Masculinity", *International Feminist Journal of Politics*, 7 (2, June 2005): 280-298; Nancy Taber, "Learning how to be a woman in the Canadian Forces / Unlearning it through feminism: an autoethnography of my learning journey", *Studies in Continuing Education*, 27 (3, November 2005): 289-300.

6   Perley-Ann Friedman, Linda Schweitzer and Leanne Karoles, "The Gender Neutral Approach of the Canadian Forces: Integrating Women into the Military", The international journal of diversity in organisations, communities and nations, 8 (4, 2008): 69-76; Jennifer M. Silva, "A new generation of women? How femal ROTC Cadets negotiate the tension between masculine military culture and traditional feminity", *Social Forces*, 87 (2, December 2008): 237-242; Rachel Woodard and Trish Winter, *Sexing the soldier. The politics of gender and the contemporary British Army*, (London/New York: Routledge, 2007); Nancy Taber, "Learning how to be a woman in the Canadian Forces / Unlearning it through feminism: an autoethnography of my learning journey", *Studies in Continuing Education*, 27 (3, November 2005): 289-300.

7   Annica Kronsell, "Gendered Pratices in Institutions of Hegemonic Masculinity", *International Feminist Journal of Politics*, 7 (2, June 2005): 280-298; Nancy Taber, "Learning how to be a woman in the Canadian Forces / Unlearning it through feminism: an autoethnography of my learning journey", *Studies in Continuing Education*, 27 (3, November 2005): 289-300.

8   Annica Kronsell, "Gendered Pratices in Institutions of Hegemonic Masculinity," 280-298.

9   Canada, *Minister's Advisory Board on Canadian Forces Gender Intergration and Employment Equity* (Department of National Defence, 2001).

10   Employment Equity Act (1995, c. 44) section 1: <http://laws.justice.gc.ca/en/showdoc/cs/E-5.401/bo-ga:s_3//en#anchorbo-ga:s_3>, accessed 13 January 2010.

11   *Supporting the Canadian Forces*, <http://www.civ.forces.gc.ca/support-appui/index-eng.asp>, accessed 13 January 2010.

12   Canadian Forces Exercise Prescription (CF EXPRES), a programme for physical fitness training and evaluation.

13   <http://www.journal.forces.gc.ca/vo7/no2/coates-eng.asp>, accessed 13 January 2010.

14   <http://www.forces.gc.ca/site/news-nouvelles/view-news-afficher-nouvelles-eng.asp?id=412>, accessed 13 January 2010.

15   Nancy Taber, "Learning how to be a woman in the Canadian Forces / Unlearning it through feminism: an autoethnography of my learning journey", 291.

16   Perley-Ann Friedman, Linda Schweitzer and Leanne Karoles, "The Gender Neutral Approach of the Canadian Forces," 69.

17   <http://www.youtube.com/watch?v=5pcsTNIBu7c>, accessed 24 April 2009.

18   <http://www.cda-cdai.ca/CDA_GMs/AGM70/CDS.pdf>, accessed 13 January 2010.

19   <http://www.earthtimes.org/articles/show/statement-by-the-minister-of,798872.shtml>, accessed 24 April 2009.

20   Perley-Ann Friedman, Linda Schweitzer and Leanne Karoles, "The Gender Neutral Approach of the Canadian Forces," 69.

21   My translation from French original: " [L'écriture du témoignage] est revendication politique d'une reconnaissance par la nation, mais aussi revendication de vérité et de dignité, revendication sociale d'existence et de visibilité dans l'espace public", Rousseau in Carole Dormier, *L'histoire en miettes*, (France: Presses Universitaires de Caen, 2004), 3.

22   Angela Febbraro, "Gender and Leadership in the Canadian Forces Combat Arms," in *Women and Leadership in the Canadian Forces: Perspectives and Experience*, Karen D. Davis (ed.) (Kingston, ON: Canadian Defence Academy Press: 2008), 102.

23   An Intelligence Branch recognized by NATO.

24   Micheal P. Leiter, David Clark and Josette Durup, "Distinct models of burnout and commitment among men and women in the military", *The Journal of Applied Behavioral Science*, 30 (1, March 1994): 78.

25   Jennifer M. Silva, "A new generation of women? How female ROTC Cadets negotiate the tension between masculine military culture and traditional femininity", *Social Forces* 87 (2, December 2008): 945.

26   Angela Febbraro, "Gender and Leadership in the Canadian Forces Combat Arms," 111.

27   Angela Febbraro, "Gender and Leadership in the Canadian Forces Combat Arms," 107.

28   Nancy Taber, "Learning how to be a woman in the Canadian Forces."

29   Nancy Taber, "Learning how to be a woman in the Canadian Forces," 292.

30   Annica Kronsell, "Gendered Practices in Institutions of Hegemonic Masculinity," 292.

31   Kimberly Hutchings, "Making Sense of Masculinity and War", *Men and Masculinities*, 10 (4, June 2008): 389-404.

32   Kimberly Hutchings, "Making Sense of Masculinity and War", 389-404; Perley-Ann Friedman, Linda Schweitzer and Leanne Karoles, "The Gender Neutral Approach of the Canadian Forces," 69-76.

CHAPTER 19

The Progress of Gender Integration in Canadian Warships: Views of the leaders

Lieutenant-Commander Lynn Bradley

Lieutenant-Commander (LCdr) Lynn Bradley, CD, MSc, (1997, University of Calgary (Industrial Organizational Psychology)) began her career as an Army Radio Operator and then a Signals Officer in the Communication Reserve. She commanded 712 (Montreal) Communication Squadron and later transferred to the Regular Force as a Personnel Selection Officer in 1991. At the time this research was conducted, LCdr Bradley was with the Maritime Staff as the Command Personnel Selection Officer, personnel policy analyst, and staff officer for all personnel applied research and military psychology issues in the navy. She has engaged in a variety of research activities over the course of her career, including those reported in this volume, and has presented at national and international forums on the topics of leadership, military culture, gender integration and employment equity. Following completion of the Joint Command and Staff Program, she has been the Personnel Operations officer in the Director General Operations group of the National Defence Headquarters Strategic Joint Staff.

The navy is a strongly gendered institution[1] where employment and occupations are sex segregated[2] and where both organizational and occupational cultures are masculine.[3] Sailing at sea in warships was long an exclusively male domain. In Canada, apart from early trials,[4] it was not until the 1989 Canadian Human Rights Tribunal (CHRT) decision[5] that the restriction limiting women's employment to support occupations was lifted and women were allowed to serve in sea-going operational (combat) roles and occupations. Nonetheless, such employment remains non-traditional for women.[6]

The past fifteen years have been a period of transition as women gained experience and demonstrated their competence in non-traditional roles, and men and women adjusted to living and working together in ships.[7] Although their numeric representation remains relatively small, at under 10 per cent,[8] women in the navy are employed in most occupations, at a number of rank levels, and in all classes of ships.[9] The navy recently opened employment access to the submarine service, which was the last remaining employment restriction.[10] However, women are not yet represented in many of the senior rank levels.[11]

Through conversations with 28 male naval personnel who had held senior leadership positions in Canada's mixed gender ships, I attempted to collect "best practices" suggestions for the benefit of future leaders of mixed gender crews. Amongst this all male group (no women had yet attained these positions in the Regular Force ships), there were 9 Commanding Officers (COs), 9 Executive Officers (XOs, the second-in-command of a vessel), and 8 Coxswains (Cox'ns) (the most senior non-commissioned member of the crew). Of the COs, two had also served as XOs in mixed gender ships and one had served previously as CO of a mixed gender ship. These conversations also revealed more general information about the progress of integrating women into previously all-male crews, which is the focus of the present article. The following topics are discussed: general attitudes toward women's integration in the navy, both at the outset and currently; influence of previous experience in mixed gender ships on these attitudes; the influence of gender integration on operational effectiveness and performance; "critical mass", and differences between mixed gender and all-male ships.

It is possible that the senior members were responding in socially desirable or "politically correct" ways. Furthermore, discussion of mixed gender issues during their tenure in a key leadership role could be considered discussion of their performance, and so could suggest discussion of more positive issues. However, members were all senior personnel whose careers would not be in any way influenced by their opinions. They were all assured that their opinions would not be attributed to them and that their identities would remain confidential, allowing them to provide their honest opinions without concern. All members appeared to be forthright in discussing these issues, providing relevant anecdotes and well-considered responses to questions regarding the leadership of mixed gender ships.

There were no systematic differences found in the comments and responses of east and west coast personnel or between anglophones and francophones. Minimal differences between officers and non-commissioned personnel seemed to reflect their relative perspectives on issues and personnel by virtue of their differing areas of responsibility within a ship's company.

Many members commented on changes in leadership styles, noting that leaders are much more likely to explain issues and decisions than in the past. Most did not attribute this change solely to the presence of women in ships, but considered that the presence of women, societal change in general, and younger people's current expectations of their leaders all affected leadership styles and best practices.

General attitudes then and now

The navy introduced women to service in ships in an incremental fashion, with only a restricted number of ships designated "mixed gender" at any given time.[12] This resulted in many men not serving with women until later in the transition, and indeed some have yet to do so. Gender integration in ships was in the late 1980s/early 1990s, which is the period considered "the early days" for this study. For some individuals, however, their personal "early days" didn't occur until the latter part of the 1990s or later, when their first tour of duty in a mixed gender ship occurred.

None of the individuals who held these leadership positions in the early days (1989-1992) had had previous experience serving at sea with women, as there had been no women in seagoing positions prior to that time. Some of those in the middle (1993-1996) or late (1997-2000) periods, however, had previously served with women while some had not. Late, therefore, does not necessarily imply previous experience serving at sea with women for individuals.

It should be noted that, while those whose first experience in a mixed gender ship was later in the transition at the *individual level*, throughout the transition period there was a gradual increase in experience serving with women *at the group level*. The posting of both men and women to different vessels over the transition period gradually increased the overall number of men who had served with women, with gradually larger representation in the ships. In the early years of gender integration, a very small percentage of the men in a mixed gender ship's company would have previously sailed with women. The men who were COs, XOs, and Cox'ns later in the transition then, while it may have been their first experience serving at sea with women, may have been leading ships' companies that had had a substantial proportion of mixed gender experienced sailors.

Comments on the early days focused on the general attitudes of members of ships' companies and on their uncertainty about how to deal with women in ships. Common perceptions were that the decision to employ women in ships was seen by many sailors of the day as "political", that most did not agree with it, and that there were personnel, including those in supervisory positions, who "were dead set against it".

It was noted that initially many members of ships' companies would treat men and women differently. In discussing typical behaviour from the early days, some members commented on being "brought up to open doors for ladies" and on a "tendency when (women) go to pick up something heavy, you want to go and give them a hand". They noted that many supervisors were "overly protective of the women" and would replace a woman having difficulty, or one they expected to have difficulties, with a man. One participant noted that most men of the day had many years of "upbringing" on how women should be treated that "You just can't change overnight". Many members commented that they also noticed this tendency in themselves and had to make a conscious effort to treat men and women the same way and to not be perceived to be showing more concern for, or paying more attention to, the women.

It was noted that helping or replacing women was neither instigated nor appreciated by the women themselves. It also tended to generate resentment among the men, as they considered that they were getting "all the dirty and heavy jobs week after week and the women were getting an easy time of it". Some of the members noted that this "annoyed the women who weren't allowed to do their jobs and weren't treated equally".

All noted that the uncertainty of the early days abated as male sailors became accustomed to working with women. Also, "people having their guard up" regarding general ways of behaving diminished, although there were, and are, specific concerns about unwarranted harassment complaints in later years.

Many of the opinions expressed towards gender integration positively explained that it is much better now than it was in the beginning; "When we started it was rough going." One member commented that: "The men, in some instances, were very suspect that the women could do a good job. I think today, the women have proven they can." Another stated that: "At first I didn't want it to happen. But after it did happen, then I was completely happy with the way things worked out."

Many noted the positive impact of more women serving in senior positions, a feature of recent times, both as evidence that progress and promotion for women is possible, and as role models. (Note that while there are more women in senior positions than in the past, the number remains relatively small.) One naval member commented that "not to say they weren't accepted before but I think they're more accepted now because they're coming on as more senior ranks".

It was noted, however, that there remained some personnel in the navy who "are hard nosed and saying, 'we don't want women here, women shouldn't be at sea'". This attitude was usually attributed to "some of the older people that haven't worked with women", as was a lingering tendency to treat men and women differently.

Influence of previous experience in mixed ships

Thirteen of the senior naval members had served at sea with women shipmates prior to attaining their position as CO, XO, or Cox'n, while nine had never previously served at sea with women, and the remaining four had had only minimal experience with women in the training system.

Many of those who had not previously sailed with women described a degree of trepidation or uncertainty at the beginning of their tour of duty. The uncertainties expressed concerned the challenges of leading a team comprised of both men and women, an area of uncertainty for some who had spent their career to date almost entirely with men. Some who did not have previous experience in mixed ships mentioned concerns generated by rumours of "horror stories" about lots of problems because of the women in the mixed gender ships. Those who had previously sailed with women mentioned no such generalized uneasiness.

Personnel who had not had previous mixed gender experience prior to their tour indicated that their concerns abated over the first few months in the job as the volume of problems suggested by the "horror stories" did not transpire and as they became comfortable in the mixed gender environment. Many commented that they realized that the basics of good leadership (such as good and frequent communication with personnel), which had served them well in single gender environments, are equally important in a mixed gender environment, and that they therefore had already developed most of the necessary skills.

Some commented that the actual experience in a mixed gender ship was somewhat contrary to their expectations: "I expected that there would be more mixed gender issues … that I would have to deal with problems. But I didn't see those sorts of problems arise", "I think I was pleasantly surprised with the effect that that many women had on the ships company."

One participant, from the latter part of the integration period, explained:

> Things have gotten a lot better. Because people are better educated and they understand it better. The guys that are XOs and COs now were in the ships in the early days, and have developed their leadership abilities such that they can apply naval policies in a practical way …while understanding that these are men and women that you're dealing with." (a former Executive Officer of a mixed gender ship.)

Operational effectiveness and performance

A couple of the members indicated that they thought that individual performance, which contributes to overall operational effectiveness, was better in mixed ships, noting specific skills and abilities of female members of their crew, such as: "quicker to pick up contacts", "more conscientious", and "didn't get in trouble". Others, particularly from the early days, noted their belief that some women were working extra hard in order to "prove themselves", which in turn sometimes incited male sailors to keep pace, resulting in improved performance for both. A couple of members noted that there could be a "slight reduction in capability in the strictly raw physical jobs", although they invariably noted that this was equally true of small men. "The women that we had at sea were excellent. They were good sailors."

Many of the senior members told stories about various women sailors who were exceptionally strong performers and "excellent sailors". It seemed that these people whose first and only experience at sea with women was in the early days noted these abilities in part because it was somewhat unexpected. That is, it was worthy of comment that it was a "female" who was the best master seaman in the ship, or the best acoustics operator, because it was to some degree surprising to them. Despite some comments that individual women excelled or that women in general were particularly skilled in some areas (e.g. the comment about picking up contacts), the overall sense of the comments from all members was that men and women generally are equally "good sailors".

Operational effectiveness is crucial to the successful accomplishment of the roles and missions of any military force. At the time of the CHRT deliberations the core of the Canadian Forces' (CF) argument against employing women in combat roles and occupations, including employment in warships, was that doing so would negatively impact on the operational effectiveness of units and ships.[13] This was a view held by most militaries in the world, and one which is still held in many countries.[14]

With both society and the CF suggesting that service at sea was not "women's work",[15] and with the suggestion that such service would have a negative impact on operational effectiveness, it is not surprising that the general attitude of sailors towards women at sea was negative. Many naval personnel did not believe that women could serve effectively at sea in combat roles and operational occupations and many people in Canadian society at large held similar views regarding suitable employment for women, which remains essentially the case today.[16]

Stewart reported the results of a survey administered to naval personnel, including those serving in the first mixed trial ship.[17] He reported that only 40 per cent of men serving in destroyers (n = 312), and 45 per cent of men serving in the trial ship (n = 65), believed that "qualified women should have the opportunity to serve at sea on destroyers".[18] He further reported that only 44 per cent of men agreed that "women can carry out tasks at sea as well as men". While 11 per cent of men in destroyers indicated a belief that women's impact on operational effectiveness would be "greatly" or "slightly improved" and 26 per cent indicated "no change", 63 per cent indicated that operational effectiveness would be "slightly" (28 per cent) or "greatly impaired" (35 per cent) if women were to be employed in destroyers.

While such beliefs may persist in some quarters, there appears to have been a marked change on the part of the key leaders who have sailed with female sailors. Not one of the members we spoke with thought that female sailors had a negative impact on operational effectiveness, which had been the fear expounded upon at the CHRT prior to the 1989 decision. Most indicated that gender was simply not a factor in the operational effectiveness of a ship:

> Operationally there is no reduction in capability because women sail in our ships. None.

Gender doesn't have any bearing at all on whether it's a good or a bad ships' company.

On the operational side, I can't think of a single incident operationally where the ship was disadvantaged by being mixed gender. I would even go as far as to say it was an advantage. There was a definite effort, a definite drive to make it all work, and to try to do better.

Stewart noted that both men and women in the first trial mixed gender ship "stated a fairly strong preference for working with males when asked: 'would you prefer to work with males, females, mixed groups or no preference?' "[19] The attitudes of the members spoken with were, again, markedly different. While not initiated by our conversations, many of the senior members with whom we spoke volunteered the statement that, if posted back to a seagoing position, they would prefer to serve in a mixed gender ship. Although this question was posed in some of the later conversations, it was not addressed directly by all participants. Many who did not address it directly made extremely positive statements about sailing in mixed ships relative to all-male ships and some commented that they had no preference for either mixed or single gender ships. Of the 28 conversations only one indicated a preference to serve in an all-male ship, with many of them expressing a preference to serve in mixed gender ships. In so stating, the "better climate" and idea that it's a "nicer place to work" that is "more normal" were invariably cited.

Early gender integration monitoring reports by external agencies[20] as well as internal research[21] indicated that integration was viewed as generally positive and there were no indications of a negative impact on operational effectiveness. These conversations confirm that, in marked contrast to the attitudes pre-integration, women were viewed as capable sailors who positively contributed to the operational effectiveness of their crews and ships. Not one person suggested otherwise. Given the very negative institutional and societal views of little more than a decade ago, it is perhaps surprising that the senior leaders of ships should unanimously express a starkly contrasting positive view.

"Critical Mass"

Its not unusual anymore to have females here. I work alongside females all the time. There's more and more of them in the Forces. I think they're becoming more accepted all the time. We are getting better at it and it's a road which is more readily acceptable now, than it was in the early days. You know, it's not uncommon anymore. They're everywhere. Just a fact of life.

A number of members addressed the issue of "critical mass", the Canadian military's term for a suitable proportion of women in the mixed ships. Personnel noted that it was good to have large numbers of women on board the ship, so that it was not unusual to see women living and working in all of the spaces on board and their presence was commonplace. While most stated that there was no optimal number, they indicated that "more is better" and some suggested that they would not like to see the proportion fall below about 10 per cent. Some attributed the fact that that they had "had no problems" to the fact that they had a large proportion of women. (Most of the mixed gender ships varied between 5 per cent and 20 per cent women, often hovering around 15 per cent. The navy's stated aim of 25 per cent was almost never achieved.)

Many of the conversations included comments on the advantages of the social support for female sailors which can be provided by larger numbers of women on board. Larger numbers allowed for, not only someone to talk to or check experiences with, but "just people to hang around with", to go for lunch with or shopping with when ashore in foreign ports. One person noted that while it may be "stereotyped", sometimes the "gals all go off together to do something" that the men may not be interested in doing. Many also noted the importance of having women at more senior levels, both in order to provide a senior voice for the issues of junior women, but also as a source of peer advice to senior male personnel who may wish to discuss an issue concerning one of their female sailors.

> You need to have the support network because sometimes a woman will just want to sit down and talk to another woman. And if there are no other women available that are of senior rank then they don't have that option and that's something that all the men have.

> I think you need to make sure (junior women) have senior representatives in the ship that they can talk to. So that they've got somebody who is in the chain of command that can take any issues from the female perspective and make sure that people are aware of them.

Many noted the "fish bowl effect" inherent in having only a few women; that is that the women felt that they were constantly being observed, and indeed assessed. This is what Kanter discusses as the high visibility of being in a skewed sex ratio group.[22] One former CO commented on the importance of "glorious anonymity" in the environment of a ship where privacy is "something we don't give you much of". It was also noted that when there were only a few women, the same women were repeatedly tasked when there are visiting groups, such as reporters or advisory board members. This served to give the impression that women were getting "special treatment".

Some noted that there had been some women who, as one of only a few in a ship's company, had no difficulties. However, all considered that this was not a good approach if it could be avoided. It was, further, suggested that having larger numbers when a ship is first converting to mixed gender is particularly important, and that the proportions could subsequently be reduced if necessary, as everyone becomes accustomed to a mixed ship.

A great deal of research has been conducted on gender integration processes. The evidence suggests that the ethnic minority group based contact and conflict models[23] were insufficient for the gender "group" context. They were largely superseded by a variety of theoretical orientations[24] which seek to explain the impact and influence of differing proportions of in- and out- or dominant/ minority groups, as well as studies addressing correlates of differing groups proportions, such as job satisfaction,[25] emergent leadership[26] and performance.[27]

Many approaches remain rooted in the generic group interaction approach, suggesting that they apply to both gender group and other "minority" group interactions. In discussing the early days, as well as in discussions of their first experience at sea with women in more recent times, the requirement to fundamentally change the way men behaved towards women was raised. The members noted that they had been socialized to treat women differently, and to engage in such behaviours as carrying heavy objects for them, or to proffer assistance for dirty or tough tasks. One noted that years of such behaviour could not be readily overcome.

In the gender integration scenario, then, the "dominant" group not only has to contend with overcoming societal stereotypes of appropriate roles and activities, which would be the case when learning about any minority group, but also confront years of actual behaviour towards women, albeit in other contexts and roles. This suggests that a good gender integration model needs to be more complex than race based models in order to account for actual behaviours and factors not accounted for by mere contact and conflict approaches, and supports Fiske and Stevens' comments regarding *"What's so special about sex"*.[28]

This deficiency has been addressed in part by researchers who have expanded the gender group proportions literature to include consideration of factors such as status, occupational sex segregation and sex-typing[29] all of which likely contribute to the process of attitude change in gender integration.

While exhorting the positive influence of large numbers, including the very positive comments of the CO whose ships' company was one-third women, most of the members had been in ships with only approximately 10 to 15 per cent women. It is therefore not possible to comment on many of the approaches which suggest different effects, both positive and negative, when larger proportions are reached.[30]

Differences between single gender and mixed gender ships

When asked, "What is the difference between a single gender ship and a mixed gender ship?" most members indicated that there is actually very little that was different between the two. Issues that were mentioned included the more "normal" atmosphere of the mixed gender ship, the potential problems of the development of personal relationships among shipmates, and the type of administrative problems, such as trying to get replacements when personnel go on maternity leave.

According to all of the conversations, the main difference between a mixed gender ship and an all-male ship is the climate or atmosphere. Using phrases like "moderating influence" and "tones down some of the macho stuff", members indicated that members of mixed ships' companies were "better behaved", and that there "was more of a family atmosphere". A couple of the members who subsequently worked in positions where they saw a number of both single- and mixed gender ships, stated that these climate differences were immediately obvious to visitors.

Some considered it simply more natural to live and work with both men and women around, as is normally the case "at home" or ashore. One noted that "having women on board gets away from the locker room kind of feeling that a lot of all-male ships have". Swearing, cursing, and other forms of "bad language" were almost invariably noted when commenting on the climate difference between single and mixed gender. It was quickly noted that women were also apt to use "foul language" but that it was more pervasive on single gender ships. "There are some females that swear worse than the males. But there are others who, if they hear it, they don't like it. So people tend to curb it."

It was noted that there are undoubtedly some sailors who prefer the all-male atmosphere, what Cheng considers "a homosocial community with other men...with hegemonically masculine norms".[31] Perhaps some prefer a "tough" climate that is different from life ashore, or consider the "more relaxed convivial atmosphere" of a mixed gender ship to be evidence of "a kinder and gentler navy", which they do not consider a positive point for combat personnel. However, most members expressed the opinion that, while those who had not yet served in a mixed gender ship would probably not agree, those who had would prefer the more comfortable climate of a mixed ship. "Maybe there's some trepidation while people are making the transition, but once they get used to it, they prefer it [the atmosphere in mixed gender ships]."

Members' comments about the positive influence of the presence of women on unit climate or "atmosphere" are not inconsistent with positive outcomes reported by others.[32] For example, Wharton and Bird reported that "perceived cohesiveness" of the workgroup, which they did not define, increased as the percentage of women increased. It may be, as also suggested by Wharton and Bird, that women's "characteristic styles" of interacting with others, communication, and supportiveness positively influenced atmosphere as well as other work attitudes. It is emphasized the "cohesiveness" as operationalized by Wharton and Baron may not be identical to "climate or atmosphere"as discussed in the present study, but may be either similar and/or related. Further research on this "atmosphere" construct needs to be conducted to consider its components as well as its effect on work attitudes and other outcomes.

Some of the "horror stories" referred to earlier relate to rumours of "all the problems" in mixed gender ships. All members indicated that there were no more problems in mixed ships than in single gender ships. They noted that the problems or "challenges" may be different but that there were definitely no more of them. They suggested, for example, that in a mixed ship there may be fewer disciplinary problems or fewer "macho incidents" like fights or people getting into trouble in a foreign port, and more problems entailing personal relationships or administrative matters because of child care requirements.

Although the conversations did not specifically discuss workplace romance, every member commented on the navy's "personal relationships policy"[33] and the potential impact of such relationships on mixed gender crews. The definition of "personal relationships" includes members of the same family but discussion of this issue or problems associated with this issue almost invariably refers to romantic or sexual relationships. While many commented that the policy applies equally to homosexual relationships and did mention lesbian relationships, it was noted that personal relationships simply had not been an issue in the all-male ships.

There was consensus that personal relationships were inevitable in mixed crews, especially considering that there are often many young, single people posted to the ships. It was noted that, despite proscriptions to the contrary, under such circumstances some dating and some more serious relationships were likely to develop. It was also noted that, depending on a variety of factors, such as the relative rank and positions of the members, their personal styles in how they handled their relationship, their discretion, etc., such relationships were not necessarily problematic.

However, It was also noted that such relationships within a crew could disrupt morale and cohesion, and could be divisive particularly when there is disagreement and shipmates "take sides", could impugn reputations where perceptions of favouritism are generated, and could affect individuals and teams within the crew.

There was no consensus on what the policy should be in this area. Many considered that prohibition of personal relationships between crewmembers and administrative, if not disciplinary action, to be appropriate while others considered this approach somewhat draconian. Others noted scenarios in which there was little to no difficulty engendered by personal relationships (such as between discrete people of the same rank level in different departments) and suggested that the complexity of possible situations required a policy that was sufficiently flexible to allow for each circumstance. Most believed that relationships between certain rank levels, and certainly between people in the same chain of command, should be prohibited but some considered that a more lenient approach could be taken to other personal relationships. Most members considered it an important policy issue for mixed ships.

> I firmly believe that the root of this thing is how we handle personal relationships. Because no matter what we do or say, they are always going to happen. So we have to be realistic, and reasonable with how we handle that eventuality. Unless they are handled in a fair, credible, and consistent manner, then we're going to cause more problems than we're going to solve. That's one of the key pillars of an integrated crew, how we handle personal relationships.

Most research on workplace romances suggests that such behaviour is not at all unusual. Quinn's seminal article noted that organizations are a "natural environment for romantic relationships"[34] that workplace romances occur frequently. As increasing numbers of women have entered the workplace, and as there has certainly been an increase in the numbers of women employed in ships, it is not surprising that the issue of romantic relationships has arisen there.

Although it is generally assumed that workplace romances have a negative impact on organizations, there is evidence that workplace romances can have positive effects, negative effects, and/or minimal effects on individuals and their job performance.[35] This is consistent with the comments provided in these conversations. Members' assessment of the impact of personal relationships depended on a number of factors such as rank of those involved, their proximity in the organizational structure, and whether or not there was a direct work relationship.

The views of these navy leaders are not inconsistent with those of civilian studies. Brown & Allgeier's found that managers tended to regard workplace romances negatively if they had negative impacts in the workplace, for example on performance, but may view them more positively if there were positive impacts.[36] Prospective managers in Powell's study were generally opposed to workplace romance, particularly between unequal organizational status participants.[37]

The navy's policy prohibits personal relationships between crewmembers but recognizes that they may still occur and provides for administrative action such as posting for personnel who do develop a relationship while in the same crew.[38] Quinn suggests that organizational policies or norms prohibiting romances have an impact on whether or not they occur, and so this policy may limit the number of such romances.[39] Some authors suggest that the range of possible scenarios requires "complex decision rules" and note that workplace romance should not be ignored because of the potential consequences in the workplace.[40]

However, it is unlikely that the navy's current or any future policies would eliminate workplace romance, especially given that naval personnel spend more time together than do most civilians. Members noted that there were almost certainly relationships that they were unaware of, which they assumed therefore had minimal impact. Further research is required to determine the extent and impact of personal relationships on ships personnel and crew cohesion.

Conclusions and recommendations

This exploration highlights the transitional or developmental nature of gender integration processes. The navy's incremental approach to mixed gender ships resulted in some personnel first working with women when no one had previously done so, while others with no previous experience entered fairly well established mixed gender units. These individual experiences parallel the overall or group level experiences and serve to further highlight the complexity of these issues. As suggested by earlier research and supported here, integrating men and women into cohesive, effective work units is much more than putting a "critical mass" of women into a work unit, even if assisted by awareness or education. The question of appropriate proportions to foster integration, which has yet to be determined, must be posed within the context of societal attitudes (e.g. occupational sex typing, stereotypes about appropriate work for women), extant organizational culture (and the extent to which it is masculine), and unit climate or culture.

Much of the research, particularly with civilian populations, is cross-sectional and compares work groups with varying sex ratios. Rarely, however, is it practical or even possible to introduce a large group of fully qualified, experienced women into a traditionally male occupation or environment. Research is, therefore, required which considers the transitions inherent in a gender integration process as progressively larger proportions of women develop over time. A comprehensive stage model, which accounts not only for the group interactions but also changes over time as team members and composition changes, as proportions changes, as members progressively achieve higher status levels (such as rank levels), and as the contextual frame of reference of societal stereotypes, occupational typing, and other factors change, needs to be developed to further inform both understanding of these issues and to assist in the practice of gender integration in organizations and institutions.

Some might suggest that it should have been assumed that women could do the job of sailors in warships, barring any evidence to the contrary. This was in fact the approach suggested by Segal[41] and taken by the CHRT in rendering its decision.[42] The reality of the day, however, was that the stereotypes of Canadian society[43] and the expectations of the sailors that were members of that society, [44] suggested that that capability remained to be proven.

This study demonstrated that, in the eyes of the leaders of the mixed gender ships, this was amply proven some time ago. It is clear that, to these leaders, the operational effectiveness of mixed gender ships and the performance of women sailors were simply not at issue. Given the generally negative attitudes of a decade or so ago, it is astounding that such a short time later many of these leaders have expressed a marked preference to serve in mixed gender ships, citing their operational capability and their better working environment or "atmosphere".

Further research is also required to explore the climate or "atmosphere" benefits, considered by many of the study participants to be, not only the major difference between single and mixed gender ships, but also a very positive aspect of serving in mixed ships. Further research is also required to consider the actual impact of personal relationships, or what the literature refers to as "workplace romance" on ships' personnel.

The views of these senior naval members represent those of personnel in key leadership positions in mixed gender ships. The results are not considered to be generalizable to all naval personnel. In fact, members noted many areas where their views are not held by all personnel in the navy. They are, however, considered accurate representations of the issues and concerns of key leaders who have been involved in the gender integration process in the Canadian navy over the past 15 years.

It is clear from them, as well as from what is reported here, that gender integration is not all positive and is not complete. This study represents no more than a mid-course review of what is an exceedingly complex process that will continue to occur and evolve for years to come. As one participant put it:

> It's a cultural change, a transition. We're well past the mid-point, I think. For anyone who's going through now, this is just the way it is. The other thing is that, for better or for worse, it's going to be remain a patriarchal society for at least the next ten years until we start getting (women in more senior leadership roles)."

1   C. Cheng, (Ed.), *Masculinities in Organizations*, (Thousand Oaks, CA: SAGE Publications, 1994); J. A. Mills, "Organization, gender and culture," *Organizational Studies*, 9 (1988) 351-369; D. Wicks and P Bradshaw. "The oppression of women in Canada: From denial to awareness and resistance," In S. E. Nancoo (Ed.), *21ˢᵗ century Canadian diversity*, (Mississauga, ON: Canadian Educators' Press, 2000), 115-142.

2   W. T. Bielby, and J. N. Baron, "A Woman's Place is With Other Women: Sex Segregation Within Organizations," In B. Reskin (Ed.), *Sex Segregation in the Workplace: Trends, Explanations, Remedies*, (Washington, DC: National Academy Press, 1984), 27-55.

3   C. Cheng, (Ed.), *Masculinities in Organizations*, (Thousand Oaks, CA: SAGE Publications, 1994).

4   R. E. Park, *Women's Sea Trial: Report of Participant Observation Study*, Working Paper, 82-6, (Willowdale, Ontario: Canadian Forces Personnel Applied Research Unit, 1982); see also R. E. Park, *Final Report of the Social/ Behavioural Science Evaluation of the SWINTER Sea Trial*, Research Report 84-4, (Willowdale, Ontario: Canadian Forces Personnel Applied Research Unit, 1984).

5   Canadian Human Rights Tribunal (CHRT). Gauthier, Houlden, Gauthier, and Brown vs. the Canadian Forces. Decision rendered on February 19, 1989 in the matter of the Canadian Human Rights Act, S.C. 1976-77, C.33, as amended, 1989.

6   Human Resources Development Canada. *Occupational Segregation and the Gender Wage Gap*, Bulletin Volume 6, Number 1, (Ottawa, ON: Author, 2001); B. F. Reskin and I. Padavic, Women and men at work, (Thousand Oaks, CA: Pine Forge Press (SAGE), 1994).

7   Chief of the Maritime Staff (CMS), *Report on Gender Integration in Maritime Command – 1989-1997*, (Ottawa: NDHQ, Maritime Staff, 1997).

8   L. Tanner, *Gender Integration in the Canadian Forces – A Quantitative and Qualitative Analysis*. (Ottawa: National Defence, Operational Research Division, 1999), Report PR 9901.

9   Chief of the Maritime Staff (CMS), *Naval Personal Relationships Policy*, (Ottawa, ON: National Defence Headquarters, 1998), CMS letter dated 12 May 98.

10   Maritime Command News Release, *Navy Opens Submarine Service to Women* (CMS: 03/01), (Ottawa, Ontario, 8 March 2001).

11   Chief of the Maritime Staff (CMS), *Report on Gender Integration in Maritime Command – 1989-1997*; Chief of the Maritime Staff (CMS), *Naval Personal Relationships Policy*, CMS letter dated 12 May 1998; and L. Tanner, *Gender Integration in the Canadian Forces*.

12   Until 2000 when this policy was changed; Chief of the Maritime Staff (CMS), *Mixed Gender Unit Policy*, CMS letter dated 14 January 2000, (Ottawa, ON: National Defence Headquarters, 2000).

13   Canadian Human Rights Tribunal (CHRT). Gauthier, Houlden, Gauthier, and Brown vs. the Canadian Forces. Decision rendered on February 19, 1989 in the matter of the Canadian Human Rights Act, S.C. 1976-77, C.33, as amended, 1989.

14   L. B. Franke, *Ground Zero: The Gender Wars in the Military*, (New York: Simon and Schuster, 1997).

15   B. F. Reskin, and H. Hartmann, *Women's Work, Men's Work: Sex Segregation on the Job*, (Washington, D.C.: National Academy Press, 1986).

16   S. E. Nancoo, (Ed.), *21st Century Canadian Diversity*, (Mississauga, ON: Canadian Educators' Press, 2000).

17   P. A. Stewart, *A Comparative Analysis of Attitudes Toward Woman at Sea: 1980 to 1982*, CFPARU Working Paper 83-7, (Willowdale, Ontario: Canadian Forces Personnel Applied Research Unit, 1983).

18   P. A. Stewart *A Comparative Analysis of Attitudes Toward Woman at Sea: 1980 to 1982*, 7.

19   P. A. Stewart, *A Comparative Analysis of Attitudes Toward Woman at Sea: 1980 to 1982*, 18.

20   K. Bindon, Report of visit to HMCS NIPIGON: 3-12 Dec & 31 Dec 1990, (St. John's, NL: Author, 1991); MABGICF, Minister's Advisory Board on Gender Integration in the Canadian Forces – Maritime Command Headquarters Visit Report, Report of 17-19 Sept 96 visit, (Ottawa, ON: Author, 1996).

21   Chief of the Maritime Staff (CMS), *Report on Gender Integration in Maritime Command – 1989-1997*, Ottawa: NDHQ, Maritime Staff, 1997; K. M. McDonald and C. D. F. Lyon, *Mixed gender integration: Feedback from the Navy 1989-1990*, Maritime Command Tech Note 02/91, (Halifax, NS: Maritime Command Headquarters, 1991).

22   R. M. Kanter, "Some Effects of Proportions on Group Life: Skewed Sex Ratios and Responses to Token Women," *American Journal of Sociology*, 82 (1977): 965-990.

23   G. W. Allport, *The Nature of Prejudice*, (Reading, Mass: Addison-Wesley Publishing Company, 1954); Y. Amir, "Contact hypothesis in ethnic relations," *Psychological Bulletin*, 71(5, 1969): 319-341;

H. M. Blalock, *Toward a Theory of Minority-Group Relations*, (New York: John Wiley & Sons, Inc, 1967); S. W. Cook, "Motives in a Conceptual Analysis of Attitude-related Behaviour," in W. J. Arnold and D. Levine, (Eds.), *Nebraska Symposium on Motivation*, (University of Nebraska Press, 1969).

24   R. M. Kanter, *Men and Women of the Corporation*, (New York: Basic Books, Inc, 1977); R. M. Kanter, "Some effects of proportions on group life"; P. M. Blau, *Inequality and Heterogeneity*, (New York: Free Press, 1977); H. Tajfel, *Differentiation Between Social Groups*, (London: Academic Press, 1978); J. C. Turner, and S. A. Haslam, "Social Identity, Organisations and Leadership," in M.E. Turner (Ed.), *Groups at Work: Advances in Theory and Research*, (Erlbaum: New Jersey, 1999); For a good review, see P. S. Tolbert, M. E. Graham, and A. O. Andrews, "Gender Composition and Group Relations: Theories, Evidence and Issues," in G. N. Powell, (Ed.), *Handbook of gender and work*, (Thousand Oaks, CA: SAGE, 1999).

25   D. L. Fields and T. C. Blum, "Employee Satisfaction in Work Groups with Different Gender Composition," *Journal of Organisational Behaviour*, 18 (2, 1997): 181-196.

26   L. Karakowsky and J. P. Siegel, "The Effects of Proportional Representation and Gender Orientation of the Task on Emergent Leadership Behavior in Mixed Gender Work Groups," *Journal of Applied Psychology*, 84 (4, 1999): 620-631.

27   V. Alexander, and P. Thoits, "Token Achievement: An Examination of Proportional Representation and Performance Outcomes," *Social Forces*, 64 (2, 1985): 332-340.

28   S. T. Fiske and L. E. Stevens, "What's So Special About Sex? Gender Stereotyping and Discrimination," in S. Oskamp & M. Constanzo (Eds.), *Gender issues in contemporary society*, (Newbury Park, CA: SAGE, 1993).

29   J. A. Jacobs, *Revolving Doors: Sex Segregation and Women's Careers*, (Stanford, CA: Stanford University Press, 1989); Marini, M. M., and M. C. Brinton. "Sex Typing in Occupational Socialization." in B. Reskin (Ed.), *Sex Segregation in the Workplace: Trends, Explanations, Remedies*, (Washington, DC: National Academy Press, 1984); O. N. Ruble and E. T. Higgins, "Effects of Group Sex Composition on Self-Presentation and Sex-typing", *Journal of Social Issues*, 32 (1976): 125-132; E. M. Ott, "Effects of the Male-Female Ratio at Work: Policewomen and Male Nurses," *Psychology of Women Quarterly*, 13 (1989): 41-57; J. D. Yoder, "Looking Beyond Numbers: The Effects of Gender Status, Job Prestige and Occupational Gender-typing on Tokenism Processes," *Social Psychology Quarterly*, 57 (2, 1994): 150-159.

30   For instance, R. M. Kanter, *Men and Women of the Corporation*; R. M. Kanter, "Some Effects of Proportions on Group Life: Skewed Sex Ratios and Responses to Token Women"; H. M. Blalock, *Toward a Theory of Minority-group Relations*, (New York: John Wiley & Sons Inc., 1967).

31   C. Cheng, (Ed.), *Masculinities in Organizations*, (Thousand Oaks, CA: SAGE Publications, 1994).

32   For instance, A.S. Wharton and J. N. Baron, "So Happy Together? The Impact of Gender Segregation on Men at Work," *American Sociological Review*, 52 (1987): 574-587; A. Wharton and S. Bird, "Stand by Your Man: Homosociality, Work Groups, and Men's Perceptions of Difference," in C. Cheng (Ed.), *Masculinities in Organizations*, (Thousand Oaks, CA: SAGE Publications, 1994); W. G. Peirce and R. Ayman, *Work-force Diversity Effects on the Quality and Strength of Organizational Climate*,

Paper presented at the 1998 annual SIOP conference, (Dallas, Texas: 1998).

33   Chief of the Maritime Staff (CMS), *Naval Personal Relationships Policy*, CMS letter dated 12 May 1998, (Ottawa, ON: National Defence Headquarters, 1998).

34   R. Quinn, "Coping with cupid: The Formation, Impact, and Management of Romantic Relationships in Organizations," *Administrative Science Quarterly.* 22 (1977): 30-45; and T. J. Brown and E. R. Allgeier, "Managers' Perceptions of Workplace Romances: An Interview Study," *Journal of Business and Psychology*, 10 (2, 1995): 169-176.

35   J. P. Dillard, & S.M. Broetzman, "Romantic Relationships at Work: Perceived Changes in Job-related Behaviors as a Function of Participant's Motive, Partner's Motive, and Gender" *Journal of Applied Social Psychology*, 19 (1989): 93-110; L.A. Mainiero, "A Review and Analysis of Power Dynamics in Organizational Romances" *Academy of Management Review*, 11 (1986): 750-762: C.A. Pierce, "Factors Associated with Participating in a Romantic Relationship in a Work Environment," *Journal of Applied Social Psychology*, 28 (18, 1998): 1712-1731; L.A. Mainiero, "Sexual Attraction in the Workplace is Often Counterproductive" in J. S. Petrikin (Ed.), *Male/female roles: Opposing viewpoints.* (San Diego, CA: Greenhaven, 1995), 284-288.

36   T. J. Brown and E. R. Allgeier, "Managers' Perceptions of Workplace Romances: An Interview Study," *Journal of Business and Psychology*, 10 (2, 1995): 169-176.

37   G. N. Powell, "What do Tomorrow's Managers Think about Sexual Intimacy in the Workplace?" *Business Horizons*, 4 (1986): 30-35.

38   Chief of the Maritime Staff (CMS), *Naval Personal Relationships Policy*, CMS letter dated 12 May 1998.

39   R. Quinn, "Coping with Cupid."

40   T. J. Brown and E. R. Allgeier, "Managers' Perceptions of Workplace Romances: An Interview Study," *Journal of Business and Psychology*, 10 (2, 1995): 169-176.; L. A. Mainiero, "A Review and Analysis of Power Dynamics in Organizational Romances", 850-762.

41   D. R. Segal, *The Impact of Gender Integration on the Cohesion, Morale, and Combat Effectiveness of Military Units*, Position Paper prepared for the Canadian Department of National Defence, 1986.

42   Canadian Human Rights Tribunal (CHRT). Gauthier, Houlden, Gauthier, and Brown vs. the Canadian Forces. Decision rendered on February 19, 1989 in the matter of the Canadian Human Rights Act, S.C. 1976-77, C.33, as amended, 1989.

43   National Defence, *Summary of Report of the Attitude Surveys on Women in Combat Roles and Isolated Postings*, (Ottawa, ON: National Defence Headquarters, Directorate Personnel Development Studies DPDS, 1978).

44   P. A. Stewart, *A Comparative Analysis of Attitudes Toward Woman at Sea: 1980 to 1982.*

CHAPTER 20

Experiences With Mixed Gender Submarine Crews[1]

Lieutenant-Commander Lynn Bradley and
Lieutenant-Commander Debbie Pestell

Lieutenant-Commander Lynn Bradley (LCdr) CD, MSc, (1997, University of Calgary (Industrial Organizational Psychology)) began her career as an Army Radio Operator and then a Signals Officer in the Communication Reserve. She commanded 712 (Montreal) Communication Squadron and later transferred to the Regular Force as a Personnel Selection Officer in 1991. At the time this research was conducted, LCdr Bradley was with the Maritime Staff as the Command Personnel Selection Officer, personnel policy analyst, and staff officer for all personnel applied research and military psychology issues in the Navy. She has engaged in a variety of research activities over the course of her career, including those reported in this volume, and has presented at national and international forums on the topics of leadership, military culture, gender integration and employment equity. Following completion of the Joint Command and Staff Program, she has been the Personnel Operations officer in the Director General Operations group of the National Defence Headquarters Strategic Joint Staff.

Lieutenant-Commander (LCdr) Debbie Pestell, CD, MD, enrolled in the Canadian Forces on 20 August, 1990. Following completion of medical school and a Family Medicine residency at McMaster University in 1995, LCdr Pestell was posted to Victoria, BC where she spent three years at sea as a ship's Medical Officer (HMCS PROTECTEUR and REGINA) with tours of duty in the Far East and Persian Gulf. From 1999-2001 she completed a Master's Degree in Public Health and a fellowship in hyperbaric and diving medicine in San Antonio, Texas. LCdr Pestell was the Consultant in Diving Medicine at Defence Research and Development Canada (DRDC) Toronto from 2001-2006 and has been working as the Consultant in Submarine and Diving Medicine in Halifax, NS since summer 2006. She is married and has two wonderful children, Lukas (6) and Emeline (4½).

Section 3 of the Canadian Human Rights Act (CHRA) prohibits discrimination on the basis of sex.[2] A Canadian Human Rights Tribunal (CHRT) held hearings between 1986 and 1988 to hear complaints against the Canadian Forces (CF) with regard to discrimination against women based on gender.[3] The Tribunal concluded that none of the risk arguments associated with physical capability, environmental conditions, social relationships, cohesion or motivation were sufficient to warrant the continued exclusion of women from combat roles, and stated that the policy was therefore discriminatory on the grounds of sex. The Tribunal, in its 1989 decision, ordered the CF to fully integrate women into all remaining combat roles, including those aboard surface warships, in combat arms, and as fighter pilots. But the CHRT issued a single exception to this order: submarines. While a *bona fide occupational requirement* (**BFOR**) did not exist with respect to combat roles (that is, combat effectiveness would not be diminished by the integration of women), the Tribunal accepted the argument that the exclusion of women from the submarine environment did constitute a **BFOR** since a lack of privacy was identified as a factor that would significantly impact operational effectiveness. In other words, the discriminatory effect was "nullified or overcome" by the occupational requirement. The Tribunal did, however, state that if a time came when the CF operated types of submarines where privacy issues were not as prominent as in the OBERON-class, this restriction could be examined again. Virtually all other allied submariner nations at the time also prohibited women from serving in submarines despite permitting them to serve in other combat environments.

With the acquisition of the new VICTORIA-class submarines in the late 1990s, many of the conditions that originally led the Human Rights Tribunal to recommend exclusion of women from submarine service were considered no longer valid. Published in 1998, the action plan for the Canadian navy's *Vision 2010: The Integrated Navy*[4] included the requirement to re-examine this policy. Fewer functions on board the VICTORIA-class submarines are performed manually, allowing for a smaller crew (on average 55 vs. 70). In addition, the new submarines are more spacious and are configured differently – there are two decks, so the main living areas and working areas are now on different decks. All of these factors allow for more privacy and personal space, and a more habitable environment for two genders.

Therefore, in 1998, the Chief of Maritime Staff (CMS) directed that a study be undertaken to determine if the presumed risk to operational effectiveness was still a valid assumption, and if there was a reason to continue to prohibit women from serving in submarines. Numerous methodologies were used in the study[5] including a search of archival data, a literature review, a two-week site visit to the OBERON-class submarine HMCS OKANAGAN while underway, a site visit to a VICTORIA-class submarine alongside in the UK, discussions and correspondence with subject matter experts, and a survey. The study concluded with the recommendation that women should now be employed in the new VICTORIA-class submarines, acknowledging that the transition would not be easy and would take time. In 2001, the recommendations made in the study were adopted by the Canadian navy and women were accepted into submarine service.

Factors affecting mixed gender crewing

Two major decision factors were considered when recommending that women be allowed to serve aboard submarines: crewing/bunk management and accommodations, and privacy. In addition, several other factors were considered that could possibly affect implementation of mixed gender crewing, including the volunteer aspect of submarine service, health and medical care issues, and psychological aspects of mixed gender crews.

Crewing/Bunk Management

Arguably the most important factor in deciding whether or not women could be integrated in to service aboard the new VICTORIA-class submarines was how crew assignment and bunk management would be dealt with. A bunk policy had to be set. The essence of the bunking problem was as follows: if the sexes were segregated, when a female member of the crew is landed or posted, finding a qualified submariner of the same occupation, rank *and* sex would be virtually impossible since the replacement pool of women is smaller – there are fewer women than men in the navy, and in particular in the submarine service, especially in the early years of mixed gender crewing. While there is some flexibility in surface vessels to accommodate women separately and generally within their rank and occupation group, it is simply not possible to reconcile these requirements with the limitations imposed by the small and specialized crew of a submarine. Also, the implications of bunks going empty are more critical in submarines, since it is less able to sail with empty billets than a surface warship where segregated bunking is practiced. Finally, designating a specific area for female bunks in the relatively inflexible crew accommodation spaces aboard the VICTORIA-class submarines would simply be impossible without major structural changes to the interior of the submarine.

Interestingly, survey results from the study indicated that there was much less resistance to the concept of mixed accommodations spaces amongst submariners than had been assumed by many senior submarine and surface naval personnel. Accordingly, it was recommended in the mixed gender crewing study that women should be employed in VICTORIA-class submarines *only* if the bunking policy was set such that bunks were assigned on a functional basis without regard to gender, that is, integrated vs. segregated bunking. This recommendation was adopted without modification, and to date there have been no problems whatsoever with mixed gender bunking.

Privacy

Privacy issues in mixed gender crewing also needed to be addressed. Some of the lessons learned during the initial integration of women on board surface warships 12 years previous were helpful during the early days of conversion to mixed gender submarine crews. Also, as previously mentioned, the structural design and configuration of the new VICTORIA-class submarines is more amenable to men and women serving together, since the main working and living spaces are on different decks; this allows for more privacy and personal space.

Short of segregating the sexes, all reasonable efforts have been made to provide for privacy requirements for the benefit of both men and women. With a smaller crew, the common practice of "hot bunking" on the old OBERON-class submarines – in which two sailors on opposite watch rotations shared the same bunk – is no longer employed in the new submarines. All submariners are now allocated individual bunks with privacy curtains. Also, a minimum attire policy (e.g. shorts/T-shirt) for sleeping and for relaxed dress in hot climates has been promulgated. In the very close quarters of the submarine environment, all crewmembers understand the need to respect each other's individual privacy whenever and as much as possible. Fraternization and inter-personal relationships between members of the boat's crew are strictly prohibited, as they have always been on board surface warships.

With respect to personal ablutions, the single heads and washplace area in the VICTORIA-class submarine which was designated for officers is used by officers and any female crewmembers on board. Doors, of course, can be latched. No other special measures were required.

Volunteer/Non-Volunteer Crewing of Submarines

In the majority of the world's navies, submarine service is voluntary in recognition of the inherently unique, austere and hazardous conditions of that environment. Submarine service in Canada was, similarly, entirely voluntary until 1 Jan 1986 when insufficient volunteers necessitated a change in policy such that naval personnel could be directed in to submarine service when required if the number of volunteers was insufficient to man the submarines. The Canadian submarine service was facing particularly difficult manning challenges in the late 1990s at the time the new VICTORIA-class submarines were coming into service.

Personnel who serve in submarines are drawn from the occupations which also serve in surface ships, both naval combat ("hard sea") and combat support occupations (although not all surface occupations are represented in submarines). In addition to basic seamanship and occupation training, members must also undergo specialized training to become submarine qualified. "Dolphins" – the badge which denotes submarine qualification – is awarded only after successful completion of the Basic Submarine Qualification (BSQ) course, training alongside in the VICTORIA-class submarine trainers, and a consolidation period aboard a submarine at sea for "on-the-job" training. Given the extensive training required to become a qualified submariner, and in part due to the small size of Canada's submarine service, submarine crewing has often been problematic due to insufficient qualified personnel. Manning shortages are critical because without sufficient qualified personnel, the submarine cannot sail.

The acquisition of the four new VICTORIA-class submarines in the late 1990s added to the historic problem of personnel shortages because now the submarine service faced the additional challenge of training enough personnel to crew a new platform. VICTORIA-class conversion training for qualified submariners who had previously served in the OBERON-class submarines began in March 1999. One of the benefits in opening up service in submarines to women is that it has helped to alleviate the chronic manning problems by tapping into a portion of the naval operational and support personnel population that had previously been unavailable to the submarine service. And by allowing women to volunteer for service in the new VICTORIA-class submarines, fewer men have to be directed in to service. Women must be employed in submarines on the same footing as their male counterparts, though. That is, volunteers are accepted as much as possible, but when the numbers are insufficient to meet manning requirements, female sailors may be directed into submarine service as well.

Health and Medical Care Issues

Several issues with respect to the medical care of female submariners needed to be considered during the implementation phase of mixed gender crewing of submarines. None of these, however, were considered "make or break" decision factors as they have been in other navies when deciding if women could serve aboard submarines. Most gender-specific medical problems in women tend to involve the reproductive and genitor-urinary systems, however, many of them can be managed or prevented entirely with proper screening and risk management. Medical emergencies in a submarine underway at sea are far more likely to arise from non-gender specific conditions (e.g. burns, appendicitis, trauma, etc.) than as a result of a female-specific problem.

Medical Care

VICTORIA-class submarines do not have a large enough crew to warrant the services of a Medical Officer, however, each submarine does have an independent-duty Physician's Assistant (PA) on board. The PA is a fully trained submariner, and since his or her medical duties do not require his or her full attention, he or she is also responsible for monitoring air quality aboard the submarines, and stand regular duty-watches as helmsmen. In as far as it is possible, consideration is given to ensuring that there are at least two women per submarine crew. Although not always possible, this allows for a female attendant should a woman require medical treatment at sea when the PA is male. To date there have been no female Physician Assistant's on board the VICTORIA-class submarines, although they have served on board surface warships for almost 20 years.

Medical facilities aboard a VICTORIA-class submarine are extremely limited and there is no specific space dedicated for a Sickbay, although a mess can be cleared and the curtain drawn to provide privacy should the PA need to conduct a physical examination on either a male or female crew member. If women are part of a submarine's crew compliment, in addition to his or her other routine medical supplies, the PA also carries a special "women's kit" on board. This kit contains medications, supplies and equipment that may be required to manage gender-specific medical problems while underway, and includes specific antibiotics and anti-fungal agents, Midol, pregnancy test kits, the birth control pill, a sterile speculum, etc.

Reproductive Health

The vast majority of female submariners are professional sailors who have volunteered for submarine service; any plans they may have for pregnancy and a family are generally carefully planned so as not to conflict with a posting to an operational submarine. Nonetheless, female members who believe they could be pregnant should be tested prior to deployment. It has been the policy in the Canadian navy that pregnant members are deemed unfit sea and unfit alongside for the health and safety of the expectant mother and the foetus ever since women began serving on board surface warships in the late 1980s. This policy also extends to women serving in submarines. Due to the unique nature of submarine operations at sea, however, there are additional risks of which female submariners must be informed.

The principles of stealth and endurance are fundamental to the very nature of submarine operations at sea. Since VICTORIA-class submarines can remain submerged at sea for long periods of time, there is the potential for lengthy deployments with limited chance of early disembarkation. Given this reality, in the event of an unknown pregnancy, female submariners may be subject to potential complications including miscarriage, ectopic pregnancy and morning sickness aggravated by motion sickness, for which definitive medical care may not be immediately available. In addition, they may be exposed to potential environmental hazards and atmospheric contaminants that could be dangerous to a developing foetus. All female submariners are briefed by the boat's PA about these risks when they join the submarine. They are then required to read and sign a *Medical Advisory Statement for Women in Submarines*;[6] this acknowledges that they have been briefed about the potential risks to themselves and a developing foetus should they be pregnant while embarked on board a submarine at sea. It is a type of "informed consent".

Infections and Hygiene

As personal hygiene on board a submarine underway is often less than optimal due to water restrictions, the lack of shower facilities, and the inability to change clothes on a daily basis, female submariners must take particular care to prevent urinary tract and yeast infections. A clean set of cotton underwear daily goes a long way to preventing such infections.

Menstruation

Many female submariners use oral or intra-muscular injections of contraceptives to minimize the risk of pregnancy and shorten or eliminate monthly menstruation. Nonetheless, products of menstruation are considered natural, biodegradable substances. According to the CF Formation Environment, all female hygiene products are to be treated as normal garbage and can be jettisoned into the ocean in the submarine's "gash gun" (garbage ejector) as necessary.

Psychological Aspects of Mixed Gender Crews

The psychological impact – both positive and negative – of integrating women in to service aboard submarines was also considered during implementation planning, however, since women had already been successfully integrated in to service aboard surface warships 12 years earlier, many male submariners had already had the opportunity to work with women in an operational environment. Efforts were made to disseminate information within the submarine community about the pending changes, and attempts were made to address any attitudinal issues including the provision of information on privacy issues, gender free performance standards and the integration process. Information about harassment, perceived harassment, harassment policies and procedures – including guidelines about what is not considered to be harassment – were also provided.

There is very little information available on women in submarine service in behavioural science databases or other research sources. NASA has done several studies on the psychological aspects of mixed gender crews,[7] and the isolation of long periods of time at sea aboard a submarine are in many ways analogous to lengthy missions in space. Women's leadership styles have been characterized by task orientation, mentoring others, and concern with the needs of other group members. All-male expeditions on the other hand, are characterized by strong competitiveness and little sharing of personal concerns among crewmembers. Some advantages that have been reported by astronauts on missions with mixed gender crews include women assuming the role of peacemaker during times of conflict, crew members feeling it is easier to express their feelings, and a sense of calmer missions. In addition, 75 per cent of men reported a reduction in rude behaviour and improved cleanliness – this would certainly be an advantage of mixed gender crews if it could be generalized to the submarine environment!

A few problem areas were also identified. Women reported being highly visible (the "fish bowl" effect), especially when it came to making mistakes. Some rated perceived acceptance by peers as lower than male crew and felt their opinions were not considered as credible. Some recommendations for shuttle and space station crews that have come out of these NASA studies include attempts to select compatible crews (not practical in the submarine environment), evaluation of crew behaviour interactions during training (this could be accomplished by the submarine sea-trainers during work-ups), more research on the ratio of women to men, length of stay, and rotation patterns on missions (again, not very generalizable to the submarine environment due to manning challenges and operational commitments), and pre-flight sensitivity training (this type of training is already mandatory for all military personnel upon entrance in to the armed forces).

Practices of Other Navies

In 2001 when Canada began accepting women into submarine service, Norway and Denmark were the only other NATO nations at the time to have successfully integrated women into this role. (Denmark no longer has a submarine service). Norway has allowed women to serve in submarines since the late 1980s, and in 1995 Solveig Krey of the Royal Norwegian Navy became the world's first female officer to command a submarine, HNoMS KOBBEN. Today several other NATO nations, including Poland and Spain, are looking at the possibility of integrating women into submarine service. Outside of NATO, women began serving aboard submarines in Sweden in 1991; as with Canada, no special provisions are made for bunking or shower facilities. In addition, Australia began training female submariners in the late 1990s. The Australian COLLINS-class submarines carry a crew of 55, and contain a six-berth bunkroom for women. Segregated bunking has created some difficulties with filing billets when a female leaves an operational submarine. In addition, there has also been a negative impact on group cohesion and a detriment to informal learning caused by accommodating women separately rather than with their work group.

Most allied nations, however, still forbid women to serve as submariners, including the United States, United Kingdom, Germany, France, Netherlands, Turkey and Israel. Some nations site safety concerns; for other nations the decision is a religious or cultural one. In the United States, combat vessels were opened to women in 1994 following congressional repeal of the "Combat Exclusion Law" with the single exception of submarines. Reasons cited for this exclusion include the prohibitive costs of berthing women and privacy arrangements (some US submarines employ the practice of "hot bunking", and the US Navy has a strict fraternization policy that it feels may be compromised if women begin serving aboard submarines). In addition, in their paper on *Medical Implications of Women on Submarines*,[8] Kane and Horn raise concerns over the length of patrols of their nuclear submarines, and the distance from coastal waters should a female crewmember require medical evacuation for pregnancy or a gynecological problem. The US Navy feels that placing women on board submarines would raise medical considerations that require critical evaluation, and that more research is needed to better elucidate the impact on, not only the individual female's health, but also on the submarine's mission effectiveness.

Germany also prohibits women from serving in submarines for bunking and privacy issues. Under British law there is also a legal requirement to provide for the care and safety of women and their unborn children at work. The Royal Navy maintains that if a female submariner does not know that she is pregnant, they cannot give assurance for the safety of an unborn child from a number of atmospheric contaminants found in the submarine environment, including elevated levels of carbon dioxide.

Conclusion

In April 1998, Canada announced the acquisition of four UPHOLDER-class submarines from the Royal Navy, subsequently renamed the VICTORIA-class submarines. The VISION 2010 Submarine Service Review project began in May 1998 to examine the feasibility of mixed gender crewing of the new submarines, and to consider potential implementation factors, since the presumed risk to operational effectiveness by employing women in the submarine service in the Canadian navy was no longer a valid assumption. Although a number of important factors such as crewing and bunk management, privacy, health and medical care issues, and the psychological aspects of mixed gender crews needed to be carefully addressed during a transition period, the study concluded that there was no longer sufficient reason to exclude women from submarine service.

Since it may take up to two years to qualify a submariner beyond basic occupation qualification due to the time required for the medical and administrative screening process, the scheduling of the BSQ course, and the limited number of training billets on board operational submarines, it was some time before the first trained female submariners were assigned to an operational unit. In 2003, a sonar operator and a naval combat information operator became the first two women to serve as trained submariners aboard HMCS WINDSOR. Today there are four female submariners serving aboard VICTORIA-class submarines and others undergoing training; all are non-commissioned members. Although one female Maritime Officer did complete the BSQ course, she did not complete the sea phase of training in order to receive her dolphins. Interviews with female submariners about their experiences serving in submarines reveals common themes: all are mature, experienced sailors who simply wish to be considered one of the crew and do not want to be singled out because they are women. They are very professional and dedicated to their careers and work hard to gain the respect of their male peers for their skills as submariners, not specifically as *female* submariners.

---

1   This study was first conducted by LCdr Lynn Bradley in 1999, then updated and presented at a NATO symposium in October 2009 (Human Factors and Medicine Panel (HFM) 158) in Antalya, Turkey by LCdr Debbie Pestell.

2   Canadian Human Rights Commission, *The Canadian Human Rights Act*, S.C. 1976-77, Section 3.

3   Canadian Human Rights Tribunal Decision. *Canadian Human Rights Tribunal*. Decision rendered on 19 Feb 1989 in the matter of the Canadian Human Rights Act, S.C. 1976-77, C.33, as amended.

4   Chief of Maritime Staff, V*ISION 2010 – The Integrated Navy: The way ahead for the next phase of integration.* (Ottawa, ON: NDHQ, Maritime Staff, 1998).

5   Bradley, B.L., *Mixed Gender Crewing of VICTORIA-Class Submarines* (Maritime Staff Research Report 99-1). (Ottawa, ON: NDHQ, Maritime Staff, 1999).

6   Canadian Forces Health Services Group Policy and Guidance 4030-71. *Medical Fitness for Submarine Service and Wet Pressurized Escape Training*, Annex C. (Ottawa, ON: Canadian Forces Health Services Group, 2008), 18.

7   Leon, Gloria R. *Men and Women in Space. Aviation, Space and Environmental Medicine*, Vol. 76 (6, 2005): B84-B88.

8   Kane, John L. & Horn, Wayne G. *The Medical Implications of Women on Submarines*, Naval Submarine Medical Research Laboratory (NSMRL), Report No. 1219, 2001.

ACRONYMS AND ABBREVIATIONS

3D	Defence, Diplomacy, Development
ACOS	Assistant Chief of Staff
Adm	Admiral
Adm Clk	Administrative Clerk
ADR	Alternative Dispute Resolution
ANDS	Afghanistan National Development Strategy
AWOL	Absent Without Leave
BFOR	Bona Fide Occupational Requirement
BSQ	Basic Submarine Qualification
BWK	Bridge Watchkeeper
Capt (N)	Captain (Navy)
CBRN	Chemical, Biological, Radiological and Nuclear
CC	Companion of the Order of Canada
CCM	Canadian Centennial Medal
CD	Canadian Forces Decoration
Cdr	Commander
CDS	Chief of the Defence Staff
CEFCOM	Canadian Expeditionary Force Command
CENTRIXS	Combined Enterprise Regional Information Exchange System
CERA	Chief Engine Room Artificer
CFAO	Canadian Forces Administrative Order
CF	Canadian Forces
CF EXPRES	Canadian Forces Exercise Prescription
CFB	Canadian Forces Base
CFLI	Canadian Forces Leadership Institute
CFSAL	Canadian Forces School of Administration and Logistics
Chiefs & POs	Chiefs and Petty Officers
CHRA	Canadian Human Rights Act
CHRT	Canadian Human Rights Tribunal
CIDA	Canadian International Development Agency
CJTF	Coalition Joint Task Force
Cmdre	Commodore
CMF	Combined Maritime Forces
CMM	Commander of the Order of Military Merit

CMP	Chief of Military Personnel
CMS	Chief of Maritime Staff
CND	Continuous Naval Duty
CNN	Cable News Network
CO	Commanding Officer
COM	Commander of the Order of Military Merit of the Police Forces
Cox'n	Coxswain
CPO1	Chief Petty Officer 1st class
CSSO	Client Services Support Officer
CTF	Combined Task Force
CWAC	Canadian Women's Army Corps
CWINF	Committee on Women in NATO Forces
CWO	Chief Warrant Officer
DBPO	Duty Block Petty Officer
DFOPS	Deputy Director Future Operations
DG	Director General
DIN	Defence Information Network
DS	Directing Staff
DVA	Department of Veteran's Affairs
FAdmO	Formation Administration Officer
FRP	Force Reduction Program
HFDF	High Frequency Direction Finding
HMCS	Her Majesty's Canadian Ship
HMY	Her Majesty's Yacht
HQ	Headquarters
IATA	International Air Transport Association
IED	Improvised Explosive Device
ISAF	International Security Assistance Force
JLC	Junior Leadership Course
JTFA	Joint Task Force (Atlantic)
KOCR	King's Own Calgary Regiment
KR & AI	King's Rules and Admiralty Regulations
LCdr	Lieutenant-Commander
LS	Leading Seaman
Lt(N)(R)(W)	Lieutenant (Navy) (Reserve) (Woman)

MARLANT	Maritime Forces Atlantic
MARPAC	Maritime Forces Pacific
MARS	Maritime Surface and Sub-Surface
MFRC	Military Family Resource Centre
MMM	Member of the Order of Military Merit
NAC	National Action Committee (on the Status of Women in Canada)
NAC Op	Naval Acoustic Operator
NASA	National Aeronautics and Space Administration (US)
NATO	North Atlantic Treaty Organization
NAVCENT	Naval Component Central Command
Nav Comm	Naval Communicator
NAVRES	Naval Reserve
NCAGS	Naval Cooperation and Guidance for Shipping
NCI Op	Naval Combat Information Operator
NCM	Non-Commissioned Member
NCO	Non-Commissioned Officer
NCSM	Navire canadienne de Sa Majesté
NMCJS	Naval Military Canadian Joint Staff
NRSSTP	Naval Reserve Summer Student Training Program
NSA	Naval Support Activity
OJT	On the Job Training
OMM	Officer of the Order of Military Merit
ONA	Operational Net Assessment
OP	Operation
OPME	Officer Professional Military Education
OPP	Operational Planning Process
PA	Physician's Assistant
PER	Personnel Evaluation Report
PMC	President of the Mess Committee
PO1	Petty Officer 1st class
PO2	Petty Officer 2nd class
POTEL	Petty Officer of Telecommunications
PRT	Provincial Reconstruction Team
PSTC	Peace Support Training Centre
Pte	Private
QGJM	Queen's Golden Jubilee Medal

RAF	Royal Air Force
RCAF	Royal Canadian Air Force
RCAF WD	Royal Canadian Air Force Women's Division
RCN	Royal Canadian Navy
RCNA	Royal Canadian Naval Association
RCN (R)	Royal Canadian Naval (Reserve)
RCN (W)	Royal Canadian Navy (Wrens)
RCSCC	Royal Canadian Sea Cadet Corps Calgary
RMC	Royal Military College of Canada
ROTO	Rotation
SAT	Strategic Advisory Team
SAT-A	Strategic Advisory Team Afghanistan
SHARP	Sexual Harassment and Racism Prevention
Sig Op	Signals Operator
SLt	Sub-Lieutenant
SNR	Senior Naval Representative
SNRA	Senior Naval Reserve Advisor
SSTP	Summer Student Training Program
STANAVFORLANT	Standing Naval Force Atlantic
SYEP	Summer Youth Employment Program
TOS	Terms of Service
TSC	Theatre Security Operations
UAE	United Arab Emirates
UK	United Kingdom
UNAMA	United Nations Assistance Mission in Afghanistan
UNDP	United Nations Development Programme
US	United States
USA	United States of America
VBIED	Vehicle-Borne Improvised Explosive Device
WAVES	Women Accepted for Volunteer Emergency Service
WD	Women's Division (see RCAF WD)
WRCNS	Women's Royal Canadian Naval Service
WRNS	Women's Royal Naval Service
XO	Executive Officer
YTEP	Youth Training and Employment Program